S0-CTW-632

HARVARD ECONOMIC STUDIES

HARVARD ECONOMIC STUDIES

PUBLISHED UNDER THE DIRECTION OF
THE DEPARTMENT OF ECONOMICS

VOLUME XXXVI

LONDON : HUMPHREY MILFORD
OXFORD UNIVERSITY PRESS

THE GREENBACKS AND RESUMPTION OF SPECIE PAYMENTS, 1862-1879

BY

DON C. BARRETT, PH.D.
PROFESSOR OF ECONOMICS, HAVERFORD COLLEGE

CAMBRIDGE
HARVARD UNIVERSITY PRESS
1931

PRINTED IN THE UNITED STATES OF AMERICA

TO

M. F. B.

PREFACE

DURING and since the Great War much attention on the part of the American public, and especially of persons interested in the subject of money and banking, has been given to the paper-money experiments of numerous countries. Those experiments have naturally caused comparison to be made with our own remarkable attempt to manage a paper currency in the Civil War period. Our experiment has never been presented as a monograph covering the whole period, although valuable contributions have been made to many aspects of the subject.

This book is an attempt to present in monographic form a critical account of the difficulties, the pitfalls, and the outcome of our experiment during the entire greenback period from 1862 to 1879.

I am indebted to the editors of the *Quarterly Journal of Economics* for the privilege of using as Chapter II an article which they published for me some years ago in that journal. The material is in part revised. As acknowledged in footnotes, Chapter III and the early part of Chapter V are based largely upon Professor Mitchell's *A History of the Greenbacks*. Chapters I and II were written before Mitchell's book appeared. These and other chapters contain considerable material which has not heretofore appeared in the literature of the subject.

I wish to thank Professor Frank D. Graham and Professor Frank W. Fetter, of Princeton University, for reading the manuscript and making many valuable suggestions.

DON C. BARRETT

HAVERFORD, PENNSYLVANIA
July, 1930

CONTENTS

THE GREENBACKS AND RESUMPTION OF SPECIE PAYMENTS, 1862–1879

CHAPTER I

THE ORIGIN OF THE GREENBACKS

THE legal tender paper money which has been an integral part of the circulating media of exchange in the United States for a period of more than sixty years is officially known as "United States Notes." But the popular term "greenbacks" has become so firmly fastened upon this element in our currency as to cause its adoption in most discussions of the subject.

EARLY LEGISLATION AND THE DEMAND NOTES

The issue of the greenbacks is inseparably connected with the existence of the Civil War. The war was formally begun on the twelfth of April, 1861, by the attack upon Fort Sumpter. The President at once issued a call for troops, and summoned Congress in extra session for July 4th in order to secure legislative action on the critical conditions of the time. In his message[1] to Congress submitted on the first day of the extra session President Lincoln stated practically nothing bearing upon the financial and monetary phases of the situation. This was presumably left to the hand of the secretary of the treasury, Salmon P. Chase. Through the "partly treacherous and largely imbecile" management in opposition to Northern interests by some of his recent predecessors, Secretary Chase, on assuming the responsibilities of his office, found the treasury on the verge of bankruptcy.[2] In his first report[3] to Congress made at an early day of the session he found that the demands upon the treasury, arising under existing appropriations and

[1] Senate Journal, 37 Cong., 1 Sess., p. 8.

[2] Under Buchanan's administration the secretaries of the treasury were: Cobb of Georgia, March 6, 1857; Thomas of Maryland, December 12, 1860; and Dix of New York, January 11, 1861. The *Boston Advertiser*, December 31, 1861, states that Dix was a faithful secretary.

[3] Senate Executive Document No. 2, 37 Cong., 1 Sess. The report was submitted July 4, 1861.

created by new exigencies altogether likely to occur, would amount in round numbers for the fiscal year ending June 30, 1862, to $318.5 millions. Laying down the principle that every sound system of finance must provide through adequate taxation for the prompt discharge of all ordinary demands of administration, for the payment of interest on the public debt, and for the creation of a sinking fund, he concluded in accordance therewith that $80 millions of revenue must be raised by taxes internal and on the seaboard, and that $240 millions must be secured through loans. Existing legislation[1] authorized the secretary to make loans amounting in the aggregate to not more than $21 millions, but even this resource was not at the time available. Chase therefore submitted a plan for raising the required loan. First, he proposed to raise not less than $100 millions by means of "seven-thirty" treasury notes[2] with three years to run, such notes, if possible, to cover the entire amount of the loan. Second, in default of meeting all requirements by this method, it was to be supplemented by an issue of $100 millions of bonds, which must be sold at a rate not less than par and with interest not exceeding 7 per cent. Third, as an auxiliary to these methods he made a recommendation, important to our purposes, that treasury notes of small denominations might be issued not exceeding $50 millions in amount, bearing a low rate of interest, and exchangeable at will for the seven-thirty treasury notes; "or, should it be found more convenient, they may be made redeemable on demand in coin and issued without interest." These treasury notes of small denominations, in either form, Chase conceived might "prove very useful if prudently used in anticipation of revenue certain to be received." However, he was fully alive to the dangers of such an expedient and realized that the greatest care would be "requisite to prevent the degradation of such issues

[1] Acts of June 22, 1860, and March 2, 1861.

[2] These notes issued as a means of borrowing bore interest at 7.3 per cent per annum, or $7.30 interest on a loan of $100, thus making 2 cents per day. Hence their popular name "seven-thirties." With interest thus easily and quickly calculated, they might pass as hand-to-hand currency.

into an irredeemable paper currency."[1] Accordingly the draft of a bill embodying these recommendations was submitted with the report for the consideration of Congress.

The result of these recommendations was finally the enactment of a law by Congress which initiated a radically new departure in the currency of the country. The National Loan Act[2] of July 17, 1861, provided for twenty-year 7 per cent bonds; for interest-bearing treasury notes with a specified time to run; and for $50 millions of demand notes without interest and reissuable. The aggregate amount of bonds and notes was limited to $250 millions. The bill was passed through both houses in the most summary manner possible, and without the slightest suggestion that, by the incorporation of the demand note clause, anything out of the usual order of things was taking place. The debate[3] in the lower house was limited to one hour, which was consumed entirely by an opponent[4] of the Northern interests, without a single reference to the provisions of the bill.[5] In the Senate, Fessenden, the chairman of the finance committee, reported the bill with the statement that it was very important that it should be disposed of at once. After a few purely verbal amendments the Senate passed the bill with no debate whatever. In this manner paper money secured, to say the least, an entering wedge into the currency system of the country, seemingly without arousing as much as the suspicion of Congress. A precedent is here established for both the demand and the non-interest-bearing character of treasury notes.

Modification of the Sub-Treasury System

On August 5, 1861, a Supplementary Act[6] authorized: first, that the demand notes of July 17th should be receivable for

[1] See report, p. 14, cited above, p. 3, for the language on the dangers of an irredeemable currency.

[2] 12 Statutes at Large, 259.

[3] See the *Congressional Globe*, July 30, 1861, p. 350, Summer Session.

[4] Vallandigham of Ohio.

[5] The vote on the bill in the House was 150 yeas to 5 nays. There was practically no opposition to the bill in the Senate.

[6] That is, supplementary to the act of July 17, 1861.

public dues; second, that these notes should be of denominations not less than $5;[1] and third, that the operations of the Sub-Treasury Act should be in part suspended. Under the pressure of the war the expenses of the government were beginning to aggregate almost one million dollars per day. The authorized loan could not be negotiated rapidly enough to supply the needed funds, hence it was considered[2] that an indispensable source of means could be secured by making the demand notes receivable for public dues, thus affording a sort of endless-chain movement of these notes into the treasury and out again in the form of disbursements. As a further indispensable aid, the provision regarding the sub-treasury system was included. That system, which in those days required all payments to and from the government to be made in specie, was to be modified so far as to permit banks lending to the government to retain on deposit for their own use the loan funds until they were gradually withdrawn by the United States treasurer in actual disbursements. The funds disbursed were naturally expected to be redeposited in the banks in due time by individuals receiving such funds. In the absence of this modification the transfer of the proceeds of loans to the government vaults was to be made at once and in the form of coin as required by the Sub-Treasury Act. Without such modification the banking institutions of the country could not hope to bring any considerable support to the government.[3]

This bill was also rushed through both houses with a minimum of debate. Some anxiety was exhibited on the part of a few members as to the suspension of this feature of the sub-treasury system, but opposition was overcome by explanations from the committees in charge of the bill of the necessity of the step and of the beneficial results flowing from it.[4] Fessenden in the Senate said: "It is thought to be exceedingly necessary

[1] The original provision was for denominations not less than $10.

[2] See speech of Stevens, *Congressional Globe*, July 25 and August 1, 1861, pp. 267, 383.

[3] See 12 Statutes at Large, 313.

[4] Fessenden was chairman of the Senate finance committee and Stevens was chairman of the ways and means committee in the House.

and wise to have this provision, and every business man acquainted with banks and their operations will see its necessity. . . . That is the opinion of the secretary of the treasury and the opinion of the committees of both houses."[1] Notwithstanding the clearness with which the proposition was set forth and the fact that it passed both houses with no material objections, we shall find Secretary Chase later refusing to assist the lending banks in this particular because, it was claimed, Congress had not clearly conferred such power upon him.

The $150-Million Loan

This brings us to the next step of importance leading up to the legal tender acts: *viz.*, the bank loan of $150 millions and, connected with this, the suspension of specie payment in December, 1861. The principal banks of the cities of New York, Boston, and Philadelphia formed an association in the late summer of 1861 for the purposc of aiding the government in placing what was at that time a loan of unprecedented extent. On August 15th the representatives of thirty-nine banks in this association were able to consummate an agreement[2] with the secretary of the treasury whereby they would take at par $50 millions of the seven-thirty treasury notes provided for by the National Loan Act of July 17th, with the privilege of taking a second sum of $50 millions on October 15th, and a third like sum on December 15th. Furthermore, the banks were to have the exclusive right of taking all of the loan so far authorized except the portion which related to the demand notes and the portion which might be placed in Europe. The secretary of the treasury agreed to make a public appeal to the people of the country soliciting them to come forward and subscribe for the loan, since of course the banks could not contemplate a permanent investment in the bonds but were to act merely as intermediaries for the government in the process of transferring the capital of private investors to the public treasury. Ten per cent of the first $50 millions was to be paid

[1] *Congressional Globe*, August 2, 1861, p. 396.

[2] *Bankers' Magazine* (New York), Vol. XI, p. 161 *et seq.*, "The Government Loan of August, 1861."

in at once and the residue credited to the government on the books of these same subscribing banks. Of the entire amount of the first subscription New York was to take $30 millions, Boston (and vicinity) $15 millions, and Philadelphia $5 millions.[1] There was a general feeling on the part of the public at large that this movement of the banks was highly creditable and would of necessity create a much-needed confidence in the government both at home and abroad.[2] At this time it was fully expected that Secretary Chase would avail himself of the opportunity under the law to modify the Sub-Treasury Act in order to ease the burden of the banks. Subscriptions for the loan on the part of the public began as early as August 20th, and throughout the next few weeks the movement in this channel gradually grew, with gratifying results. About the middle of October it was currently reported that English capitalists had decided to take $100 millions of the loan, and thereupon the associated bankers of New York resolved to confer with bankers of Boston and Philadelphia on the feasibility of taking for themselves the entire amount of the $250 millions of securities after deducting the $50 millions of demand notes.[3] Confidence in the government was perceptibly growing, and as a natural consequence its credit was gradually improving. Whether the reports of an English loan were true or false, nothing came of this hope, as events soon to occur made an immediate movement of English capital in this direction an impossibility.

In the latter part of September a second meeting of the associated bankers with Secretary Chase was arranged for the purpose of negotiating the second loan of $50 millions. In the meantime the treasury operations had been conducted in accordance with all the rigidity of the old sub-treasury system.[4] Chase refused to draw directly and gradually upon the banks

[1] Owing to the inability of the Boston banks to assume their quota, this original allotment was changed as follows: New York $35 millions, Boston $10 millions, and Philadelphia $5 millions.—*Hunt's Merchants' Magazine*, Vol. XLV, p. 331.

[2] See, for example, the *Boston Advertiser*, August 15, 19, and 21, 1861.

[3] It appears that no absolute offer was made to the government by the English capitalists. The *Boston Advertiser*, October 21 and 22, 1861.

[4] Cf. p. 6 above.

for the proceeds of their loan and insisted upon the policy of accumulating cash in the treasury vaults. The banks had been led to believe that a more flexible system would be adopted by the treasury in accordance with the act of August 5, 1861. They were therefore greatly exasperated with the secretary in his interpretation of this act. Accordingly at their September meeting they entertained a resolution in which it was held that a second loan would be made on the sole condition that the secretary should abandon the straight-jacket system of the sub-treasury and adopt a more flexible one in his dealings with them. However, the majority in the meeting, although aggrieved at the prevailing policy, contented themselves with cautioning the secretary concerning his course of action, and refused to sustain this resolution since to support it would mean the sacrifice of the opportunity to aid the government in its struggle for life.[1] Consequently arrangements were completed by which the second $50 millions of seven-thirty treasury notes were to be taken and an option for the third $50 millions reserved until the first of December following.

By the middle of November the banks changed their plan in regard to the third installment[2] of the notes and determined to take instead $50 millions of 6 per cent bonds, deferring the taking of treasury notes until January 1st. This change was welcomed by the government, since it was thus afforded an opportunity to place some of its long-term bonds provided by the National Loan Act. The limitation of the rate of interest to 7 per cent, which that law imposed, had been a subject of severe criticism since well-grounded fears were entertained that

[1] *Bankers' Magazine*, Vol. XI, p. 625, "Gallatin on the Currency." The resolutions also demanded that the secretary should limit the amount of demand notes to be issued. For resolutions, see *Boston Advertiser*, October 4, 1861.

J. E. Williams, of the Metropolitan Bank, New York, was a member of the Treasury Note Committee of the associated banks. In a letter of October 4, 1861, he states that at the critical moment he was led to move the taking of the second $50 millions because Chase's expressions to the committee indicated his willingness to draw directly on the banks.

See E. G. Spaulding, *History of the Legal Tender Paper Money Issued during the Great Rebellion*, Buffalo, 1875, Appendix, 2nd ed., pp. 96–99, for the letter by Williams.

[2] *Boston Advertiser*, November 19, 1861.

the government could not place its bonds on such favorable terms. Yet at this time the market had so improved as to lead the associated bankers to believe that a profitable investment could be made in those securities. Six per cent bonds were accordingly issued at a price which would yield a 7 per cent return.

The newspapers of the day, the December message of the President, and the annual report of the secretary of the treasury, all reflect a feeling of growing confidence on the part of the people in the stability of the government and in the success of the loans. President Lincoln stated to Congress: "The operations of the treasury during the period which has elapsed since your adjournment have been conducted with signal success. . . . The patriotism of the people has produced the large means demanded as loans. The industrial classes have confidence in the country's faith."[1] Secretary Chase stated that "beyond the expectations of the most sanguine, the country has responded to the appeals of the secretary" for loans. "The action of banking institutions in advancing funds and taking the final responsibility merits praise, but even greater praise is due the prompt patriotism with which citizens of moderate means, and working men and women, have brought their individual offerings to the service of their country."[2]

The Trent Affair

That such words indicate a condition of affairs more apparent than real is highly probable. Whether the daily press,[3] the President, and Secretary Chase were ignorant of the true situation as to currency and financial affairs, or were merely assuming a bold attitude for the sake of a favorable effect on the credit of the government, is not a matter of easy determination. It can be said, however, that during those same months of apparent growth of confidence a policy was being pursued which would destroy the vitality of the monetary system. The in-

[1] President's Message, December 3, 1861. Senate Documents, No. 1, 37 Cong., 2 Sess., Vol. I, p. 6.

[2] Report of the Secretary of the Treasury, December 9, 1861, p. 16.

[3] Reference is here made to that portion of the press which supported the government.

flexibleness of the sub-treasury system manipulated by the unyielding hand of Chase was rapidly driving the government towards a condition in which the suspension of specie payment would be almost certain if the national credit were to receive a severe shock. Such a shock was precipitated by the unfortunate event in our diplomatic relations known as the Trent Affair. The capture early in November by a United States warship of Mason and Slidell, diplomatic representatives of the Southern Confederacy who were sailing for Europe on the British vessel *Trent*, was contrary to the principle for which America had waged the War of 1812, and had the effect of arousing a storm of indignation and abuse on the part of England. News of the threatening attitude of the British government reached New York on December 16th. For the moment it seemed that the two countries would go to war. Although such extreme measures were soon put out of mind, the excitement and anxiety which their contemplation had produced quickly and profoundly affected the credit of the United States. Both Americans and Englishmen believed that our government would be subjected to burdens beyond her capacity to bear. The result was that, whatever may have been justifiably hoped in the past from the people of the United States and the capitalists of England in the way of loans, support was now jeopardized. The banks found their resources tied up in government securities for which no market was offering and none legitimately expected. The statement[1] of the transactions of these institutions on page 12 reveals their situation:

[1] See *Hunt's Merchants' Magazine*, Vol. XLVI, p. 308, in the *Commercial Review* for March, 1862.

The New York *Journal of Commerce* for January 21, 1862, makes the following statement of this transaction for that date:

(Millions of Dollars)

Amount Subscribed	Paid into Treasury	Received Back through Public Subscription	Due Government
$145.7	$136.4	$50.0	$9.3

On February 5th the same paper states that the last installment was paid the government by the banks on February 4th.

(Millions of Dollars)

Banks of	Capital	Amount of Loan Subscribed	Sold to the Public	Balance Held by Banks
New York	$69.9	$102.0	$35.0	$67.0
Boston	38.2	29.1	10.0	19.1
Philadelphia	11.8	14.5	5.0	9.5
Total	$119.9	$145.6	$50.0	$95.6

The disappointment in Chase's December report, coming as it did in the midst of alarm created by the Trent Affair, produced a marked effect which is partly revealed in the following table[1] showing the condition of banks. The statement refers to the New York banks, and it is evident that they, with large holdings of specie on December 7th, suffered a loss of over 43 per cent of those holdings in the four weeks following.

(Millions of Dollars)

Date	Loans	Specie	Deposits
December 7, 1861	$159.7	$42.3	$133.6
December 14, 1861	157.6	39.4	129.3
December 21, 1861	155.7	36.8	124.8
December 28, 1861	154.7	29.3	116.4
January 4, 1862	154.3	23.9	111.7

Suspension of Specie Payments

As early as July, 1861, suspension of specie payment was mentioned as a possibility. The insolvency of the Albany banks, due to careless management in the face of the unfortunate conditions of war, served to emphasize fears in this regard.[2] The existence of such fears should have called for double precaution. By October 1st it was apparent to many men of influence in the financial world that suspension would

[1] *Hunt's Merchants' Magazine*, Vol. XLVI, p. 309. See also letter of October 8, 1875, from George S. Coe, Spaulding, *op. cit.*, Appendix, 2nd ed., p. 93.

[2] *Bankers' Magazine*, Vol. XI, p. 2.

take place inevitably within ninety days—not because of disturbances due to military exigencies but on account of the secretary's attitude on the sub-treasury system. The associated bankers, both as a body and as individuals, on various occasions during the summer and autumn of 1861, communicated to Secretary Chase in unequivocal terms their grave fears of the outcome of his sub-treasury policy. James Gallatin,[1] son of the eminent financier, president of the National Bank, New York, and one of the most influential members of the associated bankers, was especially vigorous in his criticism of the attitude towards the banks assumed by the treasury department.

In his financial report of December 9, 1861, on the eve of suspension, Chase gave no evidence of appreciating the fact that such an event must be the logical and rapidly realized result of the existing state of affairs in case any financial shock should occur. It may, indeed, be said that it would have been highly impolitic for the secretary to acknowledge the possibility of such a catastrophe before its actual occurrence. Yet the fact remains that he had steadfastly refused to admit the validity of the reasoning on the part of the bankers relative to the ultimate consequence of his sub-treasury policy. It would seem, therefore, that Chase failed to appreciate the impending danger.[2] Moreover, the sorry showing made by the finance minister at this time caused the report itself to be a major factor in forcing suspension. These influences in addition to the military situation itself profoundly affected the public credit.

The banks in the three cities important to this matter were in excellent condition in midsummer, 1861. Their specie holdings were unprecedented in amount.[3] By the middle of Septem-

[1] *Bankers' Magazine*, Vol. XI, p. 625, "Gallatin on the Currency."

[2] In his December report, 1862, p. 8, Chase expressly states that he did not anticipate suspension at the time of writing his report of December, 1861. His memory of the situation seems to tally with the attitude indicated in the text.

[3] *Boston Advertiser*, August 21, 1861. The report of the loan committee of the New York banks for the year April 27, 1861, to April 26, 1862 (*Bankers' Magazine*, Vol. XII, pp. 135, 151), makes the following statement:

Aggregate specie held April 27, 1861....	$38.7 millions
Maximum held August 17, 1861	49.3 millions
Minimum held January 4, 1862	23.7 millions

ber the situation began to show a change consequent upon the transfer of specie to the government in connection with the first $50 millions loan. The holdings in the sub-treasury were much in excess of the immediate needs of the government, and the banks suffered a corresponding loss in specie which seriously cramped their operations. Protests against this state of affairs were met by promises of heavy disbursements by the treasury.[1] Such prospects gave hope to the bankers and partial relief was secured in this fashion during the first half of October. The disaster of the Trent Affair, as we have seen, suddenly brought to a full stop the beginnings of popular subscriptions to the loan, which the banks had temporarily assumed. The purchase of government securities by these institutions was in considerable excess of their combined capital stock, while on account of the waning credit of the government they had been able to resell only one-third of their holdings to the public at large.[2] At the same time, and in consequence of the blow to credit, the redeposit in the banks of money paid out by the treasury was checked. The banks were, therefore, stranded under the heavy weight of their undertaking, their reserves were depleted, and it was but a question of time when they should announce their suspension of specie payment. On Saturday, December 28, 1861, that step was formally decided upon by the banks of New York City, and on the Monday following it was put into effective operation. Banking institutions generally soon followed the example set by New York, and the government was of necessity forced to adopt the same policy. Henceforth the government would not redeem the demand treasury notes in coin.

Opinion as to whether the war might have been carried to a successful conclusion without a suspension of payment was divided at the time, and perhaps must always remain so. The only statement that can be made with certainty is that the sub-treasury policy pursued by Secretary Chase was destined inevitably to be a primary contributing cause of suspension of

[1] *Boston Advertiser*, September 18 and 19, 1861.

[2] See above, p. 12, for statistics.

specie payment whenever a severe crisis might overtake the government's credit. Whether the force of other circumstances might have produced a similar result at a later period in the absence of this cause it is impossible to determine.

Should Greenbacks be Issued?

In his report of December, 1861, Chase addressed himself at length to the problem of the currency. The state bank-note circulation, which in the loyal states was estimated at $150 millions[1] in amount, was regarded as so spurious in character as to call for protection against it. Accordingly it was proposed to force this circulation out of existence and to adopt one of two plans for a better currency: one calling for the further issue of demand notes, and the other the establishment of a national banking system. These proposals are interesting and important, as they show the position which Chase at that time held on the comparative advantages and disadvantages of a currency issued by the government. The advantages of a government issue, being a loan to the government without interest and affording a much-needed uniform currency for the country, were so considerable in his opinion that "if a scheme can be devised by which such a circulation will be certainly and strictly confined to the real needs of the people, and kept constantly equivalent to specie by prompt and certain redemption in coin, it would hardly fail of legislative sanction."[2] The disadvantages, however, of a temptation to overissue in times of pressure and danger; the liability to be called upon for redemption beyond the means provided even under the most careful management; the hazards of panics; the innumerable evils of dishonored public faith, were so great that they rendered it impossible for him to recommend such a plan. In his opinion, even an irredeemable state bank currency might be preferable. He strongly commends to Congress a currency to be provided by a national banking system as a far more expedient plan. With

[1] In his next annual report, December, 1862, Senate Documents, No. 1, 37 Cong., 3 Sess., Vol. I, p. 7, Chase gives the bank circulation for January 1, 1861, at $150 millions, and for January 1, 1862, at $130 millions.

[2] Report of the Secretary of the Treasury, December 9, 1861, p. 18.

this plan we are not here concerned. We are interested in knowing that, in this stage of the proceedings, Chase was emphatically opposed to a system, not only of government legal tender note issues, but of government issues in large amount in any form.

We now come to the preparation of the first legal tender act. The ways and means committee of the House at this time had turned over its most important business to two sub-committees, one having in charge affairs relating to loans, the other those relating to revenues. E. G. Spaulding of New York was chairman of the former. In accordance with suggestions in the secretary's report Spaulding, as chairman of the sub-committee in charge of loans, began in the middle of December to frame a bill for a national banking system. Chase cherished false hopes that a demand for bonds to be used as a basis for the note issues of this system might be created in sufficient amount to afford a material source of loans to the government. It was soon realized, however, that this system could not in any event be put into working order in time to give to the treasury the necessary immediate relief from the heavy pressure to which it was subjected by the demands of war. It was therefore decided to attach to the bill a section providing for the issue of $100 millions of legal tender notes which could be used for immediate exigencies. This section was then published in the *New York Tribune*, December 31st, in order to learn the attitude of the public toward the plan. It was soon seen that the passage of the banking bill must be long delayed. It was too complicated and important a piece of legislation to admit of haste. After securing a favorable unofficial decision of the attorney-general on the constitutionality of such an act, Spaulding, on December 31st, introduced in the House this legal tender section as a separate bill. On the question of introducing such a measure the committee of ways and means was equally divided. It was, however, finally reported, referred back to the ways and means committee, and again reported to the House on January 7, 1862.[1] On the eleventh of January a delegation of bankers met

[1] This bill in its form of January 7th was not considered by the House. It was displaced by another introduced January 22nd.

in conference the secretary of the treasury and the financial committees from both houses of Congress, to devise some method by which the bankers could give aid to the government. Gallatin, in behalf of the bankers, submitted a plan by which there should be: (1) adequate and immediate taxation, (2) no demand notes issued other than those authorized on July 17th, (3) $100 millions of treasury notes, with two years to run, (4) a suspension of the sub-treasury system in so far as necessary to permit the banks to become depositories of all government loans and to permit the use of checks in making the ordinary disbursements of the treasury, (5) 6 per cent bonds sold without any limitation as to price. This plan was rejected by the secretary and committees. Apparently it gave inadequate governmental control over the currency. On January 15th the bankers' delegates resorted to a second conference. On this occasion they met with the secretary alone. A second plan was proposed which provided: (1) that the banks receive and pay out the demand notes of July 17th, but that no further issue of such notes be made, (2) that the secretary pay out $20 millions of bonds at once to government creditors, (3) that Congress pass a national bank bill as recommended by the secretary, and (4) that no legal tender notes should be issued. This plan[1] met with approval at the hands of Chase and he accepted it without the concurrence of the committees of Congress. It omits the demand for modification of the sub-treasury system, accepts the demand notes, rejects the issue of legal tender paper money, and would give ultimate governmental control over bank-note currency.

In the meantime the legal tender bill, having been revised and elaborated by the sub-committee of ways and means, was submitted to the consideration of Chase. He, on January 22nd, and hence within one week of his agreement with the bankers' delegation which provided that no legal tenders should be issued, returned the bill to the House committee. The bill was accompanied by a letter[2] in which he expressed his pro-

[1] For the text of these plans see Spaulding, *History of the Legal Tender Paper Money Issued during the Great Rebellion*, Buffalo, 1869, pp. 20–22.

[2] *Ibid.*, p. 27.

found regret that it was found necessary to resort to the measure of making United States notes a legal tender but that he heartily desired to coöperate with the committee in all measures to meet existing emergencies. Although Chase had fully concluded to support the legal tender measure, the ways and means committee forced a still more positive statement from him in a letter dated January 29th. The refusal of the Boston banks to follow their delegates in accepting the plan of January 15th no doubt had an influence on Chase's attitude.[1] Having thus accomplished a complete reversal of the secretary's position on the question of legal tender issues, the committee adopted the bill and reported it to the House on the same day.

The original provisions of the bill, which ultimately became law on February 25, 1862, were: (1) the issue of $100 millions of United States notes to be made a legal tender for all debts public and private; (2) the authority to issue $500 millions of twenty-year bonds with interest not exceeding 7 per cent, or (in lieu of bonds) treasury notes of various descriptions; (3) the legal tender notes thus issued were to be convertible into bonds on demand. Before its final enactment, the bill was so amended as to increase the issue of United States notes (greenbacks) to $150 millions, to limit the legal tender quality by requiring import duties to be paid in coin, to authorize the sale of bonds at the market price, and to authorize borrowing through the means of temporary deposits made by private investors with the United States treasury.

The absence of any comprehensive plan of taxation is the most remarkable defect of these entire proceedings during the year 1861 and the beginning of 1862. Without taxation adequate to the needs of the administration it was inevitable that confidence in the government's stability should be wanting and therefore that great difficulties must be experienced in placing loans. In his report of July, 1861, Chase had recommended that $80 millions should be raised by taxation. Congress in the revenue act of August 5th attempted to comply with this

[1] *Ibid.*, pp. 45, 46.

recommendation, and in doing so levied a direct tax of $20 millions, imposed a tax of 3 per cent on incomes above eight hundred dollars, and depended largely for the completion of the amount on an increase of the customs duties. Owing to the disturbed conditions of war, the revenue from imports was insignificant, the direct tax was available in the loyal states alone, and the income tax feature was a disappointment so far as concerned receipts during the years of war. In the face of dire need for revenue almost a year passed before another act of taxation was placed upon the statute books.

The Argument of Necessity

Under such circumstances the debate on the first legal tender bill was opened in the House on January 28, 1862, by Spaulding,[1] who represented the Buffalo district of New York and was engaged in the banking business in that city. Spaulding in many respects may be considered the father of the measure. His principal argument for the bill was that of necessity. He presented what seemed to be a formidable estimate of the public debt. The actual indebtedness on that date he placed at $306.7 millions; the estimate of requirements to June 30, 1862, was $343.2 millions and for the fiscal year ending June 30, 1863, $550 millions, making a total requirement for the last date of $1200 millions. He urged that the issue of legal tenders (greenbacks) was a war measure, that the expenses of the government exceeded a million dollars per day, and that the existing session of Congress must make provision for all emergencies up to June 30, 1863. No other reasonable source than that proposed was available, and therefore the measure was one of necessity and not of choice. Bonds sold at the market price would suffer a ruinous discount, and the dignity of the nation would be brought into question by the "government's going into Wall Street, State Street and Chestnut Street, shinning for means to carry on the war." The secretary of the treasury had not been able to negotiate the last $50 millions of the authorized $250 millions loan, and could not do so except at a dis-

[1] *Congressional Globe,* January 28, 1862, p. 523 *et seq.*

count of 40 per cent. A plan for short-time treasury notes would be a worthless expedient since the government could not be in a position to redeem them when due. The demand notes of the government were already discredited by the banks, and therefore the legal tender quality was absolutely essential to make the issues circulate at par. Such were the arguments urged by Spaulding from the standpoint of controlling necessity and reiterated in slightly varying form by every advocate of the measure throughout the wearisome debate. Such an enormous requirement for expenditures in the face of existing conditions of ill success in military affairs, of patriotism untried by the test of heavy taxation, and of an extremely uncertain market for government securities, was well calculated to frighten men, necessarily untrained in the larger aspects of finance and monetary science, into legislation of a questionable character. In the midst of the perplexities of the situation in which the lower house found itself, Secretary Chase, in a letter[1] of February 3, threw his influence[2] in favor of the bill. In this letter he stated to Spaulding that "immediate action is of great importance. The treasury is nearly empty. I have been obliged to draw for the last installment of the [bankers'] November loan; so soon as it is paid, I fear the banks generally will refuse to receive the United States [demand] notes. You will see the necessity of urging the bill through without more delay." It is not too much to say that this letter, within three days after it was written,[3] coming at the precise time when it did, was the "last straw" which pressed the bill through the House. Again the secretary's influence was adroitly used upon the Senate when the bill was on the eve of coming before that body. On the seventh

[1] Spaulding, *op. cit.*, pp. 59, 60.

[2] Although Chase had lost prestige through his failure to present an adequate financial plan in his December (1861) report and although his influence over Congress was not as great as it might have been had he possessed greater ability to win friends and supporters in the Senate and House, his position as head of the treasury gave his opinions decided weight. Compare Hart's *Salmon P. Chase*, pp. 234, 235; also a letter by Conkling to Spaulding in Spaulding, *op. cit.*, Appendix, 2nd ed., pp. 83–87. Secretary Chase had submitted with his letter a bill embodying the suggestions made by him in the letter.

[3] The bill passed the House February 6th, and the Senate February 13th.

of February, while the bill was still under consideration in the finance committee of the Senate, Chase prepared the minds of senators for the necessity of immediate action by a letter to Fessenden, chairman of the committee, in which it was urged that the deplorable condition of the treasury rendered it impossible to await the Senate's action on the legal tender measure and advised that a bill be passed at once authorizing an issue of $10 millions of demand notes in addition to the $50 millions authorized the preceding July 17th and August 5th. Fessenden, although opposed in principle to a legal tender paper, stated that the emergency was known to all and asked unanimous consent to introduce the secretary's bill without notice and without sending it to the finance committee. The Senate took up the bill immediately and passed it without debate. It passed the House in similar fashion and became law on February 12, 1862. The necessitous condition of the treasury was in this manner held over the heads of the members of Congress.

Attention was turned again to the larger measure. Some brief passages from representative speeches will serve to show the state of feeling which carried it through both houses.

Spaulding said:

> The bill before the House is a war measure—a measure of necessity and not of choice, presented by the committee of ways and means to meet the most pressing demands of the treasury, to sustain the army and navy until they can make a vigorous advance upon the traitors, and crush out the rebellion. These are extraordinary times and extraordinary measures must be resorted to in order to save our government and preserve our nationality. . . . Our army and navy must have what is far more valuable to them than gold and silver. They must have food, clothing, and the material of war. Treasury notes issued by the government on the faith of the whole people will purchase these indispensable articles and the war can be prosecuted until we can enforce obedience to the constitution and laws and an honorable peace be thereby secured. This being accomplished I will be among the first to advocate a speedy return to specie payments and all measures that are calculated to preserve the honor and dignity of the government in time of peace, and which I regret are not practicable in the prosecution of this war.[1]

[1] *Congressional Globe*, January 28, 1862, pp. 523, 526.

Thaddeus Stevens, the leading figure in the House, a man of great force but ill informed upon questions of money and finance, said:

> Without the legal tender quality I do not . . . believe that such notes would circulate anywhere except at a ruinous discount. Notes not redeemable on demand, and not made a legal tender, have never been kept at par. . . . If soldiers, mechanics, contractors, and farmers were compelled to take them from the government, they must submit to a heavy shave before they could use them. The knowledge that they were provided for by taxation and would surely be paid twenty years hence would not sustain them. . . . I flatter myself that I have demonstrated both from reason and undoubted authority that such notes, made a legal tender and not issued in excess of legitimate demand, will remain at par and pass in all transactions, great and small, at the full value of their face; we shall have one currency for all sections of the country, and for every class of people, the poor as well as the rich.[1]

Senator Sherman, who has borne the reputation of being the best-informed man during those critical years upon the subjects of money, banking, and finance, took a similar position. He said:

> If you strike out the tender clause you do so with a knowledge that these notes will fall dead upon the money market of the world. . . . When you issue demand notes, and announce to the world your purpose not to pay any more gold and silver, you then tender to those who have furnished provisions and services this paper money. What can they do? They cannot pay their debts with it. They cannot support their families with it, without a depreciation. The whole then depends on the promise of the government to pay at some time not fixed on the face of the note. . . . Justice to our creditors demands that it should be a legal tender. It will then circulate all over this country. It will be the life blood of the whole business of the country and it will enable capitalists to buy your bonds.[2]

Senator Sumner said:

> Whatever may be the national resources, they are not now within reach except by summary process. Reluctantly, painfully, I consent that the process should issue. And yet I cannot give such a vote without warning the government against the danger of such an experiment. The medicine of the constitution must not become its daily bread.[3]

[1] Speech in the House, *Congressional Globe*, February 6, 1862, pp. 687, 689.

[2] Speech in the Senate, *Congressional Globe*, February 13, 1862, p. 791.

[3] *Ibid.*, p. 800.

The argument of necessity for obtaining funds for the government so dominated the minds of the majority of public men that other phases of the question were overshadowed by it. Yet other considerations were brought forward. It was at times conceded that the legal tender quality alone could not be relied upon to sustain the notes but that taxation must afford a basis for them, and it was regretted by many that a tax bill had not preceded the legal tender bill. The constitutionality[1] of the measure was touched upon in every speech of considerable length, but "necessity" seemed to be a sufficient reason to the greater number for overriding all doubts on this point. Very little was said on matters of purely monetary concern. For the most part the measure was considered as one of borrowing, and as divorced from the subject of money. Yet the stimulating effects of rising prices were pointed out by the friends of the bill, and the evil effects of inflation and contraction were pictured by its opponents. It was argued by some that a vacuum had been created in the currency by the withdrawal of specie and bank notes since suspension of specie payments and that the issue of legal tender notes was needed to supply a medium of exchange. Sherman went so far as to assert that the treasury could not sell bonds, simply because there was a lack of a medium of exchange with which to make the transactions. On this phase of the subject the debate varied from such well-taken points as "debasing the currency never added a single dollar to a country's wealth," and "a paper money régime once entered upon finds no natural check," to such fallacious notions as "the government can make a dollar out of 80 cents and it does so all the time" and "the people will not permit their paper money to depreciate because they are too wise to overthrow their own government."

[1] The constitutionality of the act will not be discussed in this volume. It was of importance then, but has now ceased to attract attention. The question of expediency was and is the important one. Pendleton of Ohio and Collamer of Vermont made the most elaborate and able arguments against the constitutionality of the greenbacks. Conkling said the bill passed without even a pretext of argument in favor of its constitutionality. While such a statement is far too strong, it is true that the opponents of the bill made much the stronger case on the constitutional point.

Enactment of the First Legal Tender Measure

With promises in both Senate and House that the first issue of $150 millions of legal tender notes would be the last, the bill was finally sent to the President, and received his signature on February 25, 1862. Those sanguine advocates of the first issue who thought that they could thus open the floodgates to legal tender paper and close them at will were disappointed. A second issue was called for within less than six months and still a third within little more than a year. The general policy of resorting to greenbacks as a financial resource was evidently determined as early as February 25, 1862.

CHAPTER II

THE SUPPOSED NECESSITY OF THE GREENBACKS

IN THIS chapter a survey of the conditions prevailing in the period beginning early in 1861 and ending about June 30, 1862, will be made with the purpose of ascertaining whether the necessity did, in fact, exist for the several issues of greenbacks during the Civil War. The period covered is the critical one for this purpose, since by its close Congress was fully alive to the importance of heavy taxation and the government had learned the necessity of paying, indirectly if not directly, a rate of interest on loans sufficiently high to attract investors. After such a stage had been reached, comparatively little danger of the inauguration, *de novo*, of a legal tender paper existed.

APPLETON AND HOOPER

The first point of evidence of the lack of necessity for the issue of the greenbacks relates to two members of the House of Representatives from Massachusetts. In the fall of 1861, as stated in the preceding chapter, a large part of the work of the ways and means committee was divided between two subcommittees, one having charge of matters relating to loans, the other of those relating to revenue. The former was composed of three members—E. G. Spaulding of New York, Erastus Corning of New York, and Samuel Hooper of Massachusetts. The legal tender legislation was initiated by this sub-committee of three. Hooper, for the first time, took his place in the House of Representatives in December, 1861, and owed his opportunity for a seat to the resignation of William Appleton, whose failing health compelled him to give up a valuable service to the country. This change of membership from the Suffolk District of Massachusetts was of the first importance in the matter of United States note issues.

Appleton had been persuaded to serve in the Congress of 1851–52, in that of 1853–54, and again in the extra session of 1861. During the entire period of his congressional career he was a member of the ways and means committee. His services in the summer of 1861 were declared to "have been of the very highest value, since his efforts, which were as devoted and active as those of the strongest political ally of the administration, were also guided by an experience and knowledge of the commerce and resources of the country such as probably no other member of the committee, or perhaps of the House, possessed."[1] The personal testimony of his contemporaries[2] informs us that the business community of Boston considered the monetary and financial interests of the nation to be much safer in his hands than in those of his successor. One of his strong characteristics was that he came to his settled opinions slowly but, having made a decision, he seldom changed his mind. All of the evidence from his contemporaries and from the results of the summer session of 1861 points to his opposition to attaching the legal tender quality to paper money.

Samuel Hooper was a man of wide business experience and of considerable information on currency questions; but his views, as expressed in 1855,[3] clearly foreshadow his attitude on the legal tender question in 1861 and 1862. He believed that the "Continental money" of the old Confederacy had "effected a good and great work at a most critical time, and the loss by its total depreciation was not much greater or less justly distributed than it would have been by any scheme of taxation."[4] He held that gold and silver only should make up the currency

[1] *Boston Advertiser*, September 30, 1861.

[2] For example, Professor Charles F. Dunbar and Mr. T. Jefferson Coolidge. Appleton never took part in debate and never, so far as I can learn, committed his opinions on monetary questions to paper. He left a diary, kept during the summer session of 1861, but it has apparently been lost. His great work was in committee and in personal contact with public men. For knowledge of his influence we must rely chiefly upon the testimony of men who knew him.

[3] *Currency or Money* (1855). These opinions, so far as important to us, were reiterated by Hooper in speeches in Congress from 1862 to 1869, and therefore may be presumed to have been held by him during the period under review.

[4] *Ibid.*, p. 25.

in times of peace, but that paper money might well be resorted to in great emergencies. At such times, he said, "it may be used for the business transactions within the country, to release the coin from that service, so that its coin may be used by the government . . . for the common welfare."[1] Being thus committed to the policy of a legal tender paper in times of emergency, having no confidence in any system of bank-note issues, and being in close sympathy with the administration, Hooper was in the frame of mind and in a position of influence to assist materially in foisting upon the country a legal tender paper money in February, 1862.

As it happened, in January the ways and means committee was equally divided on the question of recommending to the House the legal tender feature of the bill which afterwards became the act of February 25, 1862. Without changing his views, one of the members (Stratton) who was opposed to it finally consented to let the clause go before the House for consideration.[2] It was peculiarly true in those doubtful days—such was the frame of mind of congressmen—that whatever recommendation came from the ways and means committee had every chance of receiving the support of the majority in the House; hence the importance of reporting this clause. Had William Appleton instead of Samuel Hooper been a member of that committee it is not too much to say that the legal tender feature would have failed of recommendation.

Temporary Deposits

The resource of temporary deposits furnished a second point in evidence against the necessity for the greenback issues. The same pressure for means to support the government which brought about the issue of legal tender notes led also to the development of a plan for the deposit of demand notes and greenbacks as a temporary loan with the secretary of the treasury. The act of February 25, 1862,[3] provided that these notes

[1] *Ibid.*, pp. 71–75, 87. See also Hooper's speech in the House of Representatives, *Congressional Globe*, April 6, 1864, p. 1448 *et seq.*

[2] Spaulding, *op. cit.*, p. 16.

[3] 12 Statutes at Large, 345.

might be received on deposit for not less than thirty days, in sums of not less than one hundred dollars, and could be withdrawn in any sum on ten days' notice.[1] The certificates of deposit issued in return were to bear 5 per cent interest, or less at the discretion of the secretary. The comparatively small amount of $25 millions, to which the deposits were limited by the act, points to the expectation of only slight relief from this source. In fact, this provision was inserted, in the first instance, more as a means of checking the depreciation of United States notes than as a direct means of borrowing.[2] But this field proved to be comparatively fruitful in supplying funds at a critical juncture. Temporary deposits began to accumulate early and very rapidly. During the week ending March 4, 1862, they amounted to $5 millions, and during the following week to $4.5 millions. Within three weeks after this authority was given, it became necessary to amend the act by raising the limit of temporary deposits to $50 millions.[3] The table on page 29 exhibits the results of this device, by weeks, up to July 1, 1862.

We find from this table that to April 29th the withdrawals of deposits from week to week were at all times comparatively small in amount, and that the totals show a greater or less increase in every instance. Future weeks reveal a similar situation. According to Bayley, the withdrawals for the two quarters ending June 30, 1862, were less than 12 per cent of the deposits.[4] At the end of the day on May 2 the net amount lent to the government by this device at the depositories of New York, Philadelphia, and Boston was $47 millions.[5]

As early as March 5th the New York banks set on foot a project which smoothed the way to facilitate deposits.[6] In furtherance of the project, at a meeting of the Clearing House Association held on March 7th its committee reported, through George

[1] The demand notes of July 17, 1861, and of February 12, 1862, were included in this provision.

[2] *Boston Advertiser*, February 13, 1862.

[3] Act of March 17, 1862, 12 Statues at Large, 370.

[4] R. A. Bayley, *National Loans of the United States*, Washington, 1881, p. 158.

[5] *New York Tribune*, financial column, May 3, 1862.

[6] *Ibid.*, March 6, 1862.

TEMPORARY DEPOSITS TO JULY 1, 1862[1]

Week Ending	Amount of Deposits	Amount Withdrawn	Total Loans to Government
March 4, 1862.........	$5,018,455		
March 11, 1862........	4,527,693	$593,200[2]	$8,952,948
March 18, 1862........	2,706,386	665,965	10,993,369
March 25, 1862........	552,675	65,550	11,480,494
April 1, 1862..........	914,488	167,797	12,227,185[3]
April 8, 1862..........	2,371,105	622,300	13,975,990
April 15, 1862..........	7,266,130	206,905	21,035,215
April 22, 1862..........	9,164,055	487,700	29,711,570
April 29, 1862..........	7,544,500	192,400	37,063,670
	Total Amount of Loans		
On May 2, 1862........	....	....	47,000,000
On June 17, 1862.......	....	....	56,067,150[4]
On July 1, 1862........	....	....	57,746,116[4]

[1] This table is compiled from Senator Chandler's speech of June 18, 1862, *Congressional Globe*, June 19, 1862, p. 2774, except that the item for May 2 is taken from the *New York Tribune* of May 3, and the item for July 1 is taken from the Report of the Secretary of the Treasury for December, 1862. Professor Dunbar often remarked that Chandler was a keen observer and usually knew what was going on. The figures in the first column (amount of deposits) correspond roughly with those given in the daily statements of the *New York Tribune's* financial column, and hence are to be accepted as reasonably trustworthy. The *Tribune* figures, being statements for transactions at the sub-treasury at New York only, are smaller in the aggregate than Chandler's, which are for the whole country. I have not used Chandler's totals, as he seems to have confused another temporary loan with the temporary deposits in arriving at them. His figures for dates following April 29 seem confused and are not used, except the total for June 17. The temporary falling off after March 11 is due to a letter from Cisco, assistant treasurer at New York, dated March 14, stating that withdrawals would be paid in any notes which had been made a legal tender and which the government might be using at the time. Since demand notes were wanted for payment of import duties, they were withheld from deposit with the government. See *American Annual Cyclopedia*, 1862, p. 456; also pp. 454, 465.

[2] Total to date.

[3] R. A. Bayley, *op. cit.*, p. 158, states that at the end of March the net temporary loan stood at $18.8 millions. The *New York Tribune* financial column, April 14, 1862, states that on April 12th the total deposits stood at $18 millions. These are much larger amounts than those given by Chandler's figures at that date. If Bayley and the *Tribune* are correct the plan is shown to be even more effective. Chandler's figures are the more conservative.

[4] The amounts here shown in excess of the authorized limit of $50 millions are presumably due to deposits received by the treasury on authority of the secretary and before Congress authorized such additional deposits.

S. Coe, that "it had become necessary and desirable that United States demand treasury notes be made a basis for the settlement of balances at the clearing house"; and it recommended four different methods by which this could be done.[1] It was finally decided to use for such a basis, to the extent of $20 millions, the certificates of temporary deposit which, in return for the deposit of demand treasury notes, were to be issued by the assistant treasurer in convenient and special form, payable to any member of the New York Clearing House Association. The clearing house loan certificates, which were now to be displaced, bore 7 per cent interest, thus leaving the banks no inducement to expand their loans, even at 7 per cent, if thereby they became debtors at the clearing house. The effect of this new plan was to relieve the money market at once by furnishing an outlet for the demand treasury notes, and by enabling the banks to make loans at 6 per cent to 7 per cent, paying 5 per cent only on their certificates when thrown debtor at the clearing house.[2]

The interior banks were not long in learning the advantages of a loan in this form, and as early as March 12th we find their deposits with the sub-treasurer at New York making up a part of the total of $800,000 for the day.[3]

Now it is important to observe that, considered from the point of view of their supposed urgent necessity, the issue of the United States notes (greenbacks) authorized by the act of February 25 was long delayed. The contract for engraving and printing was not awarded until March 10, and no issues actually reached the sub-treasury at New York until the first week in April.[4] By April 12th greenbacks in large denominations were being issued, and, not circulating freely, accumulated in

[1] *New York Tribune*, financial column, March 10, 1862. The legal tender notes were afterwards used in the same way.

[2] The whole amount authorized by Congress at this time was $25 millions. On March 11th clearings were made exclusively in the 5 per cent certificates of temporary deposits. See *New York Tribune*, March 8 and 12, 1862.

[3] *Ibid.*, March 13, 1862.

[4] *Boston Advertiser*, April 7, 1862, and *New York Tribune*, April 7, 1862. In the *Tribune* of April 1st we find a statement that the notes are ready to forward to Washington.

the banks, which immediately placed them to the extent of nearly one million dollars on deposit with the government at 5 per cent interest. On the single day of April 21st the large sum of $2.3 millions was deposited,[1] and Secretary Chase began to consider the reduction of the rate of interest to 4 per cent. An order to that effect was issued April 25th, an exception being made in the case of clearing house banks since they extended the use of certificates of deposit for purposes of clearings from $20 millions to $40 millions, and since their deposits were likely to prove more permanent than those of other banks and of individuals.

Up to this time less than $3 millions had in the aggregate been withdrawn from deposit; and on Saturday, May 3rd, the assistant treasurer in New York ceased paying 5 per cent interest. The deposits on the preceding day were the largest any single day had yet afforded, amounting to $2.7 millions,[2] and several large lots offered on May 3rd at 5 per cent were refused by the government. From all appearances a loan from this source might have been carried on rapidly to the $100-million mark.[3] Secretary Chase had not been inclined to ask Congress to extend the $50-million limit for deposits set by the law, as he anticipated that the public would soon begin the conversion of the greenbacks into 5–20 bonds.[4] Conversions on the whole were small in amount, however, and on June 7th Chase addressed a letter[5] to the ways and means committee in which he recommended the removal of the restriction on deposits. The 5–20 bonds were not selling at that time (i.e. aside from conversions),

[1] Since the deposits were made largely after the first week in April in the new legal tender notes (greenbacks), it may seem that the temporary loan could not have existed on such a large scale without these notes. This does not, however, follow. The deposits could have been made just as advantageously in the treasury notes provided for in the plan of the minority of the ways and means committee. For this plan see *infra.*, p. 52 *et seq.*

[2] *New York Tribune*, May 3, 1862.

[3] *Ibid.*, May 5, 1862.

[4] *Ibid.*, May 6, 1862.

[5] House Misc. Docs., No. 81, 37 Cong., 2 Sess. (This document is wrongly dated. It should be June 7th and not April 7th. See *Congressional Globe*, 37 Cong., 2 Sess., pp. 2768, 2886); and Spaulding, *op. cit.*, pp. 154, 158, 159.

and the treasury was dependent upon conversions and customs receipts, both of which sources yielded but $380,000 daily, while the expenditures exceeded $1 million daily.[1] By the act of July 11, 1862, Congress raised the deposit limit to $100 millions and left the rate of interest to the discretion of the secretary.[2]

The deposit system thus created formed a savings bank of the safest description, where any person having one hundred dollars or more of greenbacks or demand treasury notes could obtain a negotiable government security which, while he kept it, paid him 5 per cent[3] interest, and could be sold or redeemed at any time after ten days' notice.[4] Moreover by patronizing the system a patriotic service was rendered. The ordinary channels of investment were more or less closed, and after the deposit limit was reached the accumulation of funds in the banks which could not be used except at very low figures proved an embarrassment.[5] The conditions prevailing during the experiment to the latter part of June, at least, make it evident that if the government had continued to pay a reasonable rate of interest the amount of deposits could have reached a large sum. The system worked much better than had been anticipated;[6] but no sooner was it evident that the people had funds to lend under proper conditions and at a proper rate than Secretary Chase, instead of having the deposit limit raised by a simple amendment, crippled the plan by reducing the rate and attempting to force holders of loanable funds to convert the greenbacks into 5–20 bonds. The desire to put the debt in a permanent form by conversions into 5–20 bonds was laudable

[1] Spaulding, *op. cit.*, p. 154.

[2] By the act of January 30, 1864, the limit was raised to $150 millions. At one time these deposits amounted to over $149 millions. See Bayley, *National Loans of the United States*, p. 158.

[3] He received 5 per cent interest until May 3, 1862, then 4 per cent on all deposits made thereafter.

[4] Cf. *New York Tribune*, April 14, 1862.

[5] *Ibid.*, May 12, 1862. Several causes, however, began to operate to relieve this embarrassment. The banks used greenbacks directly for clearing purposes, the small denominations began to circulate freely as currency, and the larger ones formed a medium of exchange between the West and the Atlantic cities.

[6] Cf. speeches by Chandler and Fessenden in the Senate, June 18, 1862.

enough in itself, but if conditions were not favorable for it the plan must be considered as ill-advised at the time. The banks were beginning to hoard the certificates bearing 5 per cent interest, and were using greenbacks directly for clearing purposes. If 5 per cent interest had been continued the banks would have continued their deposits.[1]

We conclude, therefore, that temporary deposits afforded a means of borrowing by the government on favorable terms and that the plan was similar to the operation of a bank in paying interest on deposits and using the funds so received as a source of profit.

During these operations there were finally brought into existence $150 millions of circulating treasury notes, partly legal tender (greenbacks) and partly demand notes of July, 1861. That the legal tender quality was not necessary for the success of the temporary deposit plan of borrowing is evidenced by the fact that the demand treasury notes of 1861 which were not a legal tender were used indiscriminately with the legal tender notes after the appearance of the latter in April.[2] It is safe to assume, therefore, that the non-legal-tender treasury notes proposed in the plan of the minority[3] of the ways and means committee would have served in this capacity precisely as well as the legal tender greenbacks. As these notes accumulated in the treasury in the form of temporary deposits they were sent to all parts of the Northern states in payment to troops for supplies and for other expenses of the government. It was estimated by such men as Senator Chandler that, with fair inducements to return to the treasury for deposit such as prevailed in the early spring of 1862, they should complete the circuit out from the treasury and back again in about thirty

[1] *New York Tribune*, June 28, 1862.

[2] The demand notes were sought more eagerly than the legal tenders, since the former were receivable for import duties. The non-legal-tender quality of the demand notes acted in no way as a hindrance to their use in making temporary deposits. They were the only medium used in making those deposits before the appearance of greenbacks, and were used after the appearance of the latter whenever they could be secured.

[3] See *infra.*, p. 52 *et seq.*

days. With the employment of no more than $150 millions of non-legal-tender treasury notes in this way, and with the maintenance of a reserve of 15 per cent to meet withdrawals, a loan could have been effected which would net the government more than the entire amount of the legal tender notes authorized by all of the legal tender acts of February and July, 1862, and March, 1863. In answer to a possible objection that the deposit system had worked well because the people had confidence in it, and that this confidence would have been destroyed by largely increasing the deposits, it is to be said that the authority to sell $500 millions of 5–20 bonds at the market price, and the power of Congress to make further issues of treasury notes of the description recommended by the minority of the ways and means committee, could be relied upon to meet any extraordinary demand on the part of the public and the banks for repayment of the deposits.

The certificates of indebtedness which were authorized by the act of March 1, 1862, formed another means by which the governmet was enabled, during the greater part of the calendar year 1862, to borrow on favorable terms. These certificates could be issued "in satisfaction of audited and settled demands against the United States," were payable one year after date or earlier, and bore interest at the rate of 6 per cent. The important part which they played at a time when the secretary of the treasury felt that he had no resources at hand and when none of the authorized United States notes had yet been issued can be appreciated from the fact that in the fourteen days ending April 1 they were issued to the extent of $30.2 millions in satisfaction of pressing claims against the government.[1] Selling at 96 per cent to 97 per cent, they were, at the close of the first week in April, attracting a large amount of capital from the financial centres and from the country because they were paying a higher rate of interest than was usual for investments in government securities.[2]

[1] *Boston Advertiser*, April 2, 1862. On June 30, 1862, certificates of indebtedness were outstanding to the amount of $49.8 millions. See Finance Report, 1862, p. 31.

[2] *New York Tribune*, April 7 and 17, 1862.

These two resources of temporary deposits and of certificates of indebtedness worked so well that, on the one hand, little inclination showed itself for conversion of United States notes into the long 5–20 bonds, and, on the other, they provided the treasury temporarily with means, which, with the small revenues, were its only resource for a considerable period. With more dexterous handling these devices could doubtless have rendered important service in warding off the issue of legal tender notes.

Taxation

As a more permanent and fundamental means of avoiding the issue of greenbacks still greater importance attaches to the policy of the treasury in regard to taxation. Mr. Chase was appointed to the treasury portfolio for political reasons rather than for his skill in finance. Of the duties in this field he had no knowledge and no opportunity for preparation. President Lincoln, while aware of his staunch character and great abilities, selected him as the representative of a large wing of his supporters at the election of November, 1860, and as one of his chief rivals for the presidency. Cameron, the secretary of war, did not share Lincoln's confidence to the extent which was meted out to Chase and to Secretary Seward. So it happened in the spring of 1861 when troops, especially those of the West, were to be raised and organized, it was easy for Chase to take much of the responsibility for this work upon himself. This was not distasteful to Lincoln, and Chase was spurred on by his own notion that the administration in general would fare better in his hands than in those of the President. Throughout the war he continued his interest in the movements of the army, carried on a large correspondence with commanders, and held such a position in military affairs that officers and politicians persistently sought his influence.[1]

This great amount of labor rendered outside of his own department cannot but have taken time and thought which,

[1] A. B. Hart, *Salmon P. Chase*, Boston and New York, 1889, chap. 8; and Hugh McCulloch, *Men and Measures of Half a Century*, New York, 1889, pp. 181–187.

as after events at least have proved, were sorely needed within it. Although Chase in the first months of the war did a vast amount of work in the treasury department perfecting its internal organization, he did not bring to it those larger considerations of a finance minister which would lead to a proper anticipation of future needs and to a comprehensive and well-digested scheme of finance. If in the early days of his incumbency he had brought the zeal and wisdom spent upon military matters to an analysis of the shortcomings as well as the successes in the financiering of the War of 1812, and if he had acquainted himself with some leading examples of war financiering in other countries, his services would have been greater, and his influence over Congress would not have been jeopardized within a year by want of definite and adequate plans.

It is poor excuse for this error on the part of a finance minister that few men, during the spring and summer of 1861, thought of heavy taxation as a necessity for the future. While no general anxiety was exhibited on the part of the country for heavy taxation during those months, and while general acquiescence in Chase's proposals in his report of July 4 was evident, the autumn was not far advanced when the public, represented by the press, bankers, and boards of trade, began to see earlier and more clearly than did Chase or congressmen that resort to heavy taxation was a necessary step in securing support for the government. Indeed, as early as July and August some newspapers, the most influential in their respective communities,[1] advocated this policy. On October 30 the Philadelphia *North American and United States Gazette* represented a growing sentiment when it urged the cessation of dependence upon large loans and advocated provision for a regular income sufficient to meet the wants of the government.[2]

[1] See Cincinnati *Gazette*, July 9 and 20, 1861, and *Boston Advertiser*, July 13, 1861, on the ability of the country to sustain heavy taxation. And see resolutions of the New York Chamber of Commerce, August 1, 1861, in *Hunt's Merchants' Magazine*, Vol. XLV., pp. 319, 320.

[2] Issue of October 30, 1861. On November 2 the *North American and United States Gazette* (Philadelphia) quoted from other papers—e.g. the New York *World*—in agreement with its position.

After Congress assembled in December the outside pressure was very heavy to induce it really to do something in this matter.[1] Editors pointed out repeatedly that so far there had been no real taxation, and it was declared that "this hesitancy, like timid surgery, can only lead to a fatal result." The great question of the arrangement of a system of finance, however, did not offer much scope for brilliant speeches addressed to the galleries and to distant constituencies; but it called for hard thought, close calculation, and sober reasoning. These were the efforts that the country wanted without delay. Yet Congress persisted at this crisis in spending time in criticizing military leaders and in pressing its claims of privilege to secure information on military affairs when by so doing it endangered the great movements of the war. Under these circumstances the *Boston Advertiser*[2] assured members of Congress that, if they wished to maintain their authority with the country and to earn its regard, "they must do this by addressing themselves earnestly to the great topic of government finance which oppresses every reflecting citizen. To put the truth in plain terms, however, there is a rapidly increasing feeling that Congress is afraid to deal decisively with this great subject. Taxation, heavy and universal, is felt to be the only solution for our present difficulties, and it is whispered that members dislike to come before their constituents with a long tax bill. . . . The only true prudence at such a moment lies in action. He recommends himself most to the public who grapples with questions like this boldly and confidently, and who dares to say to the people that the time has come when they must consent to feel the pressure of the war which they are carrying on."

Another argument urged in favor of heavy taxation was based upon the wasteful and corrupt expenditures by the government, of which Secretary Chase, at times, bitterly complains. There was a feeling on the part of many that increased taxation

[1] *Boston Advertiser*, January 1, 1862; New York *Journal of Commerce*, December 31, 1861; *New York Tribune*, January 15, 1862; Philadelphia *North American and United States Gazette*, January 2, 1862; New York Chamber of Commerce, January 2, 1862, in *Hunt's Merchants' Magazine*, Vol. XLVI, p. 146.

[2] Issue for January 11, 1862.

would cause the people to watch expenditures more closely and would cause officials to reduce them by an appreciable amount.[1]

It was such pressure as this, enforced by a keen sense of disappointment from the fact that Secretary Chase had failed to propose an adequate revenue system in his December report, which drove Congress, whose almost irresistible tendency was to place sole reliance upon credit devices, to pass the tardy resolution of January 15, 1862, pledging itself to raise at some future time $150 millions from internal taxation. Even in this step of promissory resolution Congress fell short of the hopes of some parts of the country and it was urged that Congress should "avail itself of the present favorable disposition of the country for the benefit of the treasury."[2] Nevertheless this was the first important step in the right direction which was taken in the matter of the financial needs of the country. Although everyone knew that the credit of the government must be relied upon to supply the immediate needs of the treasury, a thorough conviction[3] now existed throughout the country that taxation lay at the root of the whole problem, and that it must be definitely determined upon before other and immediate resources could be made properly productive.

Within a few days after Congress had pledged itself by the resolution of January 15th the fear became prevalent that, in the face of that pledge, it tended toward excessive boldness in relying upon credit and toward a corresponding timidity in taxing.[4] There seemed to be a general willingness to *enact* that 6 per cent bonds and demand notes should be worth par and a disposition to rely upon such enactments. It became necessary, therefore, that the press and other influential institutions should continue to brace up a weak-kneed Congress. Little was heard, save in the English press and in Washington,

[1] *Boston Advertiser*, January 13, 1862.

[2] *Ibid.*, January 17, 1862.

[3] *Ibid*, January 7 and 17, 1862.

[4] *Ibid.*, January 23, 1862, and the New York *Journal of Commerce*, January 29, 1862; Philadelphia *North American and United States Gazette*, January 21, 1862; *New York Tribune*, January 15 and 22, 1862; and the Report of American Geographical and Statistical Society, January 23, 1862, in *Banker's Magazine*, Vol. XI, p. 705.

as to the unwillingness of the people to be taxed; but instead of the existence of such a feeling the country presented a spectacle of a people praying to be taxed. The public had come to a clear perception of the burden it invoked, and had made up its mind to assume that burden from a deliberate consideration of the ends it was to serve.[1]

In the midst of such earnest efforts in urging Congress to action in this matter it is disappointing to find, during the first days of February and before the introduction of any measure for taxation, that Secretary Chase pressed the necessity of the immediate passage of the bill to issue United States notes (greenbacks) and that Congress finally passed it with the legal tender clause included. Bankers knew long before Congress met in December that under Chase's policy there was danger of suspension. Thus several months had gone by with nothing accomplished towards providing in taxation a basis for treasury operations. With the conditions of the case fully known for so long a period, and with the people in an attitude of praying to be taxed, it seems evident that slight excuse existed for pressing the necessity of a legal tender paper money upon the country, even with the knowledge that the treasury was almost empty.

In answer to the excuse for delay that a tax bill required time for framing, it was pointed out at the time that this excuse was "more specious than substantial," and that there was nothing to prevent the immediate preparation and passage of a bill laying an excise upon distilled spirits, malt liquors, and tobacco. These were articles that were certain to be taxed

[1] *Boston Advertiser*, February 4 and 5, and March 8; New York *Journal of Commerce*, April 29; New York *Shipping and Commercial List*, February 26; Philadelphia *North American and United States Gazette*, February 6; speech of Hooper in the House of Representatives, February 3—all of 1862. The London *Spectator* claims that its American correspondent traveled extensively over the country, and that he found the West, upon the whole, anxious for taxation. See *Spectator*, March 1, 1862. It is stated in Appleton's *Annual Cyclopedia*, 1862, p. 460, that it was the direct tax which formed the great source of complaint in the West, since it fell too heavily upon the farmer. See Thomas McI. Cooley, *Michigan*, (Commonwealth series), Boston, 1885, p. 340, for the attitude of Michigan people in favor of giving the government support.

heavily; hence there was no apparent necessity for waiting to adjust them in a complex scheme. Such a bill, drawn for the express purpose of securing revenue to be applied to the payment of interest in order to strengthen the government's credit, should have been passed instead of the less fruitful resolution of January 15, for it would have covered the case in point.[1]

The tax bill which was finally brought into the House[2] was permitted to drift until the public mind was drawn off by military successes and repelled by the undigested form in which the bill was finally passed by the House. By the latter part of April there was danger that the public, once so clamorous to see it pushed to completion, would become content to let the measure take its course.[3] This feeling was reënforced by an advance in government securities which was in greater part the result of the temporarily brighter prospects of the war. Secretary Chase himself at this late hour sent a long-promised bill for taxation to the senate finance committee, but the committee laid it aside, deeming it easier to amend the House bill than "to lick that of the Secretary into shape."[4] At this juncture the press and boards of trade began to din at Congress to remember that pay day would come even though military success continued.[5] This influence, together with changes in the fortunes of war for the worse, induced the final enactment of the bill on July 1, 1862—a twelvemonth after plans for this end should rightfully have taken shape in the hands of the secretary of the treasury.

In view of such a record of influence brought to bear by constituencies on a reluctant secretary and Congress, there is little room for doubt that, with initiative and leadership on their

[1] *Boston Advertiser*, February 11, 1862.

[2] The tax bill was not introduced until March 4, and it passed the House April 8.

[3] *Boston Advertiser*, April 24, 1862.

[4] This tax bill submitted by Chase had the merit of taxing a few articles heavily and with such a selection that the burden would be shifted to a large portion of the population. See London *Spectator*, April 5, 1862. The plan pursued by Chase in this regard had been advocated by Dunbar in the *Boston Advertiser* from the beginning.

[5] New York *World*, May 1, 1862; New York *Journal of Commerce*, April 29, 1862; New York Chamber of Commerce, April 24, 1862, in *Bankers' Magazine* for June, 1862, Vol. XI, p. 913.

part, the latter could have successfully levied heavy taxation in the autumn of 1861.

The Sale of Bonds

The policy pursued in the sale of bonds was as deplorable as that in regard to taxation. Means to support the government should have come both from taxation and from the sale of bonds. The success of the latter would have been, in any case, largely influenced by the adequacy of the former. If taxation were inadequate and the credit of the government consequently poor, the only alternative was to sell bonds at a corresponding sacrifice.

England's attitude toward the North during the early months of the war was not such as to hold out a prospect for a loan in the London market. The London *Times* exhibited great zeal in inspiring the English mind with a sense of the recklessness of the North, in view of its alleged slender resources, in attempting to quell the Southern rebellion.[1] In the earlier days of the conflict the London *Economist*, while not precisely hostile to the North, believed that it was impossible for her to overcome the South, and that to go to war "to reunite a community of free states to a set of slave states, from which Providence offered them the happy chance of an immediate disjunction," was the height of folly.[2] The tone of the English press in general was such as to afford little prospect of a foreign loan.[3] Secretary Seward's reckless language and undiplomatic proceedings in the conduct of our relations with England tended to increase the existing ill-feeling.[4] As the year wore on the attitude of the English people at large was different. Although the American diplomatic tone disgusted the taste and offended

[1] *Boston Advertiser*, September 12, 1861. For representative editorials of the attitude of the London *Times*, see issues of May 21 and 30, June 5 and 11, August 7 and 28, 1861.

[2] London *Economist*, July 27 and August 17, 1861.

[3] *Boston Advertiser*, August 17, 1861.

[4] James F. Rhodes, *History of the United States*, New York, 1895, Vol. III, p. 423 *et seq.*

the moral sense of the aristocracy, the majority of the English people, if not pro-Northern, was heartily hostile to the South.[1]

In the late summer and autumn of 1861, therefore, there was little in the attitude of a considerable section of the English investing public which prevented its purchase of our securities on the score of political or moral feeling.[2] If no market for them existed the explanation is to be found in other causes. During this same period there was a prevalent hope on our part that a considerable portion of the loans authorized by Congress in July and August might be placed in Europe and especially in England. This hope was indulged by Secretary Chase,[3] by Congress,[4] by the associated bankers,[5] and by large portions of the public.[6] In fact, we have some reports of actual purchase and shipment, on a small scale, of 7–30 treasury notes on European account and of inquiries concerning them from personages of high standing abroad. In September the great banking house of Barings expressed the opinion that the English people would be glad to take a part of the securities which the associated banks had assumed.[7]

Whatever may have been the prospect of an English loan before the middle of November, 1861, the unfortunate occur-

[1] *Spectator* (London), November 9, 1861, pp. 1225, 1226; also Rhodes's *History of the United States*, Vol. III, p. 247.

[2] London *Economist*, August 24; *Spectator*, August 3 and 17; and *Boston Advertiser*, November 25, 1861, for a letter from an English banker to a Boston friend. Also see a letter of Minister Adams, June 21, quoted by Rhodes, *op. cit.*, Vol. III, p. 430.

[3] See his report of July 4th to Congress.

[4] See the National Loan Act, July 17, 1861.

[5] That the bankers expected loans from abroad is evident from the fact that this body sought to control the entire loan then authorized when rumors were afloat that offers were coming from abroad. See *Boston Advertiser*, November 19, 1861, and London *Economist*, December 14, 1861.

[6] E.g. see *Boston Advertiser*, September 30 and December 17, 1861; Philadelphia *North American and United States Gazette*, July 8, 1861; and New York *Herald*, September 28, 1861.

[7] *Boston Advertiser*, September 16 and November 25, 1861. It was currently reported in October that English capitalists had made an offer to Secretary Chase to take a loan of $100 millions at 6½ per cent. See *ibid.*, October 21 and 22, 1861; New York *Journal of Commerce*, November 15 and 16, 1861; *Spectator* (London), November 2, 1861. There is, however, no satisfactory proof that such an offer was made.

rence of the Trent Affair shut the door, for the time being, to this resource.[1] Two months elapsed before this complication was adjusted, and then the lingering hostile feeling consequent upon disturbed relations made it difficult, even in the absence of hindrances of a purely financial nature, for Englishmen to have confidence in our securities. Foreigners were incredulous as to the ability of the American people to lay burdens upon themselves and to conquer their love of ease and improvidence.[2] To such an extent did this attitude toward us prevail that our bonds were discredited, not so much from fear that the principal would never be paid, as from doubts that we should be willing even to pay the interest.[3] The London *Economist* on February 22, 1862, stated, if "Congress had adopted an efficient system of direct taxation at the outset of the struggle, the European credit of the government might have been preserved. *At a price* they would have got some money, but now they will not get a sixpence in Lombard Street or on the continent, no matter what interest they offer."[4]

But in the early spring of 1862 a better feeling again prevailed. The English aristocracy, from motives founded in social considerations, still desired the success of the Confederate states; but large portions of the class of Englishmen engaged in manufacturing and commercial pursuits, although their chief desire was for the termination of the war that they might secure cotton, did not share this hostility toward the North. At the same time the Northern forces gained some important victories over the South, thus raising the credit of the government at Washington. As a result of these circumstances England did not present at that time an impossible market for our securities.[5]

[1] *Ante*, p. 10, and see *Boston Advertiser*, December 13, 17, and 19, 1861; and London *Economist*, December 28, 1861. The Confederate Commissioners, Mason and Slidell, were captured November 8th. The news reached New York November 16th, and London November 28th. The matter was not adjusted until January 8, 1862.

[2] *Boston Advertiser*, May 3, 1862; London *Economist*, September 7, 1861; London *Spectator*, December 28, 1861 and March 1, 1862.

[3] *Spectator*, March 1, 1862.

[4] This was written before the Northern victories of February and March were known, and applied to conditions of the winter of 1861–62.

[5] For the favorable change of English attitude, see James F. Rhodes, *History of the United States*, New York, 1906, Vol. IV, p. 76 *et seq.*, and also the financial

If England, therefore, afforded a market for our bonds within the period ending June 30, 1862, it must have done so either in the autumn of 1861, preceding the Trent Affair, or in the early spring of 1862. That the former period was the more favorable is unquestionable, and that we failed to secure the market in either period was evidently due to the absence of proper financial management.

Second only in importance to the failure to create an adequate system of taxation at the outset of the struggle was this failure to sell bonds for what they would fetch in the foreign market in the autumn of 1861. The relief derived from such a loan would have been important, the encouragement to the North of great value, and another influence would have been added to those already working in our favor abroad. No doubt such a policy would have required great sacrifice in rates. This would have been unfortunate though not discreditable. The sale of bonds at the required sacrifice would have supplied the funds needed at the time, and the associated banks which had crippled themselves with the $150-million loan to the government would have been in strong condition to give support to the treasury in the trying days of February, 1862.[1]

In relation to domestic loans, also, this same error of unwillingness on the part of the government to pay a sufficiently high rate of interest was not without great importance. There were, to be sure, some real hindrances of an administrative nature which made the progress of the popular loan difficult in the fall of 1861. It required time to acquaint the people at large with the conditions and with the desires of the govern-

column of the *New York Tribune*, March 20, 1862; and the London *Economist*, March 29, 1862. Later in the year 1862 the English attitude was not so favorable.

[1] *Boston Advertiser*, December 28, 1861. See also Fessenden's speech in the Senate, February 12, 1862, *Congressional Globe* for 1862, pp. 763, 764. Among others more obvious and familiar, there were two influences of greater or less importance—the product of narrow views—which were thrown against this policy. First, there was a suspicion that the banks would profit by it. See Hooper, speech in the House, January 19, 1863. Second, there was a feeling on the part of many that America was too great and independent to need to resort to a foreign loan. See Philadelphia *Press*, August 7, 1861.

ment relative to the loan. The establishment of local sales-agencies was slow. It became necessary to issue certificates as temporary substitutes for the 7–30 treasury notes since on account of the long delay in engraving and issuing them these notes did not appear until January, and it proved awkward to ask plain people to take the substitutes. But in spite of these hindrances, to say nothing of the larger considerations affecting the public credit, a strong sentiment existed[1] in favor of investing in bonds, thus relieving the banks of their $150-million loan. One is forced to the conclusion that at somewhat better rates than the government was then willing to offer large amounts of a popular loan could have been placed. Again in March, 1862, when government securities grew stronger with the tide of Northern victories, Chase became hopeful of procuring through loans all the means needed.[2] But at this juncture he made the surprising complaint that bonds could not be sold at their "market price." He meant that he could not sell bonds at the market price without causing a decline and that therefore he had no authority to sell at that price. That this was a gross misinterpretation of the second section of the act of February 25, 1862, is clear from the debates in Congress on that measure. As a consequence of this false notion he refused to take advantage of the favorable situation.

Thus we see that Chase and Congress in the autumn, and Chase alone in the spring, failed to take advantage of opportunities to secure necessary funds because it was considered beneath the dignity of the government to sell its bonds at a discount. The standing of bonds in the market in the period from January 1, 1861, to July 1, 1862, considered in connection with the slender basis of credit afforded by the small revenues of the government, was good and does not justify this policy. The government could have afforded a discount. An examination of

[1] *Boston Advertiser*, August 26, September 17 and 23, 1861; Philadelphia *Press*, September 14, 1861; Philadelphia *North American and United States Gazette*, September 5 and 9, 1861.

[2] *Boston Advertiser*, March 21 and 24, 1862; and *New York Tribune*, March 25, 1862.

the table given in the note below[1] shows the natural fall in the value of bonds at the outbreak of the war, touching as low as 86 on April 20, 1861. After some slight recovery another fall to $83\frac{1}{2}$ came in June. This marks the lowest quotation of the period. They rise to 90 in September and do not fall below that

[1] Table exhibiting quotations of the sixes of 1867 and 1868, and the sixes of 1881, from January 1861 to July 1862. The quotations are compiled from the *Banker's Magazine*, Vol. X, pp. 671, 839, 919, 947; Vol. XI, pp. 79, 239, 319, 479, 655, 831, 911, 973; Vol. XII, pp. 91 and 239. The quotations from January 5 to September 21, 1861, are those of the sixes of 1867 and 1868. The remainder, beginning with September 28, 1861, are those of the sixes of 1881.

Year	Month	Day	Quotation
1861	January	5	97
		11	100
		18	97
		25	98
	February	1	97
		8	95
		15	95
		22	94
	March	2	94
		16	$95\frac{7}{8}$
		23	98
		30	95
	April	6	95
		13	$93\frac{1}{4}$
		20	86
		27	$87\frac{1}{2}$
	May	4	$88\frac{1}{2}$
		11	89
		18	$88\frac{1}{2}$
		25	88
	June	1	$86\frac{5}{8}$
		8	$83\frac{3}{4}$
		15	$83\frac{3}{4}$
		22	$83\frac{1}{2}$
		29	84
	July	6	$85\frac{1}{4}$
		13	89
		20	$89\frac{1}{2}$
		30	88
	August	13	$86\frac{3}{4}$
		20	87
		27	$87\frac{1}{2}$
	September	3	88
		10	90
		21	90
		28	$91\frac{1}{8}$
	October	5	92
		12	$93\frac{5}{8}$
		23	$94\frac{1}{4}$
		30	94
	November	7	94
		14	$95\frac{1}{8}$
		21	$93\frac{1}{2}$
		27	$93\frac{1}{2}$
	December	5	$93\frac{1}{8}$
		12	$92\frac{7}{8}$
		19	89
		31	$91\frac{3}{4}$
1862	January	10	90
		20	91
	February	1	$88\frac{1}{2}$
		10	$90\frac{1}{2}$
		20	90
	March	1	$92\frac{3}{4}$
		10	$92\frac{5}{8}$
		20	94
	April	1	$93\frac{3}{8}$
		10	$93\frac{7}{8}$
		21	$93\frac{3}{4}$
	May	1	98
		10	104
		20	$104\frac{1}{8}$
	June	2	106
		11	$106\frac{1}{4}$
		21	$106\frac{1}{8}$
	July	1	$102\frac{3}{4}$

point except twice during the remainder of the period. On the first of May, 1862 the rise to 98 indicates a real improvement in the government's credit, the average premium on gold for April and May amounting to 2.4 per cent.

The following table exhibits the revenues, expenditures, and the increase of debt of the government for the fiscal years ending June 30, 1861, and June 30, 1862:

	(Millions of dollars)	
Revenues	*1861*[1]	*1862*[2]
From customs	39.5	49.0
From lands	.9	.1
From miscellaneous sources	.9	.9
From direct taxes	....	1.7
Total	41.3	51.9
Expenditures		
For ordinary civil list	23.1	21.4
For pensions and Indians	3.8	3.1
For interest on public debt	4.0	13.1
For war department	22.9	394.3
For navy department	12.4	42.6
Total	66.3	474.7

Total indebtedness, June 30, 1861, 90.8;[3] June 30, 1862, 514.2[4]

The important items of securities issued which represent the increase of indebtedness during the fiscal year ending June 30, 1862, are:[5]

7–30 treasury notes	$122.0 millions
Sixes of 1881	50.0
5–20 bonds (through conversions)	13.9
Demand notes	60.0
United States notes (greenbacks)	98.6
Temporary deposits	57.9
Certificates of indebtedness	49.8

An examination of these statistics reveals the insignificant increase in the revenues for the fiscal year 1862 over those for 1861, while the ratio of revenues for 1862 ($51.9 millions) to

[1] Annual Report of the Secretary of the Treasury, 1861, pp. 30–32.

[2] *Ibid.*, 1862, pp. 31, 32.

[3] *Ibid.*, 1861, p. 298.

[4] *Ibid.*, 1862, p. 44.

[5] *Ibid.*, 1862, pp. 31, 32.

the total expenditures for that year ($474.7 millions) is very low, not quite 11 per cent.

With the existence of such conditions it was folly to hope, as did Secretary Chase and many leading members of Congress, that United States securities bearing a comparatively low rate of interest should sell at or near par. Eighty-nine per cent of the expenditures had to be met by means of the government's credit. With these conditions and this attitude of mind prevailing it is not surprising, though not creditable, that a resort to the legal tender issues was made. Later on, however, when the greenbacks had depreciated to a sufficient degree to enable investors to purchase bonds at prices which would properly compensate them for the risk undertaken, the secretary and others were willing to sell them for seventy-five, fifty, and even thirty-five cents in gold—such was the depreciation of greenbacks for which the securities sold at par. At these prices the government sold bonds freely.

Bankers' Plans

It was obvious in the summer of 1861 that the currency needed attention. Impending political events were so absorbing that due attention has seldom been paid to the commercial crisis of 1860. Yet that crisis was severe enough to force banks, especially those in the West, into bankruptcy. Few hesitated to admit that as a consequence of the crisis an appreciable proportion of the circulating medium of the country had dropped out of existence. This produced a more or less marked vacuum in the currency. Such a condition, considered in connection with the heterogeneous character of the state banks and their issues, caused anxiety for the future. Many proposals for improvement of the currency were therefore presented to the secretary of the treasury. One of these proposals deserves attention as having offered an easy and practicable escape from embarrassments which overtook the treasury later on.

Mr. O. B. Potter, in a letter[1] of August 14, 1861, addressed

[1] This pamphlet is rare. It was published by Brown and Hewitt, New York, in 1875, with another pamphlet by Potter on the question of resumption.

to Secretary Chase, set forth a plan the important provisions of which are as follows:

1. To permit duly authorized state banks in the loyal states to deposit bonds of the United States government as security for their note issues.

2. To appoint an officer connected with the treasury department whose duty it would be to receive the bonds and issue, in return, notes so signed and stamped as to indicate their character and to differentiate them from all other bank notes.

3. To confer authority upon such superintendent, in case a bank should fail to redeem its notes, to sell the bonds and apply the proceeds to the payment of the notes.

The possibilities of this plan were important. It presented the merits of simplicity, safety, avoidance of a violent break with existing institutions, and of being based upon experience in some of the states. It was simple in its requirements, calling merely for a superintendent or comptroller who would issue uniform notes on deposit of bonds and sell the bonds for purposes of redemption when occasion demanded. The issues would have been as safe as those under the later national banking system since they would have been founded upon the same principle. It avoided any violent change because the banks would continue their existence under state charters administered by state officers. And to disarm criticism which might be justly lodged against *a priori* conceptions in the field of banking, Potter could point to the success of the system of note issues in the state of New York. Furthermore, it placed the responsibility of redeeming the circulation upon the banks and not upon the government as was the case with the greenbacks.

If this plan or a similar one had been adopted early, it would have furnished a safe medium of exchange for the country, and one by which the government could receive revenues and loans and make payments. Chase would have been deprived of the excuse for giving to the act of August 5th a faulty interpretation which prevented him from setting aside the rigid features of the sub-treasury system requiring transactions with the government to be made in specie only. He would not then have been confronted with the alternative of receiving and making payments in coin or in questionable bank notes. Chase had apparently conceived against bank issues the strong prejudice then existing among certain classes in the West. With this overcome by an acceptable and practicable system of issues, the next step would have been an easy and natural one. The problem confronting the secretary and the associated banks was to transfer, with the least possible disturbance to the existing machinery of exchange, materials of war and provisions for the army to the government from the hands of those in control of processes of production. As explained in Chapter I, different members of the associated bankers[1] repeatedly set before Chase the necessity of utilizing the check and clearing house system as a means of effecting this transfer if he would avoid draining specie from the banks and depriving them of their ability to give the very aid which he sought. Consequently they urged him to suspend the operation of the Sub-Treasury Act in so far as it interfered with this procedure and to draw directly on specified banks in favor of government creditors. His checks in this way would afford a medium of exchange, coin would be left in the banks as a basis of the system as in ordinary commercial transactions, and the tendency to hoard coin usually present in periods of disturbance would be discouraged. Chase refused to be persuaded and turned his back upon the highly developed bank-credit system which was as much an essential part of modern methods of exchange as the railway was of modern methods of transportation. It would have been easier for him to accept this system had greater familiarity with banking conditions and freedom from fear of spurious note issues been secured through the adoption and use of a system such as the Potter plan proposed. Unfortu-

[1] E.g. James Gallatin, speech at a meeting of bank officers, December 28, 1861, *Bankers' Magazine*, Vol. XI, p. 625. Also *ibid.*, p. 631, for a letter, December 14, 1861, to Fessenden in which he refers to his efforts to give information to Chase. See also G. S. Coe, letter in Spaulding, *op. cit.*, Appendix, 2nd ed., p. 91. And letters of J. E. Williams, *ibid.*, pp. 97, 98.

nately, Chase gave this plan no consideration at the time.[1] Whether this neglect was due to pressure of other duties in the treasury department, or to diverting his attention to military affairs for the sake of selfish political ends, or to the fact that he failed to see the feasibility of the plan, is now a question of minor importance.

Late in December, when suspension was close at hand, bankers, in order to continue specie payments, made an effort to institute a second plan[2] on the lines of the Potter proposal. They held $40 millions in specie and $150 millions of government bonds, and they proposed on this basis to issue notes stamped or signed by an officer of the federal government, the banks in other respects remaining under state control. With such an issue, "at once simple and expeditious," they felt that it would be practicable for them to continue their advances to the government. But this, as other proposals of those bankers who had sought to make common cause with the secretary, met with no favor and suspension was declared.

In refusing to make use of bank credit either in the form of reformed note-issues or of deposits Chase assumed that, in spite of his confessed[3] ignorance of monetary and financial matters, he understood better than men trained by long experience how to make great transfers of property with the greatest advantage to the government, the public, and the banks. In the light of later developments it is clear that undue weight was given to his opinion and that the banks would have served the nation better by pressing their desire to have the Sub-

[1] See a statement to this effect in Potter's Pamphlet of 1875, addressed to Secretary Bristow *et al.* This plan was made a part of the first National Bank Act (February 25, 1863), sections 62, 63, and 64. Hugh McCulloch, in his report of November, 1863, as Comptroller of the Currency, recommends the repeal of this feature of the act on the grounds that "it contemplates the mixing of two systems that ought to be independent." McCulloch's objection, however, would not apply to the conditions in 1861, before the national banking system was inaugurated. See Comptroller's Report, 1863, pp. 55, 56 in the Report of the Secretary of the Treasury, December, 1863.

[2] See letter of George S. Coe, Spaulding, *op. cit.*, Appendix, 2nd ed., p. 94. Chase received offers at various times to buy bonds on condition that he would receive bank checks in payment. E.g. see *New York Tribune*, June 28, 1862.

[3] See a letter of F. A. Conkling, Spaulding, *op. cit.*, Appendix, 2nd ed., p. 84.

Treasury Act modified and to have ordinary means of payment used in their transactions.

Plan of Minority of the Ways and Means Committee

The argument of necessity for the issue of legal tender paper money could not properly be urged until all other more expedient resources had been exhausted. In spite of the fact that the government had failed to improve the opportunities to secure the means for its support thus far passed in review, there still remained in February (1862), on the eve of the passage of the first legal tender act, an avenue of escape from the greenback issues.

This was offered by the plan of the minority of the ways and means committee[1] which was supported by some of the ablest men in Congress.[2] It provided:

1. For the retention of the $50 millions of demand notes of July 17th.[3]

2. For the issue of $100 millions of 3.65 per cent treasury notes, payable in two years to bearer, in denominations of five dollars and upwards, receivable for all public dues except duties on imports, payable to all creditors of the government at the option of the creditor, convertible into 7–30 coin bonds, and reissuable.

3. For the issue of $500 millions of bonds, partly bearing 7.3 per cent interest and redeemable after ten years, partly bearing 6 per cent interest and redeemable after twenty-four

[1] This minority was in fact composed of one-half of the members of the committee; *viz.*, Morrill, Horton, Corning, and Stratton. As mentioned on a preceding page, Stratton, although opposed to the legal tender issues, consented to vote in favor of reporting the bill (afterwards the act of February 25th) in order that it might be discussed by the House.

[2] Morrill, Roscoe Conkling, and Horton were among its supporters in the House. In the Senate such men as Fessenden, Collamer, and Chandler opposed the legal tender clause of the committee's bill and favored the plan of the minority.

[3] These notes were merely left undisturbed by this plan, no specific provision being called for since they were already in existence. They were considered a part of the plan by the minority.

years, and to be sold for lawful money of United States or for any treasury notes issued.[1]

4. For temporary deposits without limit and with interest at $5\frac{2}{5}$ per cent.

It is important to observe that the total issue of legal tender notes during the war bore, finally, a very small ratio to the total amount of funds received by the government. If we take the period[2] from July, 1861, to July, 1865, we find that at first the treasury was almost empty and that

	(millions)
The ordinary revenues for the period were.......	$ 753.4
The excess borrowed (including the greenback issues) was..................................	2590.1
The amount received by government............	$3343.5
The total amount of legal tender notes (greenbacks)	450.0

From the foregoing statistics we see that the legal tender issues constituted less than one-seventh of the total resources for the period. Again comparing the $2846 millions of the public debt as it stood when at its highest point on August 31, 1865, with the $450 millions of greenbacks, the latter is seen to constitute somewhat more than one-seventh of the total debt. The great bulk of the means to carry on the war came, therefore, through the increase of indebtedness in the form of bonds and interest-bearing treasury notes. The greenbacks did not play an important rôle in the long run.

In view of this situation, two arguments only can be advanced in favor of the legal tender act over the plan of the minority of the ways and means committee: first, that the United States notes (greenbacks) afforded an *immediate* relief to the treasury

[1] In this plan as proposed by the minority of the House committee there was no provision for selling bonds in the market for what they would fetch. The Senate added such a feature to the bill of the majority (i.e. to the bill which became law February 25th), and it is fair to assume that it would have added a similar provision to the plan of the minority.

[2] For revenues see the Finance Reports for the years 1862 to 1865. For statement of the excess borrowed see an announcement issued under date July 2, 1883, by the treasury department, giving an analysis of the public debt.

and therefore met the cry of pressing necessity for funds at the moment; second, that the United States notes afforded the only means of securing a proper circulating medium now that specie payment had been suspended. Neither of these reasons will bear scrutiny. The conclusive answer to the first argument is that the greenbacks did not, as a matter of fact, afford the immediate relief of which the treasury in February stood in need. As we have seen in the preceding pages, these notes did not make their appearance until the first of April, nor did they appear in considerable amounts until still later. The needs of the government were met, beyond the ordinary revenues, by the proceeds from temporary deposits, by certificates of indebtedness, and by permitting requisitions to pile up on the treasurer's desk. It was a well-settled fact as early as October 1, 1861, that severe pressure must come upon the treasury, and it was not until the following April that the greenbacks afforded a resource. The cry of pressing necessity was raised, therefore, when in fact the government had the space of six months in which to mature adequate financial plans, and when the space of more than three months remained from the time the legal tender measure was drawn up[1] by its supporters until relief came from the actual issue of the first greenbacks. In the light of these facts it cannot be said that the legal tender issues were a necessity in February to save the treasury even temporarily from embarrassment.

The second argument is no less applicable than the first to the state of facts. The supreme difficulty all along was found in devising the machinery by which the regular production of the country should be diverted from its usual objects and made available for the government's military purposes.[2] This difficulty presented a double problem—the one, the problem of the government's ability to purchase the products of the nation's industry by means of its revenues and its credit; the other, the problem of choosing a monetary medium by means of which those products might be transferred from the hands of

[1] Spaulding had the measure, in draft, completed by the last of December.

[2] Cf. *Boston Advertiser*, March 5, 1862.

producers to one another or to the army, the navy, and other public consumers. One is a problem of ability to buy goods, the other a problem of the mechanism of exchange. It is the latter question that concerns us at this point.

The commercial crisis of 1860, as we have seen, had resulted, especially in the West, in driving numerous banks to the wall, hence a portion of the bank-note circulation dropped out of existence and a vacuum in the ordinary currency of the country occurred.[1] On the other hand, as a result of the crisis and of the change and uncertainty in the channels of trade consequent upon the existence of war, stagnant conditions in ordinary commercial business prevailed, and in so far the need for currency was curtailed. We may assume that this vacuum was filled by the demand-note issues of July 17, 1861, which could be utilized until the banks were able to supply a larger circulation.

Again, after suspension of specie payment in December, 1861, gold largely although not completely disappeared from circulation. In consequence banks, such as some in New York, which preferred or were compelled to curtail their note issues rather than to refuse to redeem them in coin, tended to reduce the amount of total circulation.[2] The monetary difficulties arising from these conditions were real. The contraction of the bank-note currency thus created prevailed until the greenbacks came into circulation and were used as bank reserves for redemption purposes. Gradually the bank-note circulation and the check and deposit system both expanded.

When the productive forces of the country were fairly started towards supplying war materials, the increased need for currency was similar to a situation under normal conditions where a good year follows a poor one in the business world. In the opinion of the majority in Congress the legal tender issues were

[1] The estimated amount of this falling off varies, but not widely, according to different individuals. Secretary Chase in the Finance Report of 1862, p. 7, places the bank circulation in the loyal states for January 1, 1861, at $150 millions, and for January 1, 1862, at $130 millions. Another estimate is given by Morrill, Spaulding, *op. cit.*, p. 61.

[2] See *infra*, Chapter III, p. 74.

necessary in order to supply bank reserves and to furnish the treasury with a medium with which to purchase supplies and with which the public could buy bonds. But the plan of the minority of the ways and means committee provided for such a medium without entailing upon the public and upon the government itself all of the evils of a forced issue which were involved in the case of the greenbacks. The $50 millions of demand notes already in existence were available in large measure for this purpose, and the $100 millions of 3.65 treasury notes proposed by the minority were well fitted to serve as a medium in transactions of this character.[1] There is no reason in the nature of the cases why these notes should not have served at least as well as the legal tender issues, while withholding the legal tender quality in payments between individuals might have exercised a wholesome restraint over the tendency to excessive issues.

Conclusion

In examining the conditions under which the United States notes (greenbacks) were issued we have seen that the substitution of Hooper in the place of Appleton on the ways and means committee gave to a legal tender measure a foothold which otherwise it would probably not have secured; that it was the temporary deposits and certificates of indebtedness and not the greenbacks, long delayed in issue, which tided the government over the trying period of February, 1862, and the following weeks; that the entire issue of greenbacks bore a small and comparatively unimportant ratio to the total resources used to carry on the war; that Secretary Chase and Congress made grave mistakes in their policy on taxation and the sale of bonds; and that plans of bankers and of the minority of the ways and means committee, which might have prevented the

[1] The accumulation of interest on the 3.65 treasury notes would have influenced their circulation. They would have found their way to the banks to be used as reserves and as collateral for loans or to be funded into bonds, and they would have been placed on temporary deposit with the government at interest as were the greenbacks which were issued.

issue of greenbacks, were proposed and urged upon the government. In view of this history no adequate grounds existed for urging the necessity of the greenbacks as a means of supporting the government either in the long run or in the emergencies of February and March, 1862.

CHAPTER III

FURTHER ISSUES OF GREENBACKS AND THE STATE OF THE CURRENCY.[1]

The Second Legal Tender Act

True to the predictions of the opponents of paper money, further issues of greenbacks were soon demanded to supplement other sources needed to prosecute the war. In the interval between the first and second legal tender acts, Chase was compelled to rely chiefly upon loans. By the end of the calendar year 1861 expenditures had already reached nearly a million and a quarter dollars per day, with revenues of approximately only one-tenth of that amount. The total receipts from ordinary sources during the six months, January to June, 1862, were $36 millions, but the expenditures approached the sum of $350 millions. This shows a large margin which was in some form covered by borrowing. As we have seen during the first quarter of 1862, Chase turned to every authorized loan and to every makeshift within his reach. During the remainder of the first half of the calendar year 1862 no new financial measures were adopted, and Chase was obliged to rely upon his former resources plus the first issue of greenbacks which were now available and of which $99.5 millions were issued by the end of June. Although the ordinary receipts of the government increased by 50 per cent, nine-tenths of the expenditures had still to be secured from loans. Unfortunately the issue of $500 millions of 6 per cent bonds—redeemable after five and payable after twenty years and hence known, as already noted, as "five-twenties" (5–20s)—authorized by the first legal tender

[1] The material for this chapter is based almost entirely upon W. C. Mitchell's *A History of the Greenbacks, with Special Reference to the Economic Consequences of their Issue: 1862–65*, Chicago, 1903, Part I, chaps. 3 to 5, and Part II, chap. 2, *passim*, and in some cases points are taken verbatim from this source. Hereafter this work is referred to as Mitchell, *Greenbacks*.

act and constituting a twin resource with the greenbacks proved of little support at the time. The act had provided that greenbacks might be exhanged for these bonds at the option of the holders. Great dependence was placed by Sherman, Stevens, Spaulding, and others upon this provision for "conversion." Stevens declared the fear of enormous legal tender issues to supply war expenses was without foundation.

I do not think any more would be needed than $150,000,000. The notes bear no interest. No one would seek them for investment. . . . This money would soon lodge in large quantities with the capitalists and banks. . . . Where could they invest it? In United States loans at 6 per cent, redeemable in gold in twenty years, the best and most valuable permanent investment that could be desired. The government would thus again possess such notes in exchange for bonds, and again reissue them. I have no doubt that the $500,000,000 of bonds authorized would be absorbed in less time than would be needed by Government; and thus $150,000,000 would do the work of $500,000,000 of bonds. When further loans are wanted you need only authorize the sale of more bonds; the same $150,000,000 of notes will be ready to take them.

But the scheme of conversion of greenbacks into bonds was not to work so smoothly as anticipated. The government's credit was not good enough to tempt investors to purchase 6 per cent securities on the terms of the act as interpreted by the secretary of the treasury. In three months' time less than $14 millions was disposed of in this manner. Although, as we shall see later, the repeal of this conversion clause brought unfortunate results, the immediate authority did the treasury small service. Stevens's predictions were far from fact. Instead of a constant flow of bonds from the treasury to absorb greenbacks, thus enabling the government in an endless-chain process to take in and pay out the original amount of paper money the call became strong for a more abundant issue of greenbacks "to compensate for the small demand for bonds."

Meanwhile the first greenback issue of $150 millions placed a ready, if temporary and vicious, resource in the hands of the treasury, and Chase was able to clear away the accumulated floating debt. His December report shows that by the end of June, 1862, "not a single requisition from any department upon the treasury remained unanswered . . . and there remained in the treasury a balance of $13,043,546.81."

This comfortable condition Chase well knew would be of brief duration. When the entire greenback issue authorized by the act of February, 1862, had been paid out stringency would recur. Existing financial policy ordained that other resources would prove inadequate. In a letter to Thaddeus Stevens, chairman of the ways and means committee, Chase acquainted Congress with the prospective situation as he viewed it. The authorized limits both of greenbacks and of temporary deposits had been reached. The only available resources were customs receipts and sales of five-twenty bonds for greenbacks. These resources were entirely inadequate to meet the necessities of the treasury. Their daily average amount was not more than $380,000 in the aggregate, while the average daily expenditures exceeded one million. Chase proposed two methods to meet the deficit—the restriction to $50 millions upon the amount of temporary deposits should be raised, and a second issue of $150 millions of legal tender notes should be authorized. Minor coins were maintained in the circulating medium with such difficulty that he also proposed the issue of $25 millions of the new greenbacks in denominations less than five dollars. A bill embodying these proposals having been drawn by Chase, he laid it before Congress on June 11th with the urgent request for "prompt action." The request excited alarm among the opponents of paper money. In the Senate, Senator Chandler offered a resolution providing that the amount of legal tender notes "shall never be increased," and asserted that the mere proposal of the secretary to increase them had sent the price of gold from $2\frac{3}{4}$ to 7 per cent premium. Proper use of other resources would enable the country to avoid the disastrous consequences of fresh paper money emissions. Senator Fessenden, chairman of the finance committee, opposed though he was to further issues, induced the Senate to refer the resolution to the finance committee for fair consideration of the secretary's reasons for his request. This being done, the resolution was never reported from committee.

Meanwhile Chase's bill had been introduced into the House by Spaulding. Here the advocates of further issues assumed a bold offensive, losing the apologetic tone that marked the debate on the first legal tender bill. The legal tender notes had "worked well" and the act of February 25th had "exceeded the most sanguine expectations of its warmest advocates." Some former opponents were won over by these arguments. Others fell into line through sheer hopelessness of opposition. On the other hand, some who had voted for the original legal tender act on the plea of "necessity" opposed this one on the ground that it inaugurated a settled policy of paper money. The great need for a currency of uniform value was urged in debate, but the overpowering argument now, as in January and February, was that of "necessity of the case." Those who denied the necessity proposed "to put upon the market the small amount which will be required . . . in bonds of the government, at whatever they would bring,"[1] and they were "persuaded that it would be far better for the people of the country to sell bonds at a large discount than to further disturb the relation between price and value by a further issue of these notes."[2] As in the debate on the first legal tender bill, the advocates of the measure failed again to meet the question fairly. Instead of showing the necessity for the issues, they contented themselves with assertions that, as a method of securing revenues, it was better to issue inconvertible paper money than to sell bonds below par.

There was little desire evidenced to continue the debate at the length to which it was extended on the first act. Apparently it soon became a foregone conclusion that the secretary was to have his way and would secure additional notes with not even a promise this time that further issues would not be asked for. The bill passed the House June 24th by a vote of 76 to 47. With few exceptions members voted as they had voted on the previous act, and likewise without adhering strictly to party lines. The vote in the Senate was 22 to 13 in favor of the measure,

[1] Speech by Morrill, *Congressional Globe*, 37 Cong., 2 Sess., p. 2885, House of Representatives, June 23, 1862.

[2] Speech by Sheffield, *ibid.*, p. 2888, in the House, June 23, 1862.

and with President Lincoln's signature on July 11, 1862, the bill became law. The act authorized the issue of $150 millions of "United States notes" and raised the limit placed upon temporary deposits from $50 millions to $100 millions. The need for small change in the circulating medium was partly satisfied by a provision granting power to issue not more than $35 millions of the $150 millions of notes in denominations of less than five dollars, and partly by a subsequent supplemental act of July 17th, which authorized the use of postage and other stamps in payments of fractional parts of a dollar. Some provision of this nature was made necessary by the disappearance from circulation of small coins, but the stamps were not made legal tender between individuals, their receipt by the government for dues and their redeemability at the treasury assuring their currency. Every "private corporation, banking association, firm, or individual" was prohibited from issuing for circulation notes or tokens of any character as a substitute for these stamps.

The Third Legal Tender Act

The condition in which the treasury found itself at the beginning of the new fiscal year, July 1, 1862, was only temporary. The balance on hand of $13 millions soon disappeared. McClellen's campaign in the Peninsula proved sorely disappointing and showed plainly that the war was to be indefinitely prolonged. This meant enlargement of the army and consequent increased demands upon the treasury. On July 1, President Lincoln called for 300,000 additional troops. To meet total expenditures of $156 millions[1] for the quarter ending September 30th, receipts from taxation and miscellaneous sources had slightly increased, standing at $24 millions as compared with $21 millions in the preceding quarter. The situation compelled Chase to borrow 85 per cent of the funds required. The conversion of greenbacks into five-twenty bonds having amounted to but $2.5 millions, he relied upon issues of greenbacks ($72.5

[1] $45.5 millions of this sum were required for payment of principal of the public debt.

millions), seven-thirty notes ($3.5 millions), certificates of deposit ($23 millions), and certificates of indebtedness ($12 millions). In sum, at the end of the third quarter of the year the treasury balance of $13 millions had disappeared and unpaid warrants of $5 millions had accumulated upon the desk of the secretary. This bad situation became worse during the months of October and November. Expenditures, exclusive of those for payment of the debt, increased nearly 50 per cent, and in spite of heavy borrowing unpaid requisitions amounted to $48 millions. In the face of this discouraging outlook Chase wrote his annual report to Congress for December, 1862. He estimated that he must provide $533 millions to meet the requirements to the end of the fiscal year, June 30, 1863. Ordinary receipts plus loans of the various sorts depended upon of late, and mentioned above, would still leave $277 millions to be provided by new legislation. He proposed that no part of this large sum should be raised by an increase in the issue of greenbacks. He said:

> The easiest mode doubtless would be an issue of the required amount in United States notes; but such an issue, especially in the absence of proper restrictions on corporate circulation, would, in the judgment of the secretary, be as injurious as it would be easy. The addition of so vast a volume to the existing circulation would convert a currency, of which the benefits have thus far greatly outweighed the inconveniences, into a positive calamity. Its consequences would be inflation of prices, increase of expenditures, augmentation of debt, and ultimately, disastrous defeat of the very purposes sought to be attained by it.

But, although the secretary opposed further issues of paper money, he suggested no increase of taxation. He depended solely upon borrowing and again urged upon Congress the importance of establishing the national banking system as a means of improving the currency and of forcing the sale of bonds which were to be required of the new banks as security for their note issues.

Whatever the character of the secretary's opposition to more paper money may have been, failure to provide means to pay soldiers in the field led directly to a joint resolution of Congress which in turn made a third legal tender act inevitable. No sooner had Chase's report been laid before the House of Representatives than the ways and means committee began the preparation of a loan bill and a bank bill in accordance with suggestions in that report. Meanwhile the treasury continued to run behind and unpaid requisitions increased alarmingly. The difficulties were brought to a climax through pressing letters which poured in to members of Congress from soldiers demanding back pay to relieve the suffering of their families at home. A series of resolutions and communications passing between Congress and the war and treasury departments in December elicited the facts that unpaid claims of soldiers amounted to $28.7 millions; that the aggregate daily proceeds of $1 million from customs, internal revenue taxes, conversions, temporary deposit loans, and authorized issues of greenbacks were inadequate to meet even the more urgent demands upon the government; that the House stood ready to take "immediate steps" to pay the soldiers and to authorize by joint resolution an additional issue of $50 millions of greenbacks to enable the secretary to pay them; and that the Senate was scarcely less willing to follow the same procedure. Thereupon Chase, revealing the fact that arrears of pay to both army and navy probably approached $60 millions, and reversing his previous attitude, sent in a bill which provided for the sale, at the best rates obtainable, of $100 millions of 6 per cent ten-year bonds, a new issue of $50 millions of greenbacks, and $50 millions of two-year 4 per cent treasury notes. This bill was passed by the Senate as a substitute for the joint resolution of the House. In the meantime the House, pursuing its inquiry into the nonpayment of soldiers, demanded an explanation of the secretary's failure to sell the $500 millions of 6 per cent bonds authorized by the act of February 25, 1862. Chase lamely explained, as he had done in his annual report, that the act had only conferred power to sell bonds at "the market value thereof," that "the market value can only be ascertained by the daily quotation of sales in New York," and that large purchasers, buying to resell at a profit, could not afford to take bonds at "the market value." Thus did the secretary endeavor to shift to the shoulders of Congress the responsibility of failure to procure funds through sales of bonds at a price they would fetch on the market. But members of Congress showed little patience with such legal quibbling and insisted that the secretary should have sold bonds at the price he could obtain when offered for sale. During these days, the two great bills of the session, providing for "ways and means for the support of the government" and for the new national banking system, were taking shape in committee. The former, as introduced into the House, contained a provision for $300 millions additional issue of greenbacks "if required by the exigencies of the public service." This and other provisions of the bill the ways and means committee felt assured would in time furnish abundant funds. But immediate relief to the soldiers was deemed essential. Consequently a separate measure, in form of a joint resolution, providing simply for $100 millions additional issue of greenbacks was passed by both houses with practically no opposition. The army and navy could thus receive pay without delay. In signing the joint resolution on January 17th (1863) President Lincoln expressed his "sincere regret that it has been found necessary to authorize so large an additional issue of United States notes." Clearly a third issue of greenbacks was thus determined upon as a result of Chase's refusal to sell bonds at the price they would fetch when properly placed on sale. Funds to pay soldiers could thus have been secured and no occasion for the Joint Resolution of January 17th need have arisen.

The ways and means bill provided funds aggregating $900 millions, considered for those days a large sum. That total amount of government obligations, available partly for the current fiscal year and partly for the year beginning July 1, 1863, could take the form of 6 per cent coin bonds; or three-year treasury notes to the sum of $300 millions, bearing coin interest at 5.47½ per cent, which conveniently made 1½ cents per day on $100; or, "if required," fresh issues of greenbacks to the sum of $300 millions. The debate on this important measure was curiously sidetracked to a minor feature. Little consideration was given by congressmen either to the amount, the terms, or the various forms of the securities and currency authorized in such unprecedented abundance. The debate was consumed largely by discussions of the proposed tax on state bank notes. Opposition to an increase of irredeemable paper money had disappeared, and what references there were to the currency were generally packed with error in monetary principles. Yet, on the part of some men, "it was clearly enough seen that the bill would cause further depreciation, injure the government's credit, increase the cost of the war, work injury to recipients of fixed wages,—particularly soldiers,—to savings bank depositors, and all creditors, and that it would still further excite the 'spirit of speculation.' But this recital of ill effects which would follow the bill apparently had little influence."[1] Members found themselves in an emergency, and even the wisest of them admitted that it was "not worth while for us to be very particular."[2] "The patient has got accustomed to opiates and the dose cannot now be withheld without peril."[3] It was, however, on the warmly debated topic of whether or not the currency was "inflated" that confusion of thought was especially marked. The premium on gold was attributed to everything except the true primary cause, namely, an excessive issue of paper currency. Some persons with apparent support from Chase's annual report took the ground that further inflation was necessary to facilitate borrowing. This position was intimately connected with the policy of not selling bonds below par—a policy that was responsible for much error. When bonds could not be sold at par one of three courses was open to the government: it could increase the attractiveness of the investment by raising the interest rate and lengthening the term; it could sell bonds for what they would bring in the market; or it could depreciate the currency to a point where it would be to the investor's advantage to exchange $100 in greenbacks for $6 annual interest plus an assurance of final payment of principal

[1] Mitchell, *Greenbacks*, pp. 110, 111.
[2] Quoted by Mitchell, *ibid.*, p. 111.
[3] *Ibid.*

in coin. It was to the third of these alternatives, with all the consequences of disordered currency, that Chase and congressmen turned when they demanded more greenbacks to facilitate borrowing. Not only did they thus march into unsafe territory, but they also cut their bridges behind them by repealing the "conversion" clause which permitted holders of greenbacks to exchange them at will for 6 per cent bonds. This ill-fated action as to "conversion" prevented the currency from purifying itself by a natural process at the close of the war when, with the rise of government bonds above par, greenbacks would have flowed profitably into the funded debt and disappeared permanently from circulation.[1]

After rejecting several vicious amendments, calling for payment of interest on bonds in greenbacks instead of in coin, repealing the authority to accept deposit loans, and granting power to the secretary to issue bonds, treasury notes, and greenbacks at will within the total limit of $900 millions, the House passed the bill without a division. In the Senate several improvements were made in the measure, chief of which was the reduction in the amount of legal tenders to be issued from $300 millions to $150 millions. It then passed by a vote of 32 to 4.

The law as signed by the President on March 3, 1863, authorized a loan of $900 millions which might take three different forms. The entire amount could be issued in 6 per cent, coin interest, ten-forty bonds[2] payable in coin, at such price as the secretary might "deem most advisable." Of the whole amount $400 millions might be in three-year treasury notes, with interest at not more than 6 per cent payable in "lawful money," and the secretary was given power, "if required by the exigencies of the public service, for the payment of the army and navy and other creditors of the government, to issue on the credit of the United States the sum of $150 millions of United States

[1] The assumption here is that the favorable attitude of Congress and the general public toward contraction of the currency in the period immediately following the war would have permitted the "conversion" process to go on apace.

[2] The term "ten-forty bonds" or "ten-forties," or "10–40's," was used to indicate government securities which could be redeemed at the pleasure of the government after ten years but must be paid at the end of forty years.

notes [greenbacks] including the amount of such notes [$100 millions] heretofore authorized by joint resolution approved January 17, 1863." The treasury notes above mentioned were to be legal tender for their face value, and all bonds issuable in this and the first and second legal tender acts, as well as these treasury notes, could be sold at any price the secretary could obtain. The power of "conversion" was taken away as forecast by the action of the House. Finally, paper currency (greenbacks) for fractional parts of a dollar were issued in place of the existing postal currency. The total amount of United States notes (or greenbacks) issued under war legislation was thus $450 millions.

Issues of Greenbacks Avoided in 1864 and 1865

If, from the point of view of paper money advocates, greenbacks were absolutely necessary in the first years of the war, the question arises as to how fresh issues were avoided in 1864 and 1865, when expenditures had mounted far higher than in the earlier years. Expenditures rose from $470 millions in 1862 and $719 millions in 1863 to $865 millions in 1864 and $1297 millions in 1865. The chief reason why, under the circumstances, further resort to greenbacks was avoided is simply that an efficient revenue system had been established. The slowness of Chase and Congress in attacking the revenue problem had worked its evil results in the country's currency, but at last the old mistakes were to be corrected. The direct tax of 1861, amounting to less than $2 millions in any year of the war, brought little relief, and customs dues, although heavily laid, were likewise disappointing. But with the act of July 1, 1862, an elaborate system of internal revenue was founded which finally, improved and extended by the acts of June 30, 1864, and March 3, 1865, more than met expectations. Receipts from this last-named source in 1864 were $110 millions, in 1865 $209 millions, and in 1866 $309 millions, the receipts for 1866 representing an increase of 800 per cent over the first year of operation of the system. The benefit to the government was twofold. Receipts from taxation helped to meet expenses and, more important still, the credit of the government was vastly improved. The secretary employed Jay Cooke, private banker, to find a market for bonds. It was these receipts which afforded the best support for Jay Cooke's magnificent organization for selling the five-twenty bonds. With this advantage neither Grant's slow progress about Vicksburg nor the invasion of the North by Lee and Bragg could stop the inflow of subscriptions to his widespread agencies during the latter part of the fiscal year 1863. The gratifying result was that on June 30th of that year the treasury showed a balance of $5 millions. Encouraged by Cooke's success, Chase again in his annual report of December, 1863, pronounced against any further issue of greenbacks—this time with substantial prospect of living up to his convictions. He recommended a further increase of internal revenue taxes, and with this as a basis of credit he felt confident of receiving abundant loans at reasonable rates of interest. At last the right method of financing the war was in full swing and Congress was at one with the secretary in resolving that the total amount of greenbacks should never exceed $450 millions, albeit Thaddeus Stevens, true to his false principles, made "one more effort to save the national credit" by insisting upon paying interest on loans in greenbacks instead of in coin.

The financial embarrassments of the summer of 1864 and the enormous expenditures of 1865 threatened to force the secretary and Congress to abandon their resolution to avoid the issue of more paper money. In the spring and summer of the former year Chase found that expenditures far exceeded his anticipation. Borrowing on an immense scale had become necessary. Although Jay Cooke's success had been so marked,—$320 millions of the five-twenties were sold and the subscription books closed in January, 1864,—Chase foolishly decided to throw him overboard and to sell bonds through national banks and other agencies under the direct care of the treasury. The experiment proved a miserable failure, only $73 millions of ten-forty bonds having been disposed of by June 30th. During the same months Chase again turned to legal tender notes, but this time to a variety different from greenbacks. He issued interest-bearing legal tender notes to the amount of $163 millions with the hope that they would not enter into circulation but would be held by investors for the sake of the interest they bore. Yet, not to mention certificates of indebtedness, he ended the fiscal year with a net balance of approximately $50 millions against him in the form of unpaid requisitions.

At this juncture occurred, as has been stated, an episode which relieved Chase from his official duties. A political tangle over the appointment of the head of the New York sub-treasury gave him the tempting opportunity to show the country that his services were indispensable to the administration. He sent his resignation to the President. Much to his surprise and chagrin, the patient Lincoln promptly accepted his offer to lay down his portfolio and proceeded to the appointment of his successor. Senator Fessenden, the efficient chairman of the Senate finance committee, reluctantly consented to take the office.

The difficulties facing the new secretary seemed practically insurmountable. Besides the unpaid requisitions piled upon his desk, there were outstanding $162 millions of certificates of indebtedness to be cared for. To meet daily expenses of not less than two and a quarter millions of dollars he had but seven hundred and fifty thousand per day from internal revenues. He inherited from his predecessor failures in two negotiations for loans. In these circumstances he turned to a popular subscription for seven-thirty notes, two hundred millions of which were issuable under the act of June 30, 1864. Small results flowed from this loan and unpaid requisitions still mounted. To pay the soldiers, "who were suffering from the long delay in satisfying their just claims," he felt compelled to issue $80 millions of legal tender compound-interest notes. Fifty-three millions more from the sale of seven-thirty notes and seventeen-year bonds still left a deficit of $130 millions for the quarter ending with September, 1864. Still Fessenden was unwilling to resort to an increase of greenbacks. He was convinced, "not only of the ability of the people to furnish, at a short notice, such sums as may be required, but [also] of the entire confidence felt in the national securities." In his report of the following December he asked for authority to make further loans, increase the currency at his discretion, and extend the internal revenue duties to $300 millions per year. Fortunately the financial situation improved while this report was yet in the making. Promises of peace became more definite, and, in consequence, borrowing became less difficult. Named in the order of importance, sales of compound-interest notes, ten-forties, seven-thirties, and five-twenties yielded $187 millions during the quarter ending December 31st. In the next three months the seven-thirty notes, with sales of $185 millions, became the chief reliance of the treasury, while ten-forties brought in $56 millions.

Fessenden, having agreed to assume the responsibilities of the treasury for a limited term only, was happy to be relieved of his burdens by Hugh McCulloch, whose excellent services in private banking and in public office as comptroller of the currency strongly recommended him to the President.

With the beginning of Lincoln's second term the end of the war was in sight, and McCulloch, taking office on March 4, 1865, faced the considerable task of preparing for disbanding the army by providing for arrears of pay, bounties, and transportation of troops. Again reliance was placed upon the seven-thirty notes, and Jay Cooke, much to the secretary's credit, was once more employed to place them upon the market. By the end of July, Cooke's organization sold these securities to the amount of $530 millions and McCulloch had "the unexpected satisfaction of being able, with the receipts from customs and internal revenue and a small increase of the temporary loan, to meet all the requisitions upon the treasury."

Referring again to the rôle played by the greenbacks as a financial resource for the government, we find that it varied at different stages of the war. A comparison of the various items of receipts by the federal treasury during the fiscal years of 1861–66 shows a rapid increase in the ordinary receipts, which were composed of import duties and internal revenue taxes. Of these two items of ordinary receipts the increase in the internal revenues was by far the more important. From a tenth in 1862, the ratio they bore to total receipts rose to a quarter in 1864. Turning to the receipts from loans, they may be conveniently divided into three classes, namely: bonds, short-term interest-bearing obligations, and non-interest-bearing obligations including greenbacks. As the revenue system became more efficient a smaller proportion of the means necessary to carry on the war had to be borrowed. From nine-tenths in 1862 the proportion borrowed fell to three-fourths in 1864 and 1865. As to the method of borrowing, reliance was at first placed rather upon issues of circulating greenback currency than upon sales of bonds, but with increasing experience the secretaries of the treasury used bonds and interest-bearing notes more and greenbacks less. "The greenbacks were not an important financial resource after June, 1863. In the fiscal year 1862 more than a fifth, and in 1863 nearly half of the loans were represented by issues of United States notes [greenbacks]; but in 1864 the proportion fell to one-sixteenth, and thereafter the redemptions of greenbacks were greater than the issues." The real financial effect of the greenback policy, however, is to be found not so much in the diminishing importance of treasury receipts from the issues of United States notes, but in the influence of paper money upon the price of supplies bought by the government. As the paper money depreciated, the purchasing power represented by a thousand-dollar bond, payable eventually in gold, was diminished in equal degree. The public debt reached its maximum amount August 31, 1865, when it stood at $2846 millions.[1] Of this immense debt the careful estimates made by W. C. Mitchell in his *History of the Greenbacks from 1861 to 1865* indicate that some $589 millions, or rather more than a fifth of the whole amount, was due to the substitution of United States notes for metallic money as a common denominator of value. That is to say, the absolute loss of several hundred millions of dollars was incurred by the government on account of the depreciation of the monetary standard. When we add to this fact two further considerations,—first, that the varying depreciation of the currency continued to affect the volume of

[1] Report of the Secretary of the Treasury, December, 1866, p. 6.

both receipts and expenditures until the resumption of specie payments in January, 1879, restored the greenbacks to equality with gold, and, second, that the economic consequences of the fluctuating paper standard, as reflected in the real incomes of laborers, landlords, capitalists, and active business managers, were extremely serious,—it follows that the legal tender acts had remarkably unfortunate results.

The State of the Currency

A brief review of the various elements injected into the currency will reveal its confused and disordered state. The chief service of McCulloch lay in his work of funding the enormous public debt and in his sturdy efforts to reshape the currency in preparation for a resumption of specie payments.

The end of the war left the currency in a deplorable state. Suspension of specie payments in December, 1861, had forced the withdrawal of gold and silver coin from the ordinary channels of circulation. Various substitutes for specie had been injected into the media of exchange. When the war began the monetary circulation consisted of (1) gold coin, (2) silver coins for fractional parts of a dollar, (3) one-cent copper pieces, and (4) circulating notes issued by state banks.[1] In October, 1861, the amount of specie in circulation in the loyal states was estimated by the director of the mint to be from $255 millions to $280 millions, and bank notes had been issued to the approximate amount of $129 millions. Suspension brought confusion into the system. Gold was hoarded, and, aside from "deposit currency," the country was rapidly left with a currency of irredeemable state bank notes plus a few millions of equally irredeemable government "demand notes." Although the government paid interest on much of its debt in gold and import duties were collected in gold, that metal, except in California, whose circumstances were peculiar, practically disappeared from general circulation for a period of eighteen years.

[1] Silver dollars had long since been withdrawn because their bullion value exceeded their value as money. By law of July, 1861, treasury notes of the government payable on demand (the "old demand notes") came into use as money, and by October amounted to $33.5 millions.

During the first months of 1862 a marked contraction took place also in the bank-note circulation, New York City banks showing a decline of over 37 per cent by the first of March. With suspension one might expect the opposite tendency to have set in, but the explanation is simple. Although much looseness in method prevailed under the state bank systems, the banks of several states were required by law to redeem their notes in coin, and the law was enforced. The State Bank of Indiana, the Chemical Bank of New York, and a few others, even delayed suspension of specie payments for some time after the government and most banks had taken that step. But, since neither bank notes nor "demand notes" were then legal tender and could under no interpretation be used as reserves, and since coin became increasingly difficult to obtain for redemption purposes these banks were forced gradually to retire their note circulation.[1] As soon as the first legal tender act was passed, February 25, 1862, the situation began to change. Decisions of the courts finally satisfied the most conservative bankers that bank notes could now be lawfully redeemed in greenbacks, and by midsummer, 1863, they, as others had already done, freely issued their notes. Secretary Chase estimated the note circulation in the loyal states November 1, 1862, to have been $167 millions. This was an increase of nearly 30 per cent within a year. Bank deposits also increased from $257 millions in January, 1862, to $367 millions in January, 1863. With the introduction of the new national banking system in 1863 and 1864 many state banks were converted into national banks, and the total circulation again increased.

The demand treasury notes, bearing no interest and placed in circulation by Chase in the late summer and autumn of 1861, had an important though brief and checkered career. These were the so-called "old demand notes" to which reference has already frequently been made. The associated banks which

[1] As late as December 31, 1862, Hugh McCulloch, then president of the State Bank of Indiana, issued a statement assuring the public that under no circumstances would his bank fail to redeem its notes in coin. He proceeded, however, to retire the notes.

had subscribed for the $150-million loan received them on deposit rather hesitatingly, especially after suspension of specie payments rendered them irredeemable in coin. Yet those banks did continue to accept them as long as they could use them in paying the installments of the loan to the sub-treasury. The last installment having been paid in early February, 1862, and the notes having been refused in payment of balances at the New York clearing house, they fell to a slight discount. This condition gave great anxiety to Chase. It was to prevent discrimination against them that he urged, as one reason, the retention of the legal tender clause in the first greenback act and that he accepted them on deposit at the sub-treasuries at 5 per cent interest. These devices availed little. The notes were not made a legal tender by the law of February 25th, but, unlike the legal tender notes of that act, they were receivable for customs duties in place of coin. This superior quality increased the demand for them and sent them to a premium. When information reached New York that they were not, in fact, made a legal tender, banks again refused to receive them and they again fell to a discount. On March 7th the banks withdrew their opposition, the act of the seventeenth gave them the legal tender quality, and they advanced to par, circulated side by side with greenbacks for a few weeks, were abstracted from circulation during May by persons needing them in payment of customs duties, and remained regularly at a premium. Their use as part of the circulating medium was now at an end, and by gradual conversion into greenbacks under the law they disappeared altogether.

When the first greenbacks appeared in April, 1862, they afforded business men considerable relief from the inconvenience and uncertainty into which the currency had been thrown. True, this temporary benefit was enjoyed at the expense of other and more serious embarrassments which were later incurred by resort to paper money. One important difficulty was not at that time overcome, however. This was the disappearance of fractional coins and the lack of means to make small change. The daily life of the masses of the people was thereby constantly and

seriously disturbed. Subsidiary silver coins, containing a relatively small amount of silver metal, lingered in circulation until the greenbacks fell in value to the point where brokers found it profitable to melt or export such coins and sell them for bullion. As soon as a dollar in greenbacks was worth less than two silver half-dollars, four quarters, or ten dimes, the process of melting and exporting began. It was in June, 1862, that paper money fell sharply and subsidiary coin began rapidly to disappear. Retail trade suffered, although old Spanish quarter-dollars, worn to a light weight, came again into circulation. Numerous other devices and makeshifts were invented. A premium was charged on silver given in change for a paper dollar; dollar bills were cut into halves or quarters and passed for 50 and 25 cents; notes for fractional parts of a dollar, known as "shinplasters," were issued. These last were issued by banks in spite of laws prohibiting them, but mostly by other corporations, firms, and individuals—municipalities, hotels, restaurants, saloons, and retail shops. Unsatisfactory though it was, this "small change" had to be tolerated until Secretary Chase's action brought relief. As previously stated, Congress authorized the use of "postage and other stamps of the United States" for currency. Ordinary stamps, with their tendency to stick and crumple, were first used. Later "postage currency" composed of paper notes of small but convenient size and not gummed came into use. Again the device proved inadequate, and finally the act of March 3, 1863, provided for "fractional currency," which in fact was a currency for change less than a dollar, in the form of small greenback notes. These notes came from the printing presses in October, 1863, and at the close of the war they, with the amount of postage currency still current, aggregated $25 millions.

Inconvenience was experienced not only by the disappearance of silver minor coins but by the tendency to disappear on the part of one-cent and two-cent pieces. Curiously enough, the cents, which were made partly of nickel, went to a premium almost as soon as the minor silver coins. This fact is to be explained by the keen demand of the public for the short supply rather then by a profit to be made by melting or exporting them. "The supply was . . . so short in comparison with the demand that not less than three hundred varieties of illegal cent tokens of the same size, but less weight than the mint cent, and containing no nickel, were issued by private parties in direct violation of the law."[1] When paper currency depreciated so that the bullion value of the nickel cent was worth more than its mint value, bronze was substituted for nickel and copper by an act of 1864. The smallest fractional paper note was for three cents, and the substitution of the cheaper bronze did not give adequate relief from scarcity of small change The war over, paper dollars advanced in gold value, the cent and two-cent pieces from bronze alloys, and the nickel three-cent pieces reappeared in circulation and remained without difficulty. Then complaints were no longer heard.

The backbone of the circulating medium during the greenback period was composed of several forms of government obligations. The chief of these was, of course, the greenbacks, which, first appearing in April, 1862, displaced gold as the standard money until resumption of specie payments on January 1, 1879. Not only did they perform the price-fixing function, but they constituted, both for large and for small transactions, an important element of the media of exchange. At the close of the war they were outstanding to the amount of $431 millions. They were not, as already stated, the only legal tender notes issued by the government and used as currency. Interest-bearing legal tenders were also put forth. Under the third legal tender act, March 3, 1863, Chase issued $166.5 millions of two-year 5 per cent legal tender notes and $44.5 millions of the same kind running for one year. The treasury probably expected these notes to remain in the hands of individuals and banks as investments. Circumstances, however, forced the secretary to pay interest on them semi-annually instead of at maturity. In consequence they flowed into the currency after the interest date passed and in turn were withdrawn to enable holders to collect interest as the next such date

[1] Mitchell, *Greenbacks*, p. 168.

approached. Thus they were a disturbing and unsatisfactory element in the currency. They were gradually replaced by still another form of legal tenders, authorized also by the act of March 3, 1863, and by that of June 30, 1864. These were the compound-interest notes, running for three years, bearing interest at 6 per cent, but payable only at maturity. Since, for example, a $10 note would be worth $11.94 at the end of the third year, there was an inducement to hold it as an investment, thus preventing its use as money. Yet these same notes helped to inflate the currency. To a slight extent they went into circulation directly, but were indirectly more influential through use as reserves by banks, which held them for investment purposes as well. In this manner they set free an equal amount of greenbacks for use in hand-to-hand circulation. Non-legal tender, interest-bearing notes also helped to swell the currency. Such were the "seven-thirties"—the three-year treasury notes, bearing 7.3 per cent interest, equal to two cents per day on one hundred dollars. They were paid out directly as wages to army officers and soldiers. In a similar way millions of one-year certificates of indebtedness, bearing interest at 6 per cent, formed a part of the circulating medium.

This general review of the various elements injected into the monetary circulation of the country during the period of the war gives some conception of its confused and changing condition. The quantity of almost any given element, at a given time, is beyond definite calculation, yet the facts are clear enough to show that "not least among the unhappy consequences of the legal-tender acts was the disorder into which the circulating medium was thrown."[1]

[1] *Ibid.*, p. 181.

CHAPTER IV

EVIL EFFECTS OF PAPER MONEY

NATURE OF PAPER MONEY[1]

THE greenbacks presented a typical case of government paper money. Although on their face they were a promise to pay on demand, they were in fact fiat money, non-redeemable and dependent for their value upon the mere command of the sovereign power and upon the quantity which this same authority was pleased to emit.

General acceptability among the members of a business community is the chief characteristic of good money. Gold fulfills this prime requisite to a marked degree. But several conditions are necessary to make paper money generally acceptable throughout a community. Paper money has usually had its origin in periods of stress and difficulty for the State. It has been a tax, or, rather, a substitute for a proper form of tax. The State issues it and in return secures material goods or services. By means of it the government gets hold of property of the people and keeps it, temporarily if the currency is in due time redeemed and retired, but permanently if it becomes a definite part of the circulating medium. If resumption of specie payments takes place on any level of value below that upon which the paper money was originally paid out of the treasury, the State, in so far, retains permanently the property received. The government desires to get hold of property without paying in full for it, and paper money presents a means to this end. It secures shells, guns, soldiers, battleships, transports, clothing, etc., for nothing except strips of paper of small value. This was the case with our revolutionary continental

[1] Cf. F. W. Taussig, *Principles of Economics*, New York, 1921, 3rd ed., Vol. I, chap. 23; F. A. Walker, *Money*, New York, 1878, *passim;* Bonamy Price, articles in London *Economist*, 1866.

currency, with the French assignats, and, in a later period, with the paper issued by France, Austria, Italy, the Southern Confederacy, our own greenbacks, and the multiplicity of issues during and following the Great War in various countries in both hemispheres.

As has just been stated, to serve well as money a commodity must be one of general acceptability in a community. Ordinarily the commodity which is in such general demand as to make it a good medium of exchange, common denominator, and standard of deferred payments has assumed its position gradually. It is only after long usage as an ordinary commodity of exchange that it rises to the place of the basis itself of exchange. However, familiarity, usage, custom, widespread demand, bring into general acceptance a commodity otherwise fitted by reason of its physical and economic qualities to perform monetary functions. Thus ordinarily money is, as it were, naturally and not artificially developed. It is not placed down upon a community from above, but is developed from within. Yet a money commodity once determined upon may be influenced for efficiency, or the reverse, by political authority—for example, by imposing the legal tender quality. This quality may be attached to the commodity by law, and in consequence those persons who have refused or hesitated to receive it as money are compelled by uniformity of judicial decision to fall into line with common action and accept it in payment of debts. In the case of gold little difficulty is encountered in inducing a people to accept it in discharge of debt, since it has a high degree of exchangeability as a commodity. Such currency is regulated by the so-called intrinsic worth of the metal. Sales and purchases are carried on by a process of double barter; goods are first exchanged for coin, and the coin in turn bartered for other goods. The coined metal is the instrument used for measuring the two lots of goods, and then, either directly or through substitutes, for transferring them from one person to another. The value of the metal in the coin does not ordinarily alter much within the period comprising most commercial transactions. Business men, therefore, under a metallic currency have a relatively steady standard by which to compute and settle their accounts. On the other hand, an inconvertible currency presents quite the opposite picture. The great evil attending it is, so to say, its intrinsic uncertainty. In view of this defect and the resultant hindrance to free acceptance flowing from it, the government gives the legal tender quality to the paper. This is done not merely as signifying final approval of a satisfactory money commodity, as in the case of gold, but as a necessary prop and an influence toward securing that universal acceptability without which the money function cannot be performed. Of course, the measure carries an absurdity upon its face. A law is made to compel men to accept money, whereas no one will refuse it if it is good. The spectacle is presented of "creditors running away from their debtors and the debtors pursuing them in triumph and paying them without mercy." The uncertainty of paper money is due, however, not to the presence or absence of the legal tender quality, but to the ease of overissue. Its value, like the value of gold money, depends primarily upon its quantity. As Ricardo long ago observed, it is not necessary that paper money should be redeemable in gold in order to maintain its value. It is only necessary to restrict its amount within such limits that the money work will be done on the same level of prices as would have obtained had gold remained in circulation. But such money is unregulated by any natural conditions of production and becomes subject to purely arbitrary regulation in its quantity. Gold is produced only by much labor, and, while the conditions of production are subject to great change, a period of years is ordinarily required for changes in production to affect seriously the existing supply. Government paper money, on the other hand, may be increased indefinitely by mere resolution of political authority. It costs approximately one thousand times as much labor and capital to mine and refine 1,000,000 ounces of gold as to produce 1000 ounces. But the difference between the cost of printing $1,000,000 and $1000 of paper money is negligible. Greenbacks in America mounted from the zero point to $450 millions within the space of thirteen months; the assignats of

France increased by two or three billions of francs per month between May, 1795, and January, 1796; and the issues of German paper marks after the Great War were so large and so rapid as almost to defy comprehension. Disastrous results followed in all these instances. Only by strict limitation of issues can paper money maintain the characteristics of good money. While, therefore, the economic advantage of paper money over specie is undoubted, the political weaknesses of the case are so marked that infinitely greater abuse is possible in the one system as compared with the other. The danger of overissue never ceases. So true is it that prudence and self-restraint count for but little against a burst of popular passion that Alexander Hamilton in his "Report on the Bank" was led to say:

> The emitting of paper money by the authority of the Constitution is wisely prohibited to the individual States by the National Constitution, and the spirit of that prohibition ought not to be disregarded by the government of the United States. Though paper emissions, under general authority, might have some advantage not applicable, and be far from some of the disadvantages which are applicable, to the like emissions by the States separately: yet they are of a nature so liable to abuse, and, it may be affirmed, so certain of being abused, that the wisdom of the government will be shown in never trusting itself with the use of so seducing and dangerous an expedient. . . . In great and trying emergencies there is almost a moral certainty of its becoming mischievous. The stamping of paper is an operation so much easier than the levying of taxes that a government, in the practice of paper emissions, would rarely fail in any such emergency to indulge itself too far in the employment of this resource.

While the danger of overissue never ceases, it does not follow that excesses are ordinarily indulged to the point of causing absolute worthlessness of the inconvertible paper and of driving an entire community to revolt against its use. Such a condition was, indeed, reached in some notable instances of the past, e.g. the continental currency of the American revolutionary period, the French assignats, and the currency of the Southern Confederacy. A similar condition was also reached in several European countries in consequence of the excessive issues during and following the World War. Some rare cases could be cited in which the issues were so restrained that an inconvertible paper currency has been kept at par with gold. But overissue to the extent of causing greater or less depreciation in the value of the paper, and hence of causing a rise in prices, is the general rule. Paper money therefore tends to drive specie out of circulation. The process may take place through suspension of specie payments by government and banks. In this case specie may be hoarded by the banks and other agencies in anticipation of an early resumption of specie payments or of profits to be made from the appearance of a premium on the money metal; or the process may take place through the international flow of the precious metals. Gold is the only medium of general acceptability for the final settlement of international balances. As paper money is issued by one country and enters circulation its quantity is added to that of the specie already in circulation. The additional quantity, other conditions remaining the same, raises the general level of prices, and therefore the country of issue becomes an advantageous place in which other nations may sell commodities and a disadvantageous place in which to purchase commodities. In consequence imports of that country tend to increase and exports to decrease. Sooner or later the excess of imports must be paid for by the export of the only generally acceptable instrument of international payments, *viz.*, gold. Thus gold is expelled and prices tend to return approximately to the old level. This process will continue with further and further issues of paper money until all the gold, or specie, is driven from the circulating medium. After this point has been reached any further issues will cause a rise of prices, always provided that the amount of exchanges to be transacted and the other terms of the equation of exchange remain unaltered. With rising prices most economic relationships of society are disturbed. Creditors receive less than they lent; debtors are able to repay more easily than they anticipated; the wages of labor and other "fixed" incomes do not keep pace with increasing cost of living; business men enjoy increasing profits. Because business men are the first recipients of the product of industry and their profits increase with rising prices, industry receives a fresh impetus and prosperity seems to prevail. The stimulus wears away and readjustment of economic relationships takes place. But having tasted the delights of an intoxicating dose, the less farseeing members of society call for further issues of paper in order that the vicious round may be repeated. They feel the pressure of reaction and readjustment and loudly declare that more money is needed to insure the continuance of prosperity. No natural stopping place for this inebriating process exists. Only the final dominance of a more enlightened public opinion can eradicate the evil.

When, under a paper money régime, gold disappears from general circulation, it becomes an ordinary commodity of commerce and is bought and sold accordingly. While it ceases to perform the functions of money in general, gold is still needed to meet certain important engagements. The demand for its use in international payments, in the arts, and for the discharge of domestic obligations arising from specific contracts calling for its payment either by government or individuals makes it profitable for someone to establish a business to supply the commodity at a price, as in the case of wheat or iron or other ordinary commodity. Under such circumstances the trade of the bullion dealer is a highly speculative one and one that often brings danger to the community. A premium on gold appears at the moment paper money depreciates and is one of the first evidences of such depreciation. Because the extent of the fluctuation in the premium varies almost constantly and fundamentally independently of any influence which the bullion dealer can bring to bear, he is uncertain as to what premium is in store for him.

Such, in brief, is the nature of paper money.

Speculation in Gold and "Black Friday."[1]

Loans and taxes in some form are indispensable to organized society, but their form and nature should not be such as to vitiate or interfere with the production and transfer of the

[1] Bonamy Price, "The Apprehended Mercantile Convulsion in America," a letter dated March 21, 1866 to the editor of the *Economist*, in the London *Economist*,

products of industry from one person to another. They should have no vital connection with the monetary standard. The issue of greenbacks presented a preëminent case in which a government forced a loan or levied taxes by means of inconvertible paper. But the experiment, in addition, brought evils more severe and less defensible than even such a loan or tax. The process left a legacy of woes behind it. The country found itself burdened with a varying standard of value in the settlement of accounts and thus encountered calamity in a region altogether unconnected with loans or taxation. With wide and rapid oscillations in the value of the currency, every trader suddenly met with great fluctuations in prices; goods sold in greenbacks of a certain value were paid for a month or two later in greenbacks of a different value; every trade carried the seed of uncertainty at its core; and ruinous losses were inflicted upon innocent business men by a force which they could not control and for which they could provide no remedy.

Among the many unfortunate commercial and industrial effects of the Civil War, some would have occurred had a specie régime been maintained, but others are clearly attributable to the introduction of inconvertible paper currency. Of these latter, most resulted from the fact, just suggested, that the greenbacks not only formed in part the medium of exchange but constituted in themselves the practical standard of value. One of the most important of the effects of the greenback standard was the transfer of the control of active business from the hands of the conservative class to those of the speculative element of society. This change in control was in great part due to the fluctuations in the value of paper money, and, briefly, it came about in the following manner. The fall in the value of the greenback dollar gave the opportunity to debtors to discharge existing obligations with a smaller amount of wealth than that

March 24, 1866. M. S. Wildman, *Money Inflation in United States*, New York and London, 1905, pp. 128–133. Causes of the Gold Panic, House of Rep., Report No. 31, 41 Cong., 2 Sess. C. F. Jr. and Henry Adams, *Chapters in Erie*, New York, 1886, pp. 100–134. *McClure's Magazine*, November, 1899, p. 30, article on "Black Friday, September 24, 1869," by former Secretary George S. Boutwell. Boutwell's *Reminiscences of Sixty Years in Public Affairs*, pp. 164–182.

for which the debt was contracted. Again, the fluctuations in the standard forced dealers, wherever possible, to increase their prices in order to insure themselves against loss from unforeseen changes in the gold value of paper. In other words, individual prices changed not only in accord with ordinary changes in the demand and supply of commodities in the market, but with variations in the nominal dollar, which was itself subject to extraordinary change. Old and established business firms experienced losses from scaling down of debts and from uncertainty in trade. Many, in consequence, withdrew from active business operations and invested their capital in government securities. Thus a creditor class, more distinct than had previously been known, came into existence. The debtor class was affected in quite the opposite way. Rising prices gave welcome advantage to it. Persons of this class were able more easily to pay their debts and gain a firmer foothold in business. They were naturally more adventurous, more speculative, and perhaps more energetic than the members of the creditor class. They had little to lose and much to gain in boldly undertaking the great industrial, transport, and financial operations which were made necessary by the war. The interests of this class demanded rising prices, the interests of the other class falling prices. These influences resulted in a marked tendency to take the control of the active business of the community out of the hands of those who had property to protect and place it in the hands of those who were willing to take risks to obtain property. While it would by no means be safe to assume that under a specie régime a period of prosperity, perhaps more apparent than real, would not have been induced by the conditions of the Civil War, it is undoubtedly true that the depreciated greenback currency exaggerated the apparent prosperity and greatly strengthened speculative tendencies. It was in this atmosphere of speculation that one of the most dramatic and discreditable episodes of the greenback period was nurtured and brought to the breaking point. This was the gold conspiracy of 1869, culminating in "Black Friday," September 24, 1869.

As a conspicuous example of the evils engendered by a paper money régime it is proposed to give a brief account of the manner in which the gold conspiracy and "Black Friday" came about. In the minds of treasury officials the policy of disposing of the gold held in government vaults was intimately connected with the problems of contraction of the currency and the state of the money market. Gold was received for payment of import duties in larger amounts than were necessary to pay interest on the public debt—these being the two transactions largely requiring payment in gold. The government in the course of time became the principal holder of the gold in the country, and those persons who would benefit by the event frequently brought great pressure to bear on the administration to have it released from the treasury, or retained there, as their interests might dictate. The most noteworthy of these efforts was that of 1869. There were three methods by which the metal could be returned to the channels of business and to private hoards: one was by anticipating interest payments on the public debt; a second, by purchase of bonds with gold for the federal sinking fund; and a third, by the outright sale of gold at the market price, or premium, holding at the time of any given transaction. On occasions of real difficulty in the money market the first and second methods were in less favor and the third was put into practice. In pursuing the policy of sales of gold Secretary McCulloch was severely criticized by those who favored a speedy resumption of specie payments and for whom the accumulation of gold was essential for that event, and especially by those who desired that the accumulations in the treasury might continue in order to prevent a decline in the premium on gold. Such a decline it was argued, would afford an unjustifiable profit to bondholders, whose securities might be redeemed at a higher gold value than that at which they had been bought. Regardless of these criticisms, one of which did not run counter entirely to the secretary's real purposes and the other of which was on a low moral plane, McCulloch maintained that the surplus gold should be used when necessary to steady the money market, prevent harmful speculation in gold, and promote the movement toward a specie standard. He used his powers to accomplish these ends. This was also practically the attitude of Secretary Boutwell, who took the treasury portfolio in the spring of 1869. In 1868 the prevailing practice of disposing of gold at private sale was changed to one of selling at auction to the highest bidder. In Wall Street commercial buyers of gold for legitimate trade purposes at once objected to this change on the ground that control over the gold market was thus thrown into the hands of unscrupulous speculators and gamblers. At all events, the limited supply of gold outside the treasury vaults, together with the marked speculative tendencies of the period, led Jay Gould and James Fisk, Jr., two of the most daring speculators of that day, to attempt to corner the gold supply.[1]

When Congress met in December, 1869, the House directed the committee on banking and currency, of which James A. Garfield was chairman, "to investigate the causes that led to the unusual and extraordinary fluctuations of gold in the City of New York, from the 21st to the 27th of September, 1869." Garfield's report on the "gold panic" makes clear the fact that Gould, Fisk, and their associates entered into a combination or an understanding as early as April of that year for the purpose of forcing the premium on gold to an artificially high point. The combination was called a conspiracy, but from a legal point of view conspiracy could not be proved. Rather, this group of speculators was guilty of pursuing a policy inimical to the public interest and designed to secure large profits to themselves as holders of gold, yet a policy within the pale of lawful action, however unethical it may have been. With this plan in view the group purchased within a month large amounts of gold at prices ranging from 30 to 35 per cent premium. This seems to have been done without exciting especial speculative activity. During May and June further large purchases were made, but not without considerable fluctuation in the premium. On May 20th the price of gold in greenbacks stood at 144, then

[1] D. R. Dewey, *Financial History of the United States*, New York, 1912, 4th ed., pp. 368–370.

declined until the last of July, when it stood at 136. Secretary Boutwell sold gold and bought government bonds at this time, but to what extent he did so with the purpose of checkmating speculative ventures does not appear.

President Grant had evidently determined to leave the treasury policy entirely in the hands of Boutwell. The latter had originally declined the offer of the treasury portfolio in the President's cabinet, but, regardless of his expressed wish, Senator Washburne insisted on a confirmation of the appointment by the Senate when the nomination came before that body. Feeling under the circumstances that he had no alternative, Boutwell finally accepted the appointment and assumed his duties. Perhaps partly for this reason, Grant gave his secretary a free hand. More likely, however, was the President influenced by the military view that a subordinate officer charged with the performance of a piece of work should be left free to act and should then be held strictly accountable for results. At any rate, this latter relationship between chief and subordinate continued throughout the four years of Boutwell's incumbency, and to such extent was it carried that, according to Boutwell, only one question of policy of any considerable importance was ever presented by him to the cabinet. That question related to the effect of a prospective loan on the political fortunes of Grant in his second presidential campaign in 1872. In fact, so slightly was the President informed as to coming events in the treasury that he is known to have lost money through sales of government securities held by him as private investments when a knowledge of the secretary's contemplated action as to purchase of bonds in the open market would have rendered such loss unnecessary. Notwithstanding these facts Grant was absurdly accused of influencing the money market, during the period of disturbance, in the interest of himself and family by means of manipulating government finances.

In order to safeguard the business interests of the country as far as possible against sudden and unexpected changes in the departmental policy, Boutwell followed the practice of publishing each month the sales of gold and the purchases of bonds which were to be made by the treasury. He, himself, on the last Sunday evening of the month, or the first Sunday evening of the new month, wrote the dispatches announcing the facts and sent one copy to the sub-treasury at New York and gave one to the agent of the Associated Press in Washington. In this way he hoped that no speculators would be able to secure advance information to the detriment of the general public. In spite of this precaution the practice thus followed gave opportunity to unscrupulous men to manipulate the gold market in such manner as to lead directly to the fateful "Black Friday." They assumed that rates announced by Boutwell at which gold would sell and bonds would be purchased would hold for the space of thirty days at least, and when their lines were well laid they proceeded to advance gold. Not being content with so short a period as thirty days in which to operate under the secretary's announced program, they sought to induce Boutwell to extend the time limit to two or three months. This the secretary, whose suspicions were aroused, steadfastly refused to do. His position was difficult, for the situation was not simple, speculation was not all on one side, and many of his correspondents acted from mixed motives. The interest of some men demanded not a rise but a fall in the premium. On September 23rd a prominent New York business man wrote him: "I am actuated to again portray to you the state of financial affairs as they now exist in this city. The speculative advance in gold has brought legitimate business almost to a standstill, owing to the apprehension of a corner, which from appearances may appear at any moment." On its face, this advice and the letter from which this extract is taken seemed genuine, but unfortunately for the writer Boutwell had been supplied with a list of houses which were operating on Wall Street for a fall and those operating for rise in the premium. The writer's name appeared among those who were "short on gold."

Gould, Fisk, and associates from April until September 24th had proceeded upon the false notion that the President did not favor the policy of selling gold. To encourage him in this policy they had developed and given publicity to their appealing "crop theory" that an advance in the price of gold would cause a general advance in prices of agricultural products of the West and hence bring prosperity of which the country stood in urgent need. Their gain from this outcome was apparent. Higher prices would induce the flow of crops to the eastern markets and to Europe. This movement of grain was to them highly desirable since they were at the time large owners of railways which would naturally transport a considerable share of the crops. Although the successful application of the "crop theory" might have moved grain and increased activity in trade, it could scarcely have aided their gold scheme, since that speculation must of necessity culminate within a few days. However, the speculators felt more sure of their ground from another quarter. The President's brother-in-law, A. R. Corbin, had lent himself to their purposes and was depended upon to bring to bear upon the treasury such influences as would be favorable to their designs and against the policy of selling treasury gold. Gould and his crowd even announced that the President had ordered the secretary not to sell gold during the month of September. That this was utterly false is evident from statements of Boutwell himself.[1] One especial attempt to commit Grant to a policy of holding fast to the treasury gold took place earlier, in June, on a Fall River steamboat, when the President was on his way to the Peace Jubilee at Boston. Accidentally, on the part of Grant, but doubtless by design so far as Gould and Fisk were concerned, these men, with others, found themselves fellow passengers on the boat from New York. Fisk and Gould arranged a supper party at which they determined "to have this thing pretty thoroughly talked up, and, if possible, to relieve him [Grant] from any idea of putting the price of gold down." But the President, as usual, was a listener. Finally, in response to a direct question asking for his opinion on the policy of holding the treasury's gold, he said that the country's prosperity was to a certain degree fictitious and that the bubble might as well be tapped in one way as another. This remark fell like a high explosive in the midst of

[1] See G. S. Boutwell, *Reminiscences of Sixty Years in Public Affairs*, p. 169 *et seq.*

the gold raiders, for, as they afterwards testified, it indicated that the President was a contractionist and that he might let loose the accumulated gold. Nevertheless, having Corbin as a tool, and persuading themselves that the treasury's policy of selling limited amounts only of gold would continue, they pressed their game.

On September 22nd Boutwell was prepared to act. He had a conference with Grant at which the evidence was laid before the latter showing that Gould and Fisk had their plans laid—first, to influence the President to take such action as would advance the premium on gold; and, second, to convince their friends and their enemies that he would take that action. Corbin, who, as we now know, had no influence whatever over the President, had given assurances that the desired action would be taken. Unprincipled attempts were made through the press to strengthen the impression of the public to this effect; and in private letters to Secretary Boutwell, Gould used all the arguments, both sound and plausible, which he could bring to bear. The interests of the western farmer in securing good prices for his crops were cited. A high premium on gold was the only means to advance prices to a point where our high-priced labor and long-rail transportation to the seaboard would enable us to compete with the grain-producing countries of the Black and Mediterranean Seas. Export of our surplus products would pay our foreign debt, turn the trade balance in our favor, and thus, bringing gold to us, would eventually and safely lead to the natural decline of the gold premium. But these arguments were by no means dust in the secretary's eyes. He made either noncommittal replies or none whatever. The raiders had also fortified themselves behind the strong vaults of some New York banks. For example, it was known to Boutwell as early as September 20th that the Tenth National Bank of that city was a party to the speculation in gold and played its rôle by certifying checks drawn by brokers to vast amounts in excess of balances due them on the books of the bank. Immediate steps were taken to correct this abuse by placing that bank under the direct supervision of the Comptroller of the Currency and by trying to stop over-certification by other institutions as well. This move failed to check the speculative mania. On Thursday afternoon, September 23rd, gold was quoted at 144, and during the evening the clique, confident of the outcome, held a meeting to concoct plans for the following day. The operations at the gold clearing house, amounting on the average to about $70 millions daily, had on that date risen to $239 millions. The raiders held calls for more than $100 millions of gold, while there actually existed in New York, outside of the sub-treasury, but $15 millions of gold coin and gold certificates. They seemed to dominate the entire situation. Every man who had bought or lent gold owed it to them, and to square himself must secure the actual gold from them or settle on ruinous terms dictated by them. They had a complete list of over two hundred and fifty important New York firms who were short on gold and many of whom required gold for legitimate business purposes. They determined to put up gold still further on Friday and compel their victims to settle at 160. After business hours on that Thursday also the President and the secretary had a conference. In that conference they decided to sell a sufficient amount of gold to break the combination. The next morning Boutwell sent an order to the assistant treasurer in New York to "sell $4,000,000 gold tomorrow and buy $4,000,000 bonds." The message was not in cipher and was forwarded over each of the rival telegraph lines to New York. Within fifteen minutes after its receipt the price of gold fell from 160[1] to 133. The report came back that "half of Wall Street was involved in ruin." Although this statement proved to be an exaggeration of the facts, "the demoralization in the street was never equaled" and there was "a wholesome dread against making any obligations." On that eventful September 24th the secretary's special and trusted correspondent in New York wrote:

This has been the most dreadful day I have ever seen in this city. While gold was jumping from forty-three to sixty-one the excitement was

[1] In September the premium on gold reached 162½. See W. C. Mitchell, *Gold, Prices, and Wages under the Greenback Standard*, Berkeley, 1908, p. 8 (hereafter referred to as Mitchell, *Gold, Prices, and Wages*).

painful. Old, conservative merchants looked aghast, nobody was in their offices, and the agony depicted on the faces of men who crowded the streets made one feel as if Gettysburg had been lost and that the rebels were marching down Broadway. Friends of the Administration openly stated that the President or yourself must have given these men to feel you would not interfere with them or they would never dare to rush gold up so rapidly. In truth, many parties of real responsibility and friends of the government openly declared that somebody in Washington must be in this combination.

Grinnel, the collector of the port of New York, expressed the belief, held by many responsible persons, that had the secretary not taken the course he did "a large proportion of our most reliable merchants and brokers would have been obliged to suspend before three o'clock today, as confidence was entirely gone and the panic was becoming universal."

From April 29th, when Boutwell made his first actual sale of gold, to December 31st, the total sales were in round numbers $53 millions and the proceeds in greenbacks $70 millions. It was no part of the secretary's policy to regulate the business of Wall Street or other financial markets. It was only after the operations of the gold gamblers in New York had seriously threatened the business interests of the country and had, through the creation of conditions of panic, diminished the receipts of the federal treasury that he came forward to place a check upon those who were engaged in either forcing up or forcing down the price of gold. Excellent reasons undoubtedly can be assigned why a secretary of the treasury, or any other individual, should not be given authority to wield such enormous and uncertain powers over business interests. Yet, at the same time, Boutwell seemed to have no choice. When he entered office he found the practice in vogue and he had a crisis to meet. It was an almost inevitable penalty resulting from entangling the currency system with the financial system of the government.

It appears from Garfield's report to Congress that Gould originated the scheme and that Fisk, who from the first doubted its practical working but whose appetite was always sharpened by the scent of crooked dealing, in this instance followed the judgment of his erstwhile enemy of Erie fame. It was Fisk's infectious enthusiasm that contributed no small share to the havoc which followed. Gould, to repeat, had two main purposes in view: first, to secure large gains from a corner on gold outside the treasury vaults; second, to secure increased profits from railway traffic which he argued would be induced by a rise of gold and of prices. For selfish gain he willingly risked disaster to enemies, personal friends, and country alike. But, unfortunately for him, the scheme he built up accompolished too much. It was no part of his original plan that gold should go above 40 to 45 per cent premium. If he could have restrained his own greed and held the movement within this range, it is possible that his ends might have been consummated. When the price mounted to those quotations he and his associates forced those unfortunates who had contracted to deliver gold to make their margins good or else produce the gold. This pressure to deliver what could not be secured drove the street to panic, and, bidding against each other, the dupes of Gould carried the price to points which proved ruinous alike to them and to his own ill-conceived scheme.

So long as the greenback standard continued and a premium on specie existed, the temptations to speculate in gold were too strong to be resisted. The panic of "Black Friday" was one of the items in the great bill of costs which the country paid on account of its lapse into a paper money régime.

The Greenbacks and Price Fluctuations

Depreciation of a paper money standard marks the extent of the rise of prices—or rather, it is the reverse side of the rise of prices. The fluctuations in paper money prices are usually more frequent and more varied than those of gold prices, not only on account of ease of issue, but because paper money cannot move in and out of the issuing country under the normal influence of the monetary and commercial forces which control the international flow of the precious metals under a specie régime. Inconvertible paper is not acceptable as means of payment between nations. Being thus deprived of a natural means of adjusting the supply of money to the demand for it, inconvertible paper tends to vary widely in value. A comparison of price levels in the United States with those of England and Germany during the period 1860–80 shows a wide divergence —that in America being much higher. The chief cause of the difference and of the extraordinary advance in prices in this country during the years of the Civil War was the substitution of irredeemable greenbacks for specie as the price-making standard, and the great fall in prices from 1865 to 1879 took place as the greenback dollar gradually but unsteadily rose to par with gold.[1]

The history of the greenbacks illustrates in exemplary fashion the effects of paper money on prices of gold and of commodities. The following tables are taken from Mitchell's statistical study of the greenbacks.[2] They show, for the period 1862–78, the lowest, average, and highest price of gold in greenbacks for each year, and also the relative wholesale prices of commodities and the price of gold, by quarters, for the period

TABLE A

LOWEST, AVERAGE, AND HIGHEST PRICE OF GOLD IN GREENBACKS, BY YEARS, 1862–1878

Years	Lowest	Average	Highest	Range
1862	100½	113.3	134	33½
1863	122⅛	145.2	172½	50⅜
1864	151½	203.3	285	133½
1865	128⅝	157.3	233¾	105⅛
1866	125	140.9	167¾	42¾
1867	132	138.2	146⅜	14⅜
1868	132⅛	139.7	150	17⅞
1869	119½	133.0	162½	43
1870	110	114.9	123¼	13¼
1871	108⅜	111.7	115⅜	7
1872	108½	112.4	115⅝	7⅛
1873	106⅛	113.8	119⅛	13
1874	109	111.2	114⅜	5⅜
1875	111¾	114.9	117⅝	5⅞
1876	107	111.5	115	8
1877	102½	104.8	107⅞	5⅜
1878	100	100.8	102⅞	2⅞

[1] Cf. Mitchell, *Gold, Prices, and Wages*, pp. 31–42.

[2] *Ibid.*, pp. 4, 59, 60.

TABLE B

COMPARISON OF RELATIVE WHOLESALE PRICES OF COMMODITIES AND OF THE PRICE OF GOLD, BY QUARTERS, 1860–1880.
(Actual prices in 1860=100)

	Average Price of Gold	Median Wholesale Price
1860		
January....	100.0	100
April.......	100.0	100
July........	100.0	100
October.....	100.0	100
1861		
January....	100.0	100
April.......	100.0	96
July........	100.0	96
October.....	100.0	97
1862		
January....	102.5	100
April.......	101.5	100
July........	115.5	100
October.....	128.5	111
1863		
January....	145.1	125
April.......	151.5	137
July........	130.6	134
October.....	147.7	135
1864		
January....	155.5	156
April.......	172.7	169
July........	258.1	194
October.....	207.2	200
1865		
January....	216.2	216
April.......	148.5	190
July........	142.1	158
October.....	145.5	175
1866		
January	140.1	182
April.......	127.3	173
1866 (*Continued*)		
July........	151.6	181
October.....	148.3	173
1867		
January....	134.6	169
April.......	135.6	166
July........	139.4	150
October.....	143.5	162
1868		
January....	138.5	158
April.......	138.7	162
July........	142.7	154
October.....	137.1	159
1869		
January....	135.6	159
April.......	132.9	159
July........	136.1	158
October.....	130.2	153
1870		
January....	121.3	147
April.......	113.1	140
July........	116.8	132
October.....	112.8	135
1871		
January....	110.7	133
April.......	110.6	131
July........	112.4	130
October.....	113.2	129
1872		
January....	109.1	133
April.......	111.1	140
July........	114.3	130
October.....	113.2	133

TABLE B—*Continued*

	Average Price of Gold	Median Wholesale Price		Average Price of Gold	Median Wholesale Price
1873			1877		
January....	112.7	135	January....	106.3	114
April.......	117.8	137	April.......	106.2	108
July........	115.7	130	July........	105.4	100
October.....	108.9	131	October.....	102.8	102
1874			1878		
January....	111.4	130	January....	102.1	99
April.......	113.4	129	April.......	100.6	96
July........	110.0	130	July........	100.5	90
October.....	110.0	130	October.....	100.5	94
1875			1879		
January....	112.5	127	January....	100.0	88
April.......	114.8	125	April.......	100.0	84
July........	114.8	121	July........	100.0	85
October.....	116.4	120	October.....	100.0	95
1876			1880		
January....	112.8	117	January....	100.0	108
April.......	113.0	115	April.......	100.0	107
July........	111.9	110	July........	100.0	102
October.....	109.7	108	October.....	100.0	101

of 1860–80. The figures for commodities are Mitchell's median relative prices, and the quarterly quotations are for the months named and not for the average of the quarter.

Examination of the figures in these tables indicates a strong general tendency for the price of gold (or gold premium) and the price of commodities at wholesale to fluctuate correspondingly. When, in July, 1863, commodity prices in greenbacks rose to 134, gold stood at 130; when, in July, 1864, prices advanced to 194, gold stood at 258; prices in July, 1867, were 150 and gold 139; prices in July, 1869, were 158 and gold 136; prices in July, 1874, were 130 and gold 110. More detailed figures would show that "fluctuations in the price of gold, which attracted so much attention, were much more moderate than the extreme fluctuations in the prices of commodities,"[1] more than one-tenth of the commodities in typical series having lower relative prices than gold and more than one-tenth higher relative prices. During the war, however, the oscillations in the price of gold were more frequent and wider than those of the mass of commodities, and later even the rapid fall of prices in the spring of 1865 was outrun by the fall in gold. This fact was probably due to the more highly organized character of the gold market.[2] There were several distinct periods of fluctuations in gold during the greenback period. The first of these extended from the spring of 1862 to Lee's surrender in April, 1865, and was marked by violent fluctuations and high average premiums. During this period commodity prices were, with the difference just noted, similar in character as to fluctuations and high range. The next period extends from the spring of 1865 to "Black Friday," September 24, 1869, and, despite the riotous speculation of 1869 and other untoward events, the gold market was much quieter than during the war. The third period, from the autumn of 1869 to the spring of 1876, was characterized by a much lower average gold premium than had existed theretofore, but without much additional reduction in the premium during the period. This lower range of the premium, or improvement in the greenback currency, was due to the better financial credit of the government and to the fact that the country was "growing up to the currency." It was the period containing, on the one hand, the crisis of 1873 and, on the other, the resumption act of 1875. The last period extends from early 1876 to the resumption of specie payments on January 1, 1879, and during these three years the effective preparations for resumption gradually forced the greenback dollar to par with gold.[3]

After the war closed, the periods of fluctuation marked off for the gold premium on the one hand, and for wholesale commodity prices on the other, were not the same. For example,

[1] *Ibid.*, p. 39.

[2] *Ibid.*, p. 40.

[3] *Ibid.*, pp. 13, 14.

from 1866 to 1869 prices show a rather consistent decline, while gold, although fluctuating, maintained a comparatively consistent level. Again a turning point occurs in the gold premium in the last months of 1869 and first of 1870, but not so in commodity prices. After the first of the year 1870 gold fell to a lower level than in preceding years and then maintained that level until 1876, but commodity prices with slight exception continued their decline through these years, standing considerably lower at the end of the year 1875 than in 1870. Then, for the final period, gold consistently fell from the early part of 1876 to the date of resumption, and prices continued a still more rapid decline which was definitely begun in 1875. It is clear that the most important turning points in the gold premium were the close of 1869 and the beginning of 1876, while those of commodity prices were the speculative movements of 1872, the crisis of 1873, and the harvests of 1879.[1]

The correspondence of these two sets of fluctuations is a rough one only, yet it is sufficiently close to indicate that in large measure both are the result of the same common cause, such as changes in the quantity of money. On the other hand, these fluctuations differ widely enough to indicate the existence of separate causes operating on the gold premium itself.[2] Doubtless one such cause was the prospect of redemption in specie, as, for example, when the premium on gold rose and fell during the Civil War with the fortunes of the Northern armies and therefore with the hope, or hopelessness, that the federal government would sometime be able to redeem its promises. Again, as compared with preceding years, the generally lower level about which the premium fluctuated from Black Friday, September 24, 1869, to the early months of 1876 was influenced by the marked betterment in the public cred-

[1] *Ibid.*, p. 41.

[2] The attempt is not made here to determine the *extent* of the difference in the purchasing power of gold and the purchasing power of greenbacks. To do that would require a comparison of gold prices of commodities and greenback prices of commodities at corresponding dates. The object is to make the point clear that several causes were operating on the gold premium in addition to the quantity of greenbacks themselves.

it due to the "Public Credit Act" of 1869, successful refunding operations, and systematic payment on the public debt.[1] Another cause of special fluctuations in the premium was the demand for gold to make remittances to foreign countries. Still another influence was the various domestic calls for gold to liquidate contracts specifically payable in that metal. These and similar special causes acting on the price of gold (or the gold premium) account for its divergence from the paper money price-level, while at the same time the normal tendency to general harmony between the two sets of fluctuations was continuously impeded by the intricate processes of business by which changes in prices tend only slowly to become readjusted to each other and smoothed over. Abrupt changes in the gold premium "have led to the statement that confidence in paper money governs its value once for all, or at least mainly affects its value. It is more legitimate to say that confidence in redemption affects the value, not of paper, but of the specie. General prices do not move up and down under the influence of military or political fortunes. It is the price of specie in terms of paper that is affected; for dealers and speculators discount at once the consequences for the financial stability of the government and for the possible resumption of specie payments."[2]

During the seventeen years of the greenback standard the country experienced two conspicuous price-revolutions—first, a great rise to the first of the year 1865, then a great fall to the close of the period. In their violence, rapidity, variety, and inclusiveness, the price fluctuations of both revolutions constituted the most notable instance of the kind in the history of prices during the century preceding the Great War of 1914. Prices at wholesale, at retail, and the price of labor all fluctuated over wide ranges.[3]

The price revolutions in the wholesale markets naturally led to similar changes in the retail and labor markets. Retail prices lagged behind prices at wholesale. The former were slower than

[1] *Ibid.*, p. 14.

[2] Taussig, *op. cit.*, Vol. I, 3rd ed., pp. 311, 312.

[3] Mitchell, *Gold, Prices, and Wages*, p. 249.

the latter in rising from 1863 to 1865 and much slower in falling after 1865. Several causes explain such deviations. In the first place, retail markets are not as well organized as wholesale markets. The men concerned are usually not so able, so intent on good bargains, not given up so exclusively to purely business motives. Custom, habit, exercise more control in retail prices. Secondly, the retail dealer has on hand goods which the wholesaler disposed of some time before. If wholesale prices fall the retailers cannot reduce prices without loss and therefore resist change, and if wholesale prices rise customers bring pressure to bear to prevent the retailer from advancing his wares. Again, the retailer has other costs, such as rent, wages, and interest, which must be met in addition to the cost of his goods at wholesale. These are expenses which usually continue for some time at approximately the old rates and influence the retailers to maintain prices. Still further, the retailer buys finished products at wholesale, but prices of raw materials vary more frequently and more widely than do wholesale prices of finished products. Consequently wholesale prices in the aggregate fluctuate more than do those of finished products which influence more directly the retailer. These facts explain why "retail prices rose more slowly than wholesale prices from 1863 to 1865, reached their maximum about a year later, declined more slowly from 1866 to 1879, and rose less sharply in 1880."[1]

The price of labor was influenced by changes in the prices of commodities both at wholesale and retail. An increase of wages could be granted without a reduction of the former rate of profit, by a manufacturer whose product rose in price. If the product fell in price the usual recourse to prevent a fall in profits was to force a reduction of wages. But from his point of view, the laborer was more interested, as always, in commodity prices which affected the cost of living. During the greenback period "the cost of living corresponded rather closely with the general movements of retail prices, but rose and fell more slowly—primarily because of the sluggish movements of house rents. . . . To maintain his real wages unchanged, therefore,

[1] *Ibid.*, pp. 273–275.

and provided constancy of employment did not vary, the wage-earner must have charged a price for his labor advancing somewhat more slowly than retail prices to a maximum in 1866, and then falling somewhat more slowly to a minimum in 1879."[1] Deviations from this order of events find their explanations in the special characteristics of the labor market. That market in the sixties and largely in the seventies was one in which the laborer made his own individual bargain for wages, and, being proverbially a poor bargainer, comparatively ignorant of the possibilities of his situation, and influenced by the existence of a "customary wage," the price of his labor fluctuated more slowly than the fluctuations of the cost of living. Furthermore, the greater constancy of employment during the years of rising prices tended to increase the earnings of workmen and to make the need for an increase in the rate of wages seem less urgent to them. The outcome of the situation was that the price of labor advanced less rapidly than the cost of living up to 1866, although men left the labor market in great numbers for service in the war. It continued to advance for several years after 1866, while prices at wholesale and the cost of living were declining. After the crisis of 1873, it fell in sympathy with the movement of wholesale prices and the cost of living, and from 1874 to 1879 fell faster than the cost of living. The facts available "indicate that in degree of mobility the different classes of prices rank in the following order: gold, raw materials, finished products at wholesale, products at retail, cost of living, and labor."[2]

The social significance of the changes in the different classes of prices is found in their effects upon the welfare of different economic classes of men. The different classes of men were affected in different ways—some being benefited, some injured, by a given set of changes. The process of change was attended by serious friction, but this friction did not, upon the whole, prevent the price system from displaying a remarkable flexibility. Wholesale prices lagged behind the price of gold, re-

[1] *Ibid.*, p. 275.
[2] *Ibid.*, pp. 275, 276, 278.

tail prices lagged behind wholesale prices, cost of living behind retail prices, and wages behind cost of living. Yet, one is "much more impressed by the rapidity and system with which prices of different classes of goods were changed than by the lack of completeness in adjustment." Throughout the process of change, the flexibility which the price system displayed was so well ordered and the mutual relations of its different parts so well maintained that economic disaster was not as serious as might reasonably have been expected, and business continued to be conducted in a fairly normal fashion. Even the great business crisis of 1873 and the years of depression which followed it cannot properly be ascribed to the influence of the greenback standard. Their causes and effects operated quite as severely in European countries with a specie standard as they did in America, and they occurred years after the most violent and revolutionary price changes had taken place. The "extraordinary fluctuations of 1865, when the median of relative wholesale prices fell 58 points in six months, passed without disaster." Nevertheless these price changes had tremendously important effects upon the production and distribution of wealth. The real incomes of wage-earners and all recipients of fixed incomes were seriously affected; profits were influenced by dissimilar movements in prices and wages; lending capitalists shared in the vicissitudes of the period; and these changes in turn influenced the production of wealth.[1]

The Quantity Theory of Money

The quantity theory of money finds some support by reference to the changes in prices and in the quantity of currency in circulation during this period of 1862 to 1879. Professor Irving Fisher has given the argument succinctly in his classic, *The Purchasing Power of Money*.[2] Fluctuations in the value of the greenbacks were apparently caused by changes in the quantity of them in circulation or by anticipation of such changes. The quantity which circulated at any given time was determined by

[1] *Ibid.*, pp. 282, 283.

[2] See pp. 259–263.

confidence in the greenbacks as the monetary standard of the period. Confidence, in turn, might depend upon a number of influences, especially upon the prospect of redemption in gold and the probability of further inflation or contraction. California and a large portion of the adjoining Rocky Mountain territory distrusted paper money of any kind and, at the beginning of the paper money period, put forth strenuous efforts to prevent a circulation of greenbacks.[1] Due to the degree of success attending those efforts and to the fact that they did not circulate in the South, the circulation of greenbacks was confined to approximately two-thirds of the population of the country. The volume of trade for which they could be used, therefore, was much smaller than that exchanged by the circulating media in use before the war. This influence tended toward a rise of prices. If now, in spite of his warning as to their lack in completeness, we accept Mitchell's estimates[2] of the total circulating media for the years 1860 to 1866, as a rough approximation and the best attainable, and compare them with the average of his quarterly median prices[3] for corresponding years, we have the following table:[4]

Year	Estimated Circulation in Loyal States. (In millions of dollars)	Median Relative Wholesale Prices
1860	432	100
1861	490	97
1862	360	103
1863	677	133
1864	708	180
1865	774	185
1866	759	177

[1] See an excellent article on this subject by Professor Bernard Moses, "Legal Tender Notes in California," *Quarterly Journal of Economics*, Vol. VII, p. 1.

[2] See Mitchell, *Greenbacks*, p. 179. Also see *infra*, Chapter V, pp. 132 *et seq*.

[3] See above, p. 97.

[4] I exclude, as does Fisher, money in the treasury and interest-bearing forms given in Mitchell's estimate, since they had only a very sluggish circulation. I have used Mitchell's median figures for prices. Fisher used Falkner's prices in the Aldrich Report.

With the exception of the year 1862, when gold dropped out of circulation and greenbacks were slow in issuing, the figures in the two columns of this table show a striking correspondence in both increases and decreases. As the quantity of currency increased from 1861 to 1865, the price index increased roughly simultaneously and the fall took place in both from 1865 to 1866. For a complete demonstration of the quantity theory several important factors are not available—bank deposits, velocity of circulation, and the volume of trade. The partial evidence we have in the table given above, however, points to a confirmation of the theory.

CONCLUSION

In the present state of economic science little excuse is afforded governments of the present day to overstep the limits of paper money issues and to throw upon a people the evils of a depreciated and fluctuating currency, the almost certain speculation in gold, and the painful process of return to a specie basis. As indicated in preceding pages, several signs of approaching danger serve as dependable warnings[1] against overissues. First, we have the premium on gold. The moment excessive issues are made, bankers and other possessors of gold feel the pressure of demand for that metal as compared with the demand for paper currency, and, consequently, compelled by their business interests, they make an extra charge in terms of the paper standard for metallic money. Second, the rate of foreign exchange is affected. Foreign bills of exchange, selling in all the great commercial centers of the world, have their value fixed like any other commodity by the law of demand and supply. But these claims on foreign countries must at bottom be paid in gold since gold is the only acceptable international money. When paper money begins to depreciate the rate of exchange on foreign centers rises correspondingly because foreign bills are equivalent to gold. A third sign of danger may be the disappearance of gold from the general circulating media. In such case the flight of metallic money is in obe-

[1] Cf. Gide, *Political Economy* (Veditz translation), pp. 270–273.

dience to Gresham's law and is a characteristic phenomenon. A fourth sign of excessive issues of inconvertible paper is the rise of prices, although a rise of prices may merely be evidence of a decline in the purchasing power of gold. Excessive issue of paper causes depreciation, and depreciation is rise in prices. This sign may not be the first indicated to the public, but it is the fundamental phenomenon. While depreciation is still slight, the reluctance to disturb the equilibrium of business processes which we call custom may prevent the retailer and even the wholesaler from advancing prices. Sooner or later inflated prices appear. Finally it is observed that two different sets of prices—gold and paper—exist for all imported and exported commodities and for such domestic commodities as may still in part be exchanged by means of metallic money. The difference between the two sets of prices measures the depreciation of the paper currency. So soon, therefore, as a government perceives any of these premonitory signs it has a warning that paper money has been overissued, and it can, if it will, proceed to remedy the situation by a relative contraction of the currency.

CHAPTER V

RESUMPTION POSSIBLE, 1865–66

FOR a period of almost fourteen years after the close of the Civil War, the United States postponed the resumption of specie payments. This period of prolonged delay was characterized by a confusion of ideas on monetary affairs, by powerful political manœuvers designed to tamper with the monetary standard, and by great uncertainty in business due to fluctuating prices in terms of paper money, all of which led, in turn, to constant disturbances in the production and the distribution of wealth. The consequent misfortunes and suffering during those fourteen years were so great that one is impelled to inquire whether resumption could not have been accomplished at a much earlier date than January 1, 1879. It is not too much to say that the months of 1865–66 immediately following the close of the war presented a favorable opportunity for resumption. In this chapter, the question of the wisdom of resuming at that time will be examined. Such an inquiry will serve also to reveal important economic conditions of the period.

SPECULATIVE DEALINGS, FLUCTUATIONS IN PRICES, AND THE GOLD PREMIUM

General business conditions were sound during the period immediately following the war. Even speculative dealings were diminished and in marked contrast with those of the mid-war period. At times during the war speculation had reached a dizzy height. After the issue of paper money in 1862, prices did not advance as soon or as much as was expected. Operators in Wall Street had grown weary with waiting for the upward movement. But when the advance eventually came, so it seemed to them, the intensity of the rise in prices and the gold premium was somewhat in proportion to the length of time that the movement had been deferred. Gold and commodity prices leaped upward several points per month. Such conditions encouraged further speculation. The violent movement lasted throughout the year 1863, and by April, 1864, almost every man in the country, as seen from the viewpoint of observers in Wall Street, had become a trader and a gambler. Many had grown rich. The old maxim concerning industry and thrift was thrown to the winds and a substitute found—namely: "The way to grow rich is to buy; no matter what, or at what price—but buy."

Men realized that continuing success in business depended upon the future course of prices. They fully realized how precarious this future was. A pronounced tendency was evident to favor trade and to abandon the field of what may be called in the narrow sense productive enterprises. The pursuit of agriculture and manufactures proved to be less attractive forms of enterprise than did more purely speculative ventures. This situation led McCulloch in his first annual report as secretary of the treasury in 1865 to state:

> There are no indications of real and permanent prosperity . . . in the splendid fortunes reported to be made by skillful manipulations at the gold room or the stock board; no evidence of increasing wealth in the facts that railroads and steamboats are crowded with passengers and hotels with guests; that cities are full to overflowing, and rents and the necessities of life, as well as luxuries, are daily increasing. All these things proved rather . . . that the number of non-producers is increasing and that productive industry is being diminished. There is no fact more manifest than that the plethora of paper money is not only undermining the morals of the people by encouraging waste and extravagance, but is striking at the root of our material prosperity by diminishing labor.[1]

More explicit was David A. Wells's statement of the movement away from industry and toward speculative trading. In one of his reports as special commissioner of the revenue he said:

> During the last few years large numbers of our population, under the influence and example of high profits realized in trading during the period of monetary expansion, have abandoned employment directly productive of national wealth, and sought employment connected with commerce, trading, or speculation. As a consequence we everywhere find large additions to the population of our commercial cities, an increase in the number and cost of the buildings devoted to banking, brokerage, insur-

[1] P. 9, and quoted by Mitchell, *Greenbacks*, p. 397.

ance, commission business, and agencies of all kinds, the spirit of trading and speculation pervading the whole community, as distinguished from the spirit of production.[1]

When the spring months of 1864 arrived, most men of speculative tendencies throughout the country had bought something on credit and at prices unprecedently high. But in early summer of that year Wall Street suffered a severe panic which brought ruin to some of its most respectable houses, and the orgy of speculation received an appreciable check.

In spite of the gold bill, through which Congress had sought to control the fluctuations in gold, yet partly because of it, gold had continued to advance. As indicated in a previous chapter,[2] Secretary Chase, bitterly disappointed over his inability to control the monetary and financial situation, and peeved at fancied slights by President Lincoln concerning the appointment of subordinates in the treasury department, resigned from the cabinet. The gold bill upon which Chase had relied to stop speculation and the rapid fluctuations in the gold premium proved a failure and was repealed within two weeks after its enactment. Commodity prices at wholesale continued to rise, although the rate of advance was diminished. Mitchell's quarterly median index figures show the following range of relative wholesale prices:[3]

(Actual Prices 1860=100)

	1862	1863	1864	1865	1866
January	100	125	156	216	182
April	100	137	169	190	173
July	100	134	194	158	181
October	111	135	200	175	173

We see from this table that prices of commodities advanced almost continuously from the summer of 1862 to the early days of 1865, that the index number of July, 1864, stood at 194 as compared with the base of 100, 1860, and that it rose

[1] *Ibid.*, pp. 397–398.

[2] See above, p. 70.

[3] Mitchell, *Gold, Prices, and Wages*, p. 59.

only slightly by October following, standing then at 200. This, however, was only a temporary check. Prices continued to rise sharply during the succeeding quarter, when, standing at 216 in January, 1865, they touched the highest point reached in the greenback period. The fall in prices after January, 1865, was even more sudden and precipitous than the great rise had been. The drop aggregated 58 points from January to July of that year. The premium on gold went through a corresponding though more violent revolution. Standing in January, 1864, as low as 151.5, gold experienced a remarkable advance to 285 in the following July, and then dropped irregularly from that point to an average of 135.6 for the month of May, 1865, the lowest single quotation for this month being 128.6.[1]

As early as the second and third weeks of March, 1865, gold had fallen to the neighborhood of 150—such was the demand for greenbacks and the confidence in the government's ability to bring about an early termination of the war. The probable future of the gold premium and of prices was thus heavily discounted in spite of precaution from well-informed sources. Conservative men, such as Professor Dunbar, who was then the able editor of the *Boston Advertiser*, held that so great a reduction in the gold premium was natural only upon the fulfillment of two conditions—namely, actual relief to government credit coming from the removal of military activities and military burdens, and secondly, a relative reduction in the volume of currency. With respect to both of these influences the country had anticipated results of work yet to be done.[2] The effect of this situation was traced in the markets for merchandise. Here there was something approaching a panic. A state of affairs existed in which men were alarmed by uncertain fears and by apprehensions of what might happen if gold and prices should go still lower. In this doubtful state of affairs, uncertain whether the winding up of the long period of expansion had come, the great conservative class of business

[1] *Ibid.*, p. 6; and Bonner, "The Great Gold Conspiracy," *Harper's Magazine*, Vol. XL, p. 746.

[2] *Boston Advertiser*, March 24, 1865.

men, and even the speculative and trading portion of the community, had been indisposed to move and to place themselves under obligations which it might be ruinous to meet.

Effects of Price Fluctuations on Incomes of Different Economic Classes[1]

The violent price fluctuations during the war period caused far-reaching disturbances in the economic relations of the different economic classes of society. The paper currency had been issued for fiscal reasons, but the results of the issue extended to every corner of the economic organization and affected for good or ill the income of every person in the country. The decline in the specie value of the greenbacks indicated an extraordinary rise in paper money prices.[2] Since production and distribution of wealth take place by a process of money payments, the division of the real income of society—necessities, comforts, and luxuries—in the first instance is seriously affected by price changes. Business men obtain the use of land, labor, and capital by paying money prices for these factors of production to the landowner, the wage-earner, and the capitalist. They reckon their own profits in money. But the system of money and exchange is only a convenient means of distributing the total real income of society among the various economic classes which have produced that income. In other words, when the price level changes, the effect is to disturb the proportions of the good things of life which flow to landowners, laborers, capitalists, and business men as their reward for assistance in producing consumable commodities. The rise of prices in greenbacks decreased the purchasing power of a given money income and hence decreased the real income. The

[1] See *passim*, Mitchell, *Greenbacks*, Part II, chaps. 1 and 5 to 10. It is proper here to make this blanket reference to Mitchell on this part of chap. 5. Specific references will also be made. His purpose was, however, different from mine. He was interested to explain the losses men sustained during the war from the overissue of greenbacks, while I am interested to show that all classes were in fairly comfortable condition in the months following the close of the war.

[2] The fluctuations in the price level which would have taken place under a specie standard are not here considered.

inconvenience and suffering caused by diminishing the accustomed quantity of satisfactions to any group of persons led that group to demand an increase in money income in order to offset losses incurred from rising prices. Hence we find laborers struggling for higher wages, landowners for higher rents, capitalists for higher interest. At the same time, to resist the demands of the other economic classes was the rôle of business men, whose money incomes (and real incomes) were initially, as always, increased by rising prices. In sum, the effort was made to restore the same relative distribution of wealth among the different economic classes as had prevailed before the disturbance in prices took place.

Many obstacles stood in the way of this readjustment. Legal contracts in existence when the rise of prices began, for the payment of specified rates of wages, interest, and rent, tended, until their termination, to prevent the recovery of losses incurred. Customary prices such as street-car fares, given types of clothing, fees for special kinds of service, etc., were difficult to change. And even though difficulties of contracts and customary prices were overcome, changes in the amount of certain money payments tended to produce friction, since any change whatever set on foot other changes which were resisted by persons who would be injured by them. "Persons whose products or service do not at once rise in price, oppose, so far as they can, changes which increase their money expenditures."[1] The situation was further complicated because the readjustments necessitated under the greenback standard, especially for the period of the war and immediately following were very numerous. No sooner was one readjustment well under way than a change in the value of a dollar and a corresponding shift in prices made another process of adjustment necessary.

We may conclude that the most important consequence of suspending specie payments and establishing a paper money standard during the Civil War was the serious alterations which

[1] Mitchell, *Greenbacks*, p. 139.

took place in the real incomes of business men, landowners, capitalists, and laborers.

Professor Mitchell, in his *History of the Greenbacks*, was interested to reveal and explain the losses which each economic class in the country sustained as a result of the excessive issue of paper money, while here, in the pages immediately following, the purpose is to show that when the period of the summer and autumn of 1865 was reached each economic class had, in substantial degree if not fully, recovered its comfortable economic position and was then in a fair condition to undergo the process of resumption of specie payments.

Condition of each Economic Class and Resumption in 1865–66

What, then, was the financial condition of each economic class in the community in 1865–66: (1) the business man, (2) the landowner, (3) the capitalist, and (4) the wage-earner?

Business Men

First, as to the business man. The more sober-minded portions of the business man's class bore the principal burden of the economic progress of the nation. Upon their financial and economic status, more than upon that of the more purely speculative portion, depended the ability of the country to resume specie payments soon after the close of the war. We need more particularly to see how they stood at that time. They also, of course, had been affected by fluctuations in gold and in prices. But they had been remarkably cautious in certain phases of their financial undertakings. Although there had been some departure from the system of cash payments into which the war had led the non-speculative element of the community and although private credits had, to some extent, been increased, most men in the ordinary channels of business had due regard to the old maxim that a period of inflation is not the time in which to contract debts. During practically the entire period of the war great uncertainty prevailed concerning the future course of prices.[1] When men were

[1] *Ibid.*, pp. 374, 376.

enjoying profitable business they were well aware that profits were frequently due to the depreciation of the greenback standard. If prices should drop suddenly, as might happen at any time owing to a change in the military situation and consequent relative contraction of the greenback circulation, business affairs might easily be quickly and adversely affected. With such a possibility in view cautious men refused to enter into contracts which would involve them in repaying large amounts in so uncertain a future. A debtor facing falling prices might be compelled to make disadvantageous sales of products or other property in order to meet his obligations. The man who kept within the narrower field of operations with his own capital would enjoy a safer position. The noticeable decline in credit operations during the war is evidence that business men of the non-speculative class gave heed to considerations such as these. As credit operations declined business on a cash basis increased. "Even the West, which has long been wont to strain credit to its utmost, is now buying and selling for cash to an unprecedented degree," the *New York Times* stated in November, 1863.[1] The next year Dun's Mercantile Agency expressed the opinion that the small number of bankruptcies at that time was to be attributed to "rigid action" in dispensing credits.[2] McCulloch adds the weight of his belief that in the latter part of 1865 trade was "carried on much more largely for cash than was ever the case previous to 1861," and, further, that individuals are free from debt in greater degree than in previous years.[3] A survey made by the *Commercial and Financial Chronicle* in the autumn of 1865 brings the same conclusion. In so far as these conditions affected the financial status of business men, they tended to place them on a sound footing during the months following the close of the war.

Furthermore, we have evidence tending to show that the

[1] Cited by Mitchell, *Greenbacks*, p. 375.

[2] *Ibid.*

[3] Annual Report of the Secretary of the Treasury, 1865, pp. 11–13, and Mitchell, *Greenbacks*, p. 375.

profits of business men were uncommonly large and their prosperity pronounced. David A. Wells in his reports as special commissioner of revenue presents statements of "most anomalous and extraordinary" profits in several industries. Dun's annual circular for 1864 tells us that "the average profits of trade range from 12 to 15 per cent" and this agency is also authority for the statement that a marked decrease took place both in the number and the amount of liabilities of bankrupt firms from 1857 to the close of the war. Thus evidence is afforded that business men in general found themselves in sound condition in 1865. In view of the instability of the currency and the extreme and sudden fluctuations in prices during the preceding years, with the accompanying hazards in business, the small number of failures is surprising. Yet the unusual dangers to which men were exposed seem to have proved a substantial safeguard. They knew that, the war once over, both gold and prices measured in the greenback standard would fall. They therefore exercised great care in undertaking obligations which a sudden fall in prices might ruin them to meet. Under ordinary circumstances the revolutionary drop in prices which occurred from January to July, 1865, would have caused a business crisis of the first magnitude. But the prudence of business men had its reward and failures were fewer in that year than in any other except one since 1857.[1]

Many specific experiences made up the aggregate of forces which led men finally to pursue the policy of safety which they adopted. One of these influences operating to induce them to place business upon a solid foundation related directly to the head of the federal treasury. In midsummer of 1864, Senator Fessenden had reluctantly assumed the secretaryship of the treasury under circumstances more extraordinary than those which had surrounded any secretary since the days of Alexander Hamilton. He was called to it with the unanimous consent of the country, and in the early spring of 1865 it was still fresh in the minds of thoughtful men that his acceptance of the great burden was followed by a universal revival of

[1] See Mitchell, *Greenbacks*, pp. 389, 390.

confidence. His name and recognized capacity were a powerful support to the treasury during the latter half of 1864. But in the critical military, financial, and monetary situation prevailing in the early weeks of 1865 there was abatement of the first flush of popular enthusiasm even in Fessenden's favor. The feeling became widespread that he had not succeeded in the great task of properly financing the war. Doubtless Fessenden's predicament was due to the intrinsic difficulties and embarrassments of a position in which under existing circumstances he who effected most seemed to have done little.[1] Nevertheless this was the feeling accumulating against the secretary, and its weight was added to the force of uncertainty with which men regarded the business situation.

As a result of such conditions and such feelings, the prudent heeded the signal which had been given by the shift in gold and in prices, and attempted to arrange their business on a solid and trustworthy basis.[2]

The whole situation was struck off clearly and pithily by a New York business man writing in *Harper's Monthly Magazine*:[3] "When the war ended, we all knew we should have a panic. Some of us, like Mr. Hoar, expected that greenbacks and volunteers would be disbanded together. Others expected gold to fall to 101 or 102 in a few days. Others saw a collapse of manufacturing industries, owing to a cessation of government purchases. But we all knew a 'crisis' was coming, and having set our houses in order accordingly, the 'crisis' of course never came."

As the residual claimant of money incomes in the first instance, the business man had been in a favored position during the greater part of the war. His prosperity was increased by virtue of holding this pivotal position. So long as money wages, money interest, and money rent which in the natural course of business he had to pay to other parties in the process of producing goods rose less rapidly than the prices which

[1] *Boston Advertiser*, January 7 and March 24, 1865.

[2] *Ibid.*

[3] Vol. XL, p. 747. Also cited by Mitchell, *Greenbacks*, pp. 390–391.

he received for his products, his profits grew by an increasing margin. As will be shown later, the other economic classes—namely, landlords, lending capitalists, and wage-earners—had begun, by 1865–66, in an appreciable degree to recover from the unfavorable condition from which they had suffered during a large part of the war. But they had in the meantime been placed at a disadvantage as compared with the active business man. What they lost was so much gain to the business man or employer. Moreover, rising prices produced a feeling of prosperity. The higher prices mounted the more business men thought they were profiting by their enterprises. In so far as this attitude of mind led to increased zeal for their work, it resulted in an actual increased production of wealth, and, other things being equal, an increase of profits to employers. At any rate, this prosperous feeling was not altogether a superficial appearance. "Business was in reality as well as in appearance rendered more profitable by the issue of the greenbacks. There is therefore no error in saying that the business of the country enjoyed unwonted prosperity during the war."[1]

We may conclude, therefore, that, during the period following the end of the war, business men as a class were on a fairly solid footing. The uncontrollable and unpredictable variations in prices had led them to exercise caution in using their credit and to transact business to an increasing extent upon a cash basis. The testimony of some of the keenest contemporary observers indicates that business profits were satisfactory. The position of residual claimant to money incomes gave business men an advantage throughout the period of rising prices. They had proved themselves able to survive the revolutionary drop in prices from January to June, 1865, and they were as a class in a favorable condition to face the task of resumption of specie payments at that time.

Landlords

We now turn to the other economic classes of the community to learn if their condition in 1865–66 could have permitted the burden which resumption might involve.

[1] *Ibid.*, p. 395.

First, as to the landlord class. The landlord's condition can be shown fairly well by the rentals paid for urban real estate and for farm lands. The following table presents Mitchell's index figures for relative house rents of a certain type of cheaper dwellings. It shows the relative rents for a considerable number of towns in eastern and western states, the relative rents in five important cities (Boston, Philadelphia, Cincinnati, Louisville, and St. Louis), and, for comparison the median relative wholesale price of commodities.

RELATIVE HOUSE RENTS AND MEDIAN RELATIVE WHOLESALE PRICES, BY YEARS, 1860–80.

Year	Average Relative Rents in Eastern and Western States[1]	Average Relative Rents in Five Typical Cities[2]	Median Relative Wholesale Prices[3]
1860	100	100	100
1861	98	101	97
1862	104	101	103
1863	114	123	133
1864	130	166	180
1865	135	173	185
1866	138	185	177
1867	134	166	162
1868	139	177	158
1869	142		157
1870	144		138
1871	147		131
1872	148		134
1873	145		133
1874	145		130
1875	141		118
1876	133		112
1877	132		106
1878	132		95
1879	130		88
1880	133		104

[1] Mitchell, *Gold, Prices, and Wages*, p. 90.

[2] Mitchell, *Greenbacks*, p. 357.

[3] Compiled from Mitchell's quarterly median index; see his *Gold, Prices, and Wages*, pp. 59, 60.

Mitchell, in his *Greenbacks*, showed that during the war urban landlords suffered on account of depreciated paper money. Their income from rents lagged behind prices in the general advance at that time. "The figures . . . establish a presumption that relatively few owners of urban real estate escaped injury."[1] But for our purpose, we are here concerned to point out that in the years 1865–66 this economic class was making great progress toward recovery from its previous unfavorable position.

The figures in the table show that relative prices reached the high point of 185 as an average for the year 1865, while relative rents in towns and cities throughout the country rose only to 135. But the figures also show that prices began their long and and continuous decline at that time and that rents, with the exception of the year 1867, continued steadily to rise until, in 1870, their relative index number stood higher than that of prices. From that point onward through the greenback period rents stood higher than prices and made rapid gains over them. If we compare the rental figures for five large cities, mentioned above, the results show a still more favorable recovery of the comfortable position of the landlord. By the year 1865, when the general level of prices stood at an average of 185, the average of rents for those cities stood at 173, and in 1866 the index for rentals was actually higher than that of prices. The more detailed quarterly figures would show still more encouragement for landlords in 1865, since the enormous drop of 58 points in prices from 216 in January to 158 in July reduced temporarily the margin of difference between prices and rents from 81 points to 23 points.[2] The urban landlords' position was, therefore, in 1865–66 an encouraging one.

[1] Mitchell, *Greenbacks*, p. 357.

[2] Median relative wholesale prices for 1865–66. See Mitchell, *Gold, Prices, and Wages*, p. 59.

Base 1860 = 100

Year	Month	Price	Year	Month	Price
1865	January	216	1866	January	182
	April	190		April	173
	July	158		July	181
	October	175		October	173

Looking now to the owners of farm lands,[1] we find that they did not, upon the whole, suffer so much disadvantage during the war as was the case with the majority of urban landlords. Those who let their land for money rents did, indeed, suffer because money rents did not advance so rapidly as general prices. But owners of farms in America have never followed to any great extent the policy of letting their land for money rents. Today it is a common custom to let farming land for a share of the products. In the Civil War period that custom was followed even more tenaciously than at present. It is safe to conclude, judging from the best evidence[2] attainable, that three-quarters of rented farms were let in those days, not for a fixed money payment, but for a payment in kind. In the case of this large proportion of rural landlords no great injury was inflicted by depreciated greenbacks. The higher prices mounted, the more they received from rents in kind. Any advance in price of agricultural products due to changes in the greenback standard was an advantage in assisting them to retain their relative financial position because their incomes increased simultaneously with the advance in the prices of farm products, which followed, although lagging somewhat behind, the rise in the general level of prices.

We may fairly assume, therefore, so far as the evidence has significance, that the landlords as a class were in a position to bear a share of the strain which might have been occasioned by a resumption of specie payments in 1865–66.

Lending Capitalists[3]

As an economic class lending capitalists found themselves in a trying position for at least a part of the Civil War period. Those who made loans in the earlier part of the war and were later repaid in greenbacks suffered loss by reason of the diminished purchasing power of the principal of the loan. When the principal was returned to the lender after the monetary standard had depreciated, it did not command an amount of

[1] Mitchell, *Greenbacks*, pp. 358, 359, 386–388. [2] *Ibid.*, p. 358.
[3] *Ibid.*, Part II, chap. 7, *passim.*

goods or services equal to that placed at the disposal of the borrower at the time the loan was contracted. This was the situation in regard to almost all loans made before the summer of 1864 and repaid before the early part of 1865. But the condition of capitalists making loans in the summer of 1864 or later was quite different. As a rule they made gains instead of losses. The effect of the great fall in prices was such that loans made in January, 1865, and repaid six months later would show an increase in purchasing power of the principal of more than 40 per cent.

It is an accepted principle of monetary science that losses incurred by lending capitalists during a period of depreciation of the monetary standard tend to be offset, in some measure, by increases in the rate of interest which they secure, and, likewise, that the gains accruing to this class in a period of appreciation tend to be offset, in some measure, by a progressive lowering of the rate of interest. But during the Civil War period this principle seems almost entirely to have failed of application. The creditor was able to secure only slight advances in interest rates as depreciation of the paper standard proceeded. The price changes were so rapid and so violent and the future course of the monetary standard so uncertain that the lender was unable to exact from the borrower an adjustment of the rate of interest which would counterbalance continuous market changes in the level of prices. Until the decline in prices began in 1865 persons who derived their income from capital lent at interest for short terms were seriously injured by the issue of greenbacks. Persons making long-time loans in the first years of the war found their real income reduced by half, late in 1864 and early in 1865. The borrower, of course, reaped a decided benefit because, securing higher prices for his products, he could pay interest and eventually principal more easily.

Although lending capitalists suffered losses while prices were rising from 1862 to January, 1865, they were in a much more fortunate position in the spring and summer of 1865, and indeed, for the most part, during all the remaining years of the greenback period. It is impossible to state the extent of the losses to this class in the earlier and shorter period, or the extent of their gains in the later and longer period. But it is clear that in 1865–66 the position of this economic class was decidedly improving and that, regardless of the losses it may have sustained in the past, its ability to bear its share of the burden of resumption was increasing. In fact, there was good reason for numerous lending capitalists to support a movement for resumption in 1865–66. As we have seen, the uncertain conditions of the war period induced business men to transact their affairs as nearly as possible with their own capital and on a cash basis. The field of employment for the funds of lending capitalists was therefore considerably restricted so far as trade and industry were concerned. It follows that losses incurred by this class on account of a fluctuating monetary standard were much less than at first blush we might expect—i.e., lending being restricted, losses from lending naturally were fewer. Failing to lend to business men, many of them were led by their economic interest as well as the dictates of patriotism to make loans to the government. In lending to the government they had invested in the public funds. Evidently, any influence which would tend to increase the value of government securities would have been advantageous to this economic class as holders of such securities. Resumption of specie payments in 1865 would have accomplished this result. Confidence in the government would have been created by its ability and willingness to pay its debts in coin. United States bonds would have risen in value and the position of lending capitalists would have been improved. This economic class, we may conclude, was in a position to share in the burdens which might have been involved in a resumption of specie payments in 1865–66, and its real interest demanded that resumption should take place.

Wage-earners

Coming to the wage-earners, what do we find? Was this economic class in a position to bear a burden which might have been entailed by resumption in 1865–66?

The best way to discover the economic fortunes of wage-earners is to compare variations in the cost of living in the period under review with the variations which took place in wages. The issue of greenbacks undoubtedly seriously affected the welfare of this class. As the paper standard depreciated and prices rose, wages, obeying a familiar economic law, lagged behind. Real wages became less and less for the time being. The struggle on the part of the wage-earner was to readjust money wages to the increased cost of living.

The following table shows the changes in the relative real wages of employees of manufacturing industries in eastern states. The computation is based upon Mitchell's figures for relative cost of living, in which the arithmetic average is used,[1] and his figures for relative rates of wages of employees in manufacturing industries of eastern states, in which the median index is used.[2]

RELATIVE REAL WAGES

Year	Wages	Year	Wages
1860	100	1865	85
1861	90	1866	93
1862	82	1867	102
1863	81	1868	102
1864	80		

The figures in this table do not tell the whole story, as will be apparent directly. They indicate that the purchasing power of money wages touched its lowest point in 1864, when it stood at 80 as compared with the base 100 in 1860, and that a rapid recovery ensued, bringing the real wage to 85 in 1865, to 93 in 1866, and to 102 in 1867 and 1868. The recovery in 1865 and later was due partly to the remarkable fall in commodity prices beginning in January, 1865, and also partly to a continuation of the rise in relative money wages. The use of cost of living figures instead of prices of commodities at wholesale in arriving at the purchasing power in the hands of workmen evidently gives more accurately the condition of laboring men.

[1] Mitchell, *Gold, Prices, and Wages*, table 68, pp. 242–244.

[2] *Ibid.*, table 65, p. 231 *et seq.* This table presents the relative wage for January and July of each year. I have used the average of the two.

The decline in prices at wholesale after January, 1865, was much more sudden than the decline in the cost of living, and therefore to use wholesale prices would result in exaggerating the comfortable situation of this economic class. That a decided improvement in its condition took place is unmistakable, and it was more substantial than appears upon the surface. The prices which are used to arrive at the cost of living index probably exaggerate in one respect the suffering to wage-earners consequent upon the existence of a high price-level. The reason is that the prices used include those of many articles no longer found in the list of consumable goods bought by the ordinary workman's family. The principle of substitution in supplying the wants of a family was extensively applied during the war and after, with the result that commodities whose prices had undergone extraordinary advances were no longer purchased but gave way to cheaper substitutes in the family supplies. Thus, cotton goods, having risen abnormally on account of the loss to the world's market of the American cotton crop, gave way to manufactures of wool and linen; tea and coffee gave way to chicory, sassafras tea and other cheap beverages. Many workmen's families even used dandelion roots as a substitute for coffee. Although these cheaper substitutes afforded a diminished amount of well-being to the wage-earning class, it still remains true that an index number of cost of living which includes some extraordinarily high-priced articles no longer purchased by a particular economic class overestimates the inconvenience in meeting an advancing cost of living to that class.

Furthermore, it is altogether probable that the wage tables used in arriving at changes in the cost of living underestimate the increase in money wages actually received by the laboring class. That this is true appears because labor was more fully employed during the war than it was in the preceding years with which comparison is naturally made.[1] The income of a wage-earner is affected vitally by two factors. It is a result of both the rate of wages and the degree of constancy of employment. What were the facts as to employment? The army

[1] Mitchell, *Greenbacks*, pp. 349, 350.

made large drafts upon the labor supply of the Northern states, drawing off in 1864 and 1865 approximately one million men from a total of almost seven million persons estimated to be gainfully employed.[1] Since the labor supply of the North was thus diminished by one-seventh, and since we may properly assume that the demand for labor was not decreased, it follows that those who remained at home during the war could find more constant employment than they had found in ordinary times. The resort to strikes also proved to be a means of improving the laborer's condition. The *Springfield Republican*[2] tells us that in the spring of 1863 workmen in almost every branch of industry had their strike and in almost every instance the demands of the employees were granted. This testimony indicates at once an active demand for labor and probably a good degree of constancy of employment. During the greater part of the war, however, the men who stayed at home did not succeed, in spite of these favoring circumstances, in securing advances in wages commensurate with the increased cost of living. But, during the year 1864, the arithmetic average for relative cost of living slackens its rate of increase, and from the first of the year 1865 begins its long and continuous decline. On the other hand, the index number for relative wages still rises, and continues to rise until July, 1872.[3] That is to say, prices and wages moved in opposite directions for several years from 1865, and by 1872 the median index number for wages stood 43 points above the median index number for wholesale prices, and 33 points above the median index number for retail prices.[4] This situation indicates that the condition of wage-earners was improved by midsummer of the year 1865 and continued to improve for some years to follow.

Another method of statement shows, similarly, the improvement in the wage-earner's condition. Up to the summer of

[1] *Ibid.*, p. 348 (footnote).

[2] *Ibid.*

[3] See Mitchell, *Gold, Prices, and Wages*, chart IX, opposite p. 244, and also chart XII, opposite p. 280.

[4] *Ibid.*, p. 230 *et seq.*; chart VII, opposite p. 236; table 74, p. 279; and chart XII, opposite p. 280.

1864 the cost of living was relatively above the money incomes of .9 of the employees of the manufacturing industries of the eastern states, in 1867 it was above less than .4, and in 1873 above less than .2 of such incomes.[1] Moreover, constancy of employment was well maintained during this period. Now, if we may assume that the position of laborers in the eastern states is typical for all the states of the North, this situation seems to indicate that in spite of the return of the soldiers to the ranks of labor at the close of the war, and in spite of the necessary readjustment in the industrial and commercial affairs of the nation from a war basis to a basis of peace, the condition of the laboring class as a whole continued to improve from the months toward the close of the war up to the crisis of 1873.[2]

"The working men of the North were receiving considerably more than a bare subsistence minimum before the war." During the war a "reduction of consumption was possible without producing serious want,"[3] and now in midsummer of 1865 they were rapidly regaining their *ante bellum* relative wage.

In view of these facts small doubt can exist that wage-earners in the summer and autumn of 1865 and in 1866 were in a position to bear some burdens which might have been involved in a resumption of specie payments at that time. In fact, they were as a class in a more favorable condition than they were during the years 1876 to 1878, when the treasury department, led by Sherman, did actually prepare for resumption under the act of 1875.

It may well be that the wage-earners might have suffered through resumption at this earlier period. The process may have resulted in driving down the rate of money wages due to a sudden shift to a monetary standard of higher value, while, with a money which was slowly increasing in value, the nominal wage level would have tended to remain unchanged and the real wage level to rise. This latter situation affords a great stim-

[1] This statement is based upon Mitchell's figures, *ibid.*, table 68, pp. 242–244

[2] Cf. *ibid.*, pp. 247, 248.

[3] Mitchell, *Greenbacks*, p. 351.

ulus to invention, efficient management, coöperation between worker and employer, and like expedients devoted to the purpose of keeping the nominal wage unchanged while prices are falling.

Undoubtedly all economic classes would have suffered more or less from the process of resuming specie payments in 1865–66, but hardship is always involved in movements to a money of higher value—such was the case in 1875–79, when resumption was actually accomplished. It is a penalty which must be paid in recovering a normal position after indulgence in abnormal excesses. Neither can it be maintained that individual losses which would have been sustained would have balanced in large part undeserved gains which had been realized during the period of inflation. Such matters are incapable of proof. Yet upon the whole, and in view of the record set forth in the preceding pages, we may fairly conclude that all of the various economic classes of the Northern states were in fair condition to undertake resumption in the latter half of the year 1865 or in 1866.

Without going into a detailed account of conditions in the Southern states, it can be said that, in the transition from the Confederate currency to a new circulating medium, no greater disturbance would have occurred by bringing them back immediately to a gold standard currency than did occur in bringing them back to the greenback standard, which was indeed inflated, but which was very far from having sunk to the depths which marked their own experiment with paper money.

The Way to Resume is to Resume

Assuming, then, that the different economic classes could have borne the burden of resumption at this earlier date, let us inquire what other forces were necessary in order to place the country upon a specie basis.

Former Secretary Chase and the *New York Tribune* represented a section of opinion in the country favorable, at various points of time from 1865 to 1879, to immediate resumption. Their policy was boldly to undertake the task, believing that payment in specie, once fairly launched, could be maintained through the natural operation of economic laws which control the international flow of the precious metals. "The way to resume is to resume" was their favorite way of stating their plan. It has been the custom in many quarters from that day to this to consider the method of resumption represented by this slogan as naïve and ineffective, but it is not to be so lightly rejected.

One of the chief sources of mistakes in the affairs of the treasury as managed by Secretary Chase was his firm belief that the war would be a short one.[1] This largely explains his timidity in taxation, his refusal to sell bonds for what they were worth on the market, and, above all, it in part explains why he permitted himself to be drawn into the plan of making government notes a legal tender. On the other hand, this misplaced optimism as to the brief duration of the struggle exerted a strong influence on a point of excellence in Chase's loan policy. His policy was to issue short-time loans, whether of bonds or of notes, in order that, with the war ended and the government's credit improving toward a normal basis, he could borrow on terms more and more favorable. He correctly conceived that the state of the public credit and the possibility of resumption would be closely related. He was convinced that his policy of short-term loans would tend to facilitate an easy and prompt resumption of specie payments at the close of the war, and had he remained in the treasury he would have attempted resumption within a few months after Lee's surrender. He considered this policy practical and safe at any time within a year after peace was concluded and that it might have been effected then with far less embarrassment and danger than at any later time. In his judgment every year's delay added to the difficulties of regaining a sound currency, since greater obstructions were certain to arise as the period of inconvertibility was prolonged. "The way to resume is to resume,"[2] he wrote in a letter to Horace Greeley in the early

[1] Cf. A. B. Hart, *Salmon P. Chase*, Boston and New York, 1899, p. 237.

[2] While we know from his biographer (Schuckers) that Chase was from the beginning in favor of an early resumption, this famous phrase, which became so

part of the year 1866. What his method of procedure would have been has not been placed definitely on record.[1] As early as May, 1864, a letter to a friend indicates Chase's attitude. He wrote: "I agree in the opinion that an inflated paper currency is a great evil, and should be reformed as soon as possible." He saw already the dangerous results of the legal tender clause, and when the war was over and he saw the notes still continued in circulation he took alarm and began to urge speedy resumption.[2]

In general, we can hold with Noyes that the theory of the men responsible for the legal tender act in 1862 was clearly understood. They, upon the whole, regarded the greenbacks as the creation of a government floating debt, and they saw in the legal tender quality given them an endowment of special privilege only in order that they might be kept in circulation. They held that resort to legal tender powers was an evil, but justified it by the extreme emergency, and they regarded the circulation of government notes in any form as a comparatively temporary measure. The public drew the logical inference that these notes would be paid for and cancelled as soon as the emergency had passed. Indeed, the national banking system was established in 1863 on the express theory that one of its prime objects was to supply bank notes, instead of government notes, as the requisite currency of the future. With a few notable exceptions, the general position of our public men at the close of the war was the same. Government notes, in their view, constituted a temporary scheme, and when the country was at peace the first financial resolution adopted by the Congress meeting in December, 1865, was a definite and sincere promise to abolish legal tender paper money.[3] The

popular, seems to have been first expressed by Chase in his letter of May 17, 1866, and was not original with Greeley in a *New York Tribune* editorial, as is generally believed.

[1] J. W. Schuckers, *Life and Public Services of S. P. Chase*, New York, 1874, pp. 409, 410.

[2] Hart, *Salmon P. Chase*, Boston and New York, 1899, pp. 389–390.

[3] A. D. Noyes, *Forty Years of American Finance*, New York and London, 1909, pp. 7–9; and see *infra*, Chapter VII.

Boston Advertiser, whose wise and careful editor, as already stated, was at that time Professor Charles F. Dunbar, expressed the belief that nine men out of every ten in the country desired an early resumption. It appears, therefore, that the attitude of mind of both statesmen and the general public was favorable for immediate steps toward resumption in 1865–66.[1] With so much in its favor, the difficulties of the movement were already largely surmounted. That men should earnestly desire resumption and should be united in expecting it to come in the immediate future was of great importance. The fear of contraction of the currency had not yet troubled them. In so far, the situation can be said to have been more favorable at least than it was in 1877–78, when preparation for resumption was actually undertaken.

Necessary Preliminary Preparation

But evidently it would not have been wise merely to announce that the government would resume on a given day with no action taken by the administration to insure the success of the movement. Even with the existing favoring conditions it would have been necessary to smooth the way for a return of greenbacks to a parity with gold. To accomplish this result it would have been necessary, first, to withdraw from circulation a small amount of some parts of the media of exchange; second, to require the banks to coöperate by preparing also for resumption according to a specific plan; third, to ascertain whether our foreign trade situation would render success impossible; and fourth, to assure ourselves of a reasonably certain market—especially a foreign market—for our government bonds in order to secure a supply of gold.

As to the first point. Doubtless a withdrawal of any amount of the currency would soon have aroused opposition in some quarters. It always does. But under the influence of the prevailing state of mind in 1865 the task of contracting the currency to some extent should not have been a great one.

[1] E.g. see *New York Tribune*, December 18, 1865, and *Boston Advertiser*, March 3 and December 4, 1866.

The withdrawal of a comparatively small percentage of the currency would have brought the greenbacks to par with gold. The total amount of currency in the loyal states in 1865 cannot be accurately known. Mitchell's estimates are the nearest approach to a satisfactory statement that has been made. His table,[1] comprising numerous separate items, is as follows:

Currency of the Loyal States at the Close of the Fiscal Year 1865.
(Millions of dollars)

I. Specie:	
1. Gold coins	22.0
2. Silver dollars	None
3. Subsidiary silver	3.0
4. Minor coins	3.3
II. Postage and fractional currency:	
1. Postage currency	9.9
2. Fractional currency	15.1
III. Non-interest-bearing legal tender treasury notes:	
1. Old demand notes	.5
2. Greenbacks	431.1
IV. Bank notes:	
1. Notes, state banks	142.9
2. Notes, national banks	146.1
V. Interest-bearing legal tender treasury notes:	
1. One-year 5 per cent treasury notes of 1863	None
2. Two-year 5 per cent treasury notes of 1863	42.3
3. Compound-interest notes	193.8
VI. Government obligations not a legal tender:	
1. Certificates of indebtedness	115.8
2. 7–30 treasury notes of 1864	234.4
3. 7–30 treasury notes of 1865	437.2
VII. Coin, bullion, and paper money in the treasury:	55.4

It is impossible to know what proportion of several of these government obligations was at any given time in actual use as media of exchange and what proportion was held out of circulation by investors, and for this reason Mitchell cautiously warns us against casting up the sum of the separate items in order to arrive at the total amount of actual currency for the Northern states. It is likewise impossible to know with any approach to accuracy what amount of contraction of the cur-

[1] Mitchell, *Greenbacks*, p. 179.

rency would have caused the greenbacks to appreciate to par with gold. Statistical calculation is on this head, therefore, out of the question. But if we make reasonable allowance[1] for the use as currency, both directly and indirectly, of interest-bearing legal tender treasury notes and governmental obligations not a legal tender (items V and VI of Mitchell's table), and if we may accept McCulloch's figures of December, 1865,[2] as the best possible estimate of the requisite contraction of the currency in order to bring greenbacks to par, we shall find that the percentage of the total currency necessary to be withdrawn from circulation for this purpose must have been small. If, now, we add to the circulating media the item of $544 millions of national bank deposits, which is McCulloch's esimate[3] of these deposits for September 30, 1865, but which naturally is omitted in Mitchell's table, the percentage of the currency necessary to be withdrawn is seen to be still smaller.

The contraction of the currency would have caused a fall in prices, and would in consequence have affected business interests adversely, but business interests had survived the great fall from January to July, 1865, without disaster, and in the face of that experience public opinion was now in favor of sufficient contraction to make way for resumption. Upon the whole, the conclusion seems justified that the requisite contraction could have been made with fortunate permanent results for the nation and without temporary disaster.

The second requirement—the necessity to smooth the way for resumption by securing the coöperation of the banks with the government—should not have presented difficulty. The adroitness with which Sherman[4] accomplished coöperation be-

[1] *Ibid.*, pp. 173–178.

[2] Report of the Secretary of the Treasury, p. 14. McCulloch estimated that the withdrawal of all of the compound interest-bearing notes ($193.8 millions) and the cancellation of $100 millions (or at most $200 millions) of greenbacks would be such a contraction of the currency as would bring the greenbacks to par with gold.

[3] *Ibid.*, 1865, p. 11. McCulloch tells us he had no reliable information on the deposits of state banks. The addition of their sum to the amount of circulating media would still further reduce the percentage.

[4] *Infra*, Chapter IX.

tween the banks and the treasury in 1878–79 would have been equally successful in 1865–66.

As to the third point—was the foreign trade situation in 1865–66 such as to render resumption impossible? McCulloch stated in his annual reports of December, 1865,[1] and December, 1866[2], that specie payments could not be resumed so long as the balance of trade was against us, because gold would necessarily be exported and we could not accumulate and maintain a gold reserve for the redemption of the greenbacks. He found that the balance was against us at that time, and quotes the imports and exports of merchandise and certain invisible items to substantiate his statement. His inference from the figures, that resumption was impossible under the circumstances, is, however, of questionable validity. The adverse balance of trade in that period was no bar whatever to resumption. The inflow or outflow of specie is not a necessary consequence of an excess or deficiency of exports. For three-quarters of a century preceding the year 1865 the United States had been a borrowing country. She placed loans in various foreign countries, especially in England. During a great part of the period her merchandise imports exceeded her exports, and continued to do so until 1874.[3] Yet she was able to retain her share of the precious metals so far as abnormal conditions of the currency would permit. An adverse balance of trade in a gold-producing country is, other things being equal, an inevitable result of the adoption and retention of an inconvertible paper currency. No market exists at home for the gold produced, therefore it must seek a market abroad, and the gold exports will form a part of the payments for commodity imports. That is, disregarding financial transactions, a gold-producing country on an inconvertible paper basis will always have an adverse balance of trade. Of course, in our situation in the greenback period other factors were involved. The volume of our borrowing abroad was so great as to lead to an

[1] P. 13.
[2] Pp. 11, 12.
[3] *The Review of Economic Statistics* (Harvard), Vol. I, pp. 215–224.

adverse balance of trade in any case. But there is no reason to believe that the adverse balance would have persisted if gold payments had been resumed, unless continued borrowings had forced such a balance. The movement of trade followed foreign loans in the period from 1860 to 1878. When the United States placed foreign loans she had an excess of merchandise imports; when foreign loans ceased to be floated or were repaid, the tendency to excess of merchandise exports appeared.[1] Under the greenback standard heavy borrowing abroad would tend to depress the premium on gold, making it relatively cheap. The net export of gold under such circumstances would be large. But it is also true that with a restoration of specie payments the tendency would have been toward an inflow of gold.[2] Resumption would have required some contraction in the existing volume of currency and credit, and this would have quickly reduced the price level in the United States. It would then have been easier for foreigners to buy in this country than it had been before, and the adverse balance, so far as it was due to the necessity for selling gold abroad, would have disappeared.

No doubt the return to specie payments would have been easier with a comfortable excess of exports over imports, but the process was not impossible even though this was not in the beginning the case. We know that, although an unfavorable balance of merchandise existed in the years 1865 and 1866, the total debits and credits in our foreign trade were kept in approximate balance—and this was true from period to period, of a year or two each, throughout the years 1860 to 1878. The balance was effected through the influence of specie movements and of the invisible items of trade, especially the item of loans floated in foreign countries. Professor Frank D. Graham has compiled an international trade balance sheet for the United States in account with foreign countries, covering the years 1860 to 1878.[3] The following table presents his results for the fiscal years 1865 to 1867.

[1] Frank D. Graham, "International Trade under Depreciated Paper. The United States, 1862–79." *Quarterly Journal of Economics*, Vol. XXXVI, p. 272.

[2] *Ibid.*, p. 232.

[3] *Ibid.*, p. 231.

FIGURES FOR YEARS ENDING JUNE 30 (IN THOUSANDS OF DOLLARS)

Item	1865	1866	1867
Merchandise imports.......	$238,745	$434,812	$395,761
Gold and silver specie and bullion imports.........	9,810	10,700	22,070
Freights payable...........	17,417	32,247	30,062
Net interest payments......	24,000	30,000	36,000
Repayments on loans.......	....	....	....
Total debits...........	289,972	507,759	483,893
Merchandise exports.......	166,029	348,859	294,505
Gold and silver specie and bullion exports.........	69,643	86,043	60,868
Freights receivable.........	4,956	15,483	13,079
Sales of ships..............	5,333	....	....
Loans floated.............	75,000	70,000	74,000
Total credits	320,961	520,385	442,452

Such evidence as is available in regard to invisible items not mentioned in this table shows that their debits and credits tend to counterbalance one another, and they are omitted.[1] The figures here presented show that we had an excess of merchandise imports amounting to nearly $73 millions in the year ending June 30, 1865, to $86 millions in 1866, and to $101 millions in 1867. McCulloch assumed that so long as this unfavorable merchandise balance continued resumption would be extremely difficult if not impossible. But the figures also show that the total credits to the United States exceeded the total debits by more than $30 millions in 1865, and $12 millions in 1866, while for 1867 the debits exceed the credits by $41 millions. That is, upon the whole we were in one way and another balancing our international account, chiefly through loans. Our credit abroad was such as to carry us along. As we should expect, our total debits and total credits for the entire period 1860–78 approximately balance each other.[2] Nat-

[1] *Ibid.*, p. 230.

[2] Graham's table shows the total debits for the period to have been $10,082,910,000 and the total credits $9,981,099,000. *Ibid.*, p. 231.

urally, we could not go on forever borrowing from foreign nations, but being a new and richly endowed country we were sure in time to develop our excellent resources to the point of having an excess of exports.

We conclude that the adverse balance of trade should not have been allowed to stand in the way of resumption of specie payments in 1865–66, provided we could find a sustained favorable foreign market for our government bonds, whose proceeds, in addition to those sold at home, would afford opportunity to accumulate the gold reserve necessary to insure coin payments.

Did, then, a foreign market exist for our securities? This is our fourth condition for a successful movement to resume. It is the important question discussed in the following chapter.

CHAPTER VI

POSSIBILITY OF BRITISH LOANS, 1865–66

THE question of a foreign market for American securities was not so much a problem of making loans *per se* as it was of floating government securities on a scale sufficiently extensive to enable us to maintain a reserve fund for resumption. We had been borrowers for decades past, and as the event proved we borrowed in the fiscal year 1865 $75 millions, in 1866 $70 millions, and in 1867 $74 millions.[1] But in order to secure a reserve fund for resumption purposes, in addition to the sums for ordinary requirements, we should have been compelled to place foreign loans for more than twice as much as we had received in any one of those years, and the greater part of the increased amount must come in the form of gold from abroad. This was a huge sum for the government at that time to contemplate. The ability to float loans in Europe was the outstanding problem of such an undertaking. It was a great problem for Sherman in 1877–79, when resumption was actually accomplished. Could it have been done in the earlier period?

The evidence is quite sufficient for the belief that in 1865–66 America could have borrowed in the British market adequate additional funds to see her through a resumption of specie payments at that time.

SOURCES OF INFORMATION

Interviews during the summer of 1914 with several elderly Englishmen who in 1865–66 were young men of promise and held positions of importance in government and financial institutions yielded some evidence on this question. The chief among these persons were Lord Welby and Mr. Alexander J. Wilson. The former, at the close of our Civil War and for most

[1] Graham, *Quarterly Journal of Economics*, Vol. XXXVI, p. 231.

of a long lifetime, held a position in the British Treasury, and in 1914 he was still freely consulted by officials of government and editors of the most important British financial periodicals. Mr. Wilson was for many years associated with Walter Bagehot on the editorial staff of the *Economist* (London), and in 1914 was editor of the *Investors' Review*. These men were in a position to know financial conditions at the close of our Civil War. In their opinion, as well as in that of other men of similar type who were consulted, the United States could, with proper effort, have borrowed all that she needed for purposes of resumption.

But better, as a source of information, than the memories of able men whose perspective might possibly be influenced by the remarkable financial growth and prosperity of the United States during intervening years is the contemporaneous editorial comment of the greatest weekly financial journal of the time—the *Economist* (London). Walter Bagehot's editorial activities on that journal covered the years under review and many more. In his searching analyses Bagehot brought to bear on the economic and financial conditions of his time such range of knowledge, keenness of observation, and sanity of judgment as to induce English bankers and investors to rely upon his opinions and guidance in matters concerning the money and investment markets. The "leading article," as the English call the principal editorial, was almost always from his pen.[1] His position as the active London representative of his Bristol banking house placed daily in his possession the intimate facts of the world's financial and banking center, and enabled him with his rare ability to speak to "the City" and to the financial world with an authority vouchsafed to no one else of his generation. Contemporaries of Bagehot who held positions of responsibility in his day, as well as those Englishmen of the present day who are students of that period, are of one opinion in regard to the accuracy with which Bagehot portrayed the real attitude of English bankers and investors.[2] Opinions,

[1] Interview in 1914 with Mr. A. J. Wilson, Bagehot's associate.

[2] Interviews and opinions from Lord Welby, Alexander J. Wilson, Sir Inglis Palgrave, and others.

therefore, expressed in the *Economist* are of the first importance in determining the question of America's opportunity to secure loans in order to resume specie payments. To the records of that journal, accordingly, we turn. Did the *Economist* believe that England had both the ability and the willingness to lend sufficient funds to America?

Ability of English to Lend

First as to her ability to lend. Whether England could successfully lend or not depended primarily upon her ability to accumulate savings, and secondly upon the ability of her bankers to transfer loans of those savings to America without undue disturbance to the money market and to the exchange situation. The problem of transfer, granted reasonable circumspection, should not have presented much difficulty. It presented little, if any, in 1877–79, when Sherman imported gold for resumption purposes. The question of savings—volume of capital accumulation—was the important one. The amount of savings depended upon the condition of trade and industry, the attitude of mind of Englishmen on spending versus saving, and upon their confidence in borrowers.

Condition of Trade and Industry

The condition of trade and industry during the two years 1865 and 1866, although subject to considerable fluctuation and misgiving, showed upon the whole an upward tendency. Attention in London was centered upon three fields of activity—the cotton trade, the harvest, and the aggregate of trade and industry without reference to special lines.

It was natural that cotton and the cotton trade should come in for a due share of solicitude.[1] Now that the American Civil War was ended both manufacturers and traders were compelled to readjust themselves to a larger but uncertain supply of cotton fiber from America and a corresponding diminution of imports from Egypt, India, China, and elsewhere. Price fluc-

[1] London *Economist*, April 29, 1865, pp. 499–500, and November 18, 1865, pp. 1396–1397.

tuations for the year ending November, 1865, were great and grievous, as shown by the adjoining table:

(Quoted in Pence per Pound)

	Middling Orleans	Fair Egyptian	Fair Surat
November, 1864	27½	28½	20
April, 1865	13½	13	10
November, 1865	20	21	16½

The price of middling Orleans dropped from 27½ pence per pound in November, 1864, to 13½ pence in the following April, and rose again to 20 pence in November, 1865. Men naturally asked themselves how long such disconcerting variations would continue. The event proved that the panic of April which seized upon Liverpool merchants and which depressed cotton prices unduly had nothing to warrant it. At the time warning was given by the *Economist* that the increased American supply of raw cotton after the declaration of peace in April, 1865, though welcome, would no more than approximately offset the decrease in supply from the East. And toward the end of the year arrivals from America, though increasing and helpful, were still scanty in comparison with the exaggerated expectations of those who thought the Southern states held great reserves. Well-informed persons knew that the future supply must be uncertain until at least the autumn of 1866, when the first crop planted after the establishment of peace had been gathered. It was everywhere recognized, however, that "America must always determine and rule the cotton market."[1] When eventually the cotton crop of 1866 began to move the sources for England were largely revolutionized. For the year ending October 1st of that year £28 millions had been imported from the United States, as compared with £650,000 for the preceding year,—an increase of more than forty-fold,—while every other country, except Egypt and Bra-

[1] *Ibid.*, November 18, 1865, pp. 1396–1397, and December 2, 1865, pp. 1454–1455.

zil, sent notably diminished supplies. Thus the total import of raw cotton was £53.5 millions in 1866, as against £24.5 millions for the preceding year, with practically the entire increase coming from the United States.[1] These conditions resulted in the twofold effect of stimulating English industry in marked degree and of placing America on the verge of receiving gold in payment for her increased exports.[2]

Harvests

Coming to the harvest situation, what do we find? In neither 1865 nor 1866 was the English harvest[3] up to the average yield. Apparently this fact was bound to supply conclusive evidence against ability on the part of Englishmen to accumulate savings and to lend to America. Such, however, was not the case. Wheat and other crops of 1865 had indeed passed through a very hard winter, and, in spite of genial weather in April and May, the unfavorable weather conditions of the autumn brought results which were not the best. While no ground existed for alarm or serious apprehension as to the state of the country on this score, it was impossible for Englishmen not to harbor the feeling that their trade and their comfort were not likely to be so favorably circumstanced as they had been of late. Over the commercial world grain had been cheap, and this cheapness had every where induced a good market for English clothing and other plain necessities. But now, unfortunately, as they thought, they were to "suffer from still dearer meat and be aided by less cheap corn." For the year 1866 harvests were no better. Bad weather again affected the crops, and by October of that year a large increase in the importation of foreign breadstuffs was noticed, amounting to 72 per cent more than that of a similar period in the year previous.[4] But

[1] *Ibid.*, October 6, 1866, p. 1161.

[2] *Ibid.*, and also November 17, 1866, p. 1333.

[3] *Ibid.*, July 15, 1865, pp. 848–849; August 26, 1865, pp. 1025–1026; September 9, 1865, p. 1091; October 6, 1866, p. 1161.

[4] The imports, chiefly wheat, flour, barley, and oats, were £9.3 millions for 1865, and £16 millions for 1866, both the first nine months of the year. London *Economist*, October 6, 1866, p. 1161.

these conditions were not seriously detrimental. It must be borne in mind that an inferior harvest was not so much a calamity to the England of those years as it had been in earlier times. That country was already habitually a large importer of food, and a sudden falling off of the domestic supply did not disturb it as was the case when it depended almost solely upon its own agricultural production. For this reason, unfavorable, yet not disastrous, harvests need not have stood in the way of England's ability to make larger loans to America. On the contrary, the prospects were in favor of greater importations of food from America, and, since loans tend to follow trade, a natural drift of English capital to American should have been expected.

Industry and Trade in General

In like manner, we find that the circumstances of trade and industry in general were not unfavorable to British savings and investments abroad. Recovering from the crisis of 1857, the English nation continued to prosper until the cotton industry was for a second time almost ruined by the effects of America's Civil War. In Lancashire the cotton famine deprived 800,000 wage-earners of their livelihood. But again this industry recovered from what had been a very severe blow, and its progress in 1865, after the close of the Civil War, gave an impetus to new business which was accompanied by considerable development in English trade with China, India, and Australia. Even the sudden and for the most part unexpected failure of the great banking house of Overend, Gurney and Company the next year, although causing some uneasiness, did not prevent the continuation of an increasing prosperity during several succeeding years.[1] Trade and industry in the aggregate were so profitable that Newmarch[2] estimated the annual savings of the country to be not less than 130 million pounds sterling. These savings had been a steady, gradual, accumulating force, going on much at the same pace for years.[3] It was not true, therefore,

[1] H. de B. Gibbins, *Industry in England*, New York, 1903, pp. 465–466.
[2] London *Economist*, October 21, 1865, p. 1270, and October 23, 1866, p. 731.
[3] *Ibid.*, January 21, 1865, p. 61.

as some persons in Lombard Street imagined, that because the national capital seemed to be fully employed the country was unable to furnish means for new enterprises such as loans to their own or foreign governments or to domestic or foreign construction of factories, ships, etc.[1] The business of the country was of two sorts: first, the necessary common business for the supply of the ordinary wants of life; and second, the "optional business" by which new channels of trade were developed and desires gratified, the mere existence of which was before all but unknown.[2] To the amount of these annual savings England was therefore prepared during each year to repair and replace capital in her existing undertakings and to take up new enterprises and new investments among which her capitalists selected the most promising.[3]

Temporary disturbances in the money market were no indication of inability to supply capital for new enterprises. For the Britisher there is one cardinal difference between a bullion drain and a demand for capital in their effects upon the money market. A bullion demand—for example, one arising from an unfavorable balance on account of imports of American cotton—is a catastrophic phenomenon. It jerks the money market out of its place, to which it may as suddenly return when the spasmodic cause is eliminated, while the demand for the more general forms of capital is a steady force going on week by week and month by month. It is not the former perturbing influence but the latter more settled influence which is related to the accumulation of savings. The London money market in years immediately preceding the close of the American Civil War was considerably affected in consequence of the necessity of supporting the change in trade which was developed to replace that of America. This trade required an export of bullion, since it was carried on with less advanced countries such as India and Egypt, where the tastes and habits of the people called for large consumption of the precious metals.

[1] *Ibid.*, October 21, 1865, p. 1270.
[2] *Ibid.*, October 20, 1866, p. 1217.
[3] *Ibid.*, October 21, 1865, p. 1270.

Thus British bank reserves were affected and discount rates disturbed. But this disturbing influence, connected as it was with the ordinary eating and drinking of the nation, had righted itself in the natural course of events. The annual savings had been large and apparently unaffected by fluctuating bank rates. On the other hand, the means of employing capital received a simultaneous augmentation from several causes. First, England's foreign trade was rapidly growing year by year. Second, English investors were increasing in intelligence. They now dared to take investments from which they formerly shrank. They thought of outlets of which they had never before dreamed. The increase of intelligence of the capitalist acted upon the value of capital as the coming of a great captain of industry after an inefficient one acts upon the value of a business organization. It increased the achievements though not the amount of capital. Third, opportunities for English capital increased as well as the intelligence of the capitalists. There were outlets in foreign countries such as had never existed before. All parts of the world which the British race either colonized or influenced had arrived, some parts suddenly, at a stage of progress where peace was sufficiently secure and human abilities sufficiently developed for a greater commerce. In England, as in other countries, the very organization of industry, too, was in a state favorable to the lender. It produced for him securities. In an earlier stage of England's economic development securities had been rare. "The land" and "the funds" were then the important phrases, and they represented accurately enough the sort of things which exclusively presented to the British investor the qualities of security—viz., permanence and profitableness. Formerly, when an Englishman once left the soil and the debt of his country, no other things existed which were sure to last and sure to pay. But now railways, telegraph companies, canals, and other enterprises, as well as foreign governments in increasing numbers, competed with the land and the state for loanable capital. Railway companies and other "limited liability" companies, of which so much was said in the sixties, were more or less effective devices to reinforce the bankers' efforts to collect capital from those who wished for a fixed income, and they gave in return bonds or stocks, as best suited the temperament of the lender. In either case they took out of the loan market capital which formerly overloaded it and pressed it down. With such conditions prevailing we should expect to find fluctuating rates in the money market, but on the other hand it must also be clear that fluctuating rates did not necessarily, nor usually, mean a real dearth of capital. Those fluctuations meant, among other things, that many and urgent demands were developing to absorb the huge annual accumulation of savings.[1]

The New Trade of Lending

Lending to foreign countries assumed such magnitude so suddenly at this period that the *Economist* frequently referred to it as "the new trade of lending."[2] "We have taken up a new trade, the trade of lending," Bagehot writes. "England is now, by a machinery more refined and efficient than it ever had before, with a regular magnitude which was never before approached, lending to the industrial organization and the governments of foreign countries. If anyone wants a large sum of money at *once* he comes to London for it, and if anyone wants permanent capital he may expect to find much of it in England if he pays an adequate interest and gives what will be thought good security for it." The lending propensity was a propensity likely to be accelerated rather than retarded. Agencies which temporarily reduced the rate in the money market might be more powerful at the moment, but the "new" cause was one of lasting character and would tend, as compared with past years, to increase that rate. Nevertheless, in spite of prospective increased value of money, "adequate interest" and "good secur-

[1] *Ibid.*, January 21, 1865, pp. 61, 62; November 4, 1865, pp. 1329, 1330.

[2] *Ibid.*, February 25, p. 217; June 3, p. 653; July 22, p. 877; July 29, p. 909; August 12, p. 969; October 14, pp. 1233–1234; November 4, pp. 1329, 1330; December 16, p. 1517—all for the year 1865; April 14, 1866. Also the London *Times*, January 10, 1866, p. 12, for the opinion of a New York importer that the heavy exports from England to the United States in the last half of 1865 were met by United States 5–20 bonds and other securities.

ity" would take capital abroad. These were the qualities which America must furnish, and, having furnished them, she could borrow all she needed. Adequate rates of interest she was abundantly able to pay, and a sense of good security could in no wise have been produced so well as by resumption of specie payments at that time.

Overend-Gurney Failure

The statement has often been made that the failure of Overend, Gurney and Company in May, 1866, stood in the way of England's ability to lend. But that was not true. The bankruptcy of that erstwhile great house, destructive though it was, is apt to be credited with greater influence upon the prosperity of England than it in fact wielded. For fully three months before the event the *Economist* had expected[1] the downfall of the firm, but, with due regard to the well-being of Lombard Street, had not dared give utterance to its belief. Early in the year there had been no signs of a collapse in industry—not even a mitigated and minor collapse, far less one such as those which occurred as results of the financial difficulties of 1847 and 1857.[2] Knowing that this private banking house was a mere shell of its former greatness, all really instructed people were surprised at the intensity of the immediate panic which its failure precipitated. It could hardly in its most reputable days have produced a greater immediate effect. It was a signal illustration of how much an old name, with its virtue lost, still retains its magical power over the multitude. Lombard Street was thronged and almost stopped by curious wonderers. The collapse of credit for the moment was diffused and complete. Overends deserved to go, but many firms which did not deserve it were likely to be drawn into the current. Over-speculation in shares of the new limited liability companies had indeed imparted a certain taint to many transactions, and such financial companies as indulged in this activity speedily realized that firms which live by credit, as all banks must, should avoid

[1] See issue for May 12, 1866, p. 553.

[2] London *Economist*, February 3, 1866, p. 121.

even the suspicion of evil.[1] However, suspension of the Bank Act worked a cure for the panic of 1866. This was merely a happy turning to account of a widespread delusion. Most men in the finanical district believed that what their banks were accustomed to lend was coin and bank notes, and that when loans were scarce nothing more was needed than to make plenty of notes. When, therefore, these people heard that the Bank Act was temporarily set aside and notes in abundance were coming out they quieted themselves and left their deposits in the bank. The gain was real, but it was achieved by a process of the imagination, for not a single note was set to work.[2] The panic was purely and simply a bankers' panic.

The fabric of credit may be disturbed in any one or more of several ways, three of which were especially in the minds of men of that day. First, it may be disturbed by attempting to transact too much business and to engage in more undertakings than are capable of support by the capital at the disposal of business men. But England in 1866 did not suffer from the lack of capital or other commodities. The general state of trade in the country was sound. Business had been carried on with a view to profit and was profitable. With the exception of particular branches of speculative trade, as cotton or pig iron, or ship-building and ship-owning, her business was hardly ever sounder.[3] The consumption of the country and the demand for all articles of manufacture went on as usual. The crisis of 1866, unlike others, was practically confined to England, and therefore neither the foreign demand for her products nor the foreign means of supplying her wants were likely to be affected by it.[4] A second kind of disturbance may arise from an external drain of gold. The ultimate object of all contracts is to obtain capital and consumption goods, but the universal language in which contracts are expressed is money. Promises must be kept not only in articles but also in money. A scarcity of gold dis-

[1] *Ibid.*, May 12, 1866, pp. 553–554.

[2] *Ibid.*, May 19, 1866, p. 588, for a letter by Bonamy Price, "The Suspension of the Bank Act."

[3] *Ibid.*, May 12, 1866, p. 554; May 19, 1866, p. 581 *et seq.*

[4] *Ibid.*, August 18, 1866, p. 965; October 20, 1866, p. 1217.

turbs credit and may produce panic. But neither did England in 1866 suffer from a drain of bullion. In comparison with former panics the Bank held much bullion, and it had often held less without a panic. Yet credit was injured even though capital was not exhausted and though bullion was kept in adequate supplies. The injury proceeded from still another source, the third cause above referred to. This was in the form of a blow to confidence in banking houses. Confidence is a feeling generated at first by the display of sound judgment, continued often by blind habit, but always liable to be dispelled by evidence of misjudgment. Overend, Gurney and Company, the most notable borrowers of the community's capital and users of credit, had conspicuously shown themselves unworthy of confidence.[1] Their reputation for having done bad business impaired confidence in others until such time as men could again learn whom to trust. The continuance of the unsettled feeling, at least from early May to the middle of August, 1866, was partly due to a mistaken policy of the Bank of England in maintaining the high discount rate of 10 per cent after the necessity of such extreme action had disappeared. This policy caused country bankers and foreigners to persist in the belief that the Bank directors held secret some dreadful disaster yet to break over "the City."[2] This mistake was in time corrected, and as the year wore on a more comfortable feeling prevailed.[3] Moreover, the panic, unlike its predecessors, occurred in the spring instead of the autumn, and had therefore not added its force to the annual autumnal period of stringency in the money market. The realization of this fact had a quieting effect. By the middle of November the Bank of England was able to free itself from the exceptional discount business which had fallen upon it as a result of the Overend failure.[4] During the autumn the low prices of English financial and industrial securities continued to excite remark, but only from those who

[1] *Ibid.*, June 23, 1866, p. 731.

[2] *Ibid.*, June 30, 1866, p. 761; August 4, 1866, p. 905; August 18, 1866, p. 965.

[3] *Ibid.*, August 18, 1866, p. 965; October 6, 1866, p. 1162; October 20, 1866, p. 1217.

[4] *Ibid.*, November 17, 1866, p. 1333.

failed to consider that in this as in every panic loans previously contracted could not be paid until the panic had passed away. Securities upon which loans were effected could not, for the time, be realized. In time lenders began to require them to be turned into cash. They called in their loans and at some price securities had to be sold. The investors in securities—the peculiarly propertied class—were injured and were in consequence reluctant to make fresh investments in English companies.[1] But they were inclined to look elsewhere. Here was America's opportunity.

England passed through some difficult and trying experiences during these years, but in view of the situation here reviewed, including the condition of trade and industry, the panic of 1866, and the insistence of both Newmarch and Bagehot that the annual national savings were very large and that the ordinary routine business of the country was for the most part prospering, the conclusion seems justified that England during the years 1865 and 1866 was able to advance funds to America or to any people who satisfied her capitalists in regard to the permanence and the profitableness of the investment.

Willingness of English to Lend

Even though the evidence presented may go to show that English investors had the ability to make considerable loans to the American government, their willingness to make such loans on a large scale was quite another matter. Were they willing to do so?

While the Civil War continued English feeling was alienated by reason of exaggerated statements and attacks against England by officials of our government and by numerous other persons of the North. England had helped the North by export of arms and warlike stores twenty to one as against exports to the South, yet the North was bitter when two vessels[2] escaped the vigilance of British authorities and destroyed American merchantmen. The plain truth was, however, that "the head and front of Britain's offending"—the real reason why it was

[1] *Ibid.*, October 20, 1866, p. 1217; October 27, 1866, p. 1249.
[2] The *Alabama* and the *Shenandoah*.

so impossible for her to pacify the people of the North—was that the views of England and the North as to the wisdom and righteousness of the war in which the latter was engaged were so radically at variance. Some able orators, writers, and journalists in England embraced the cause of the Northern states, but, notwithstanding, the North had a conviction, half instinct, half observation, that the English nation as a whole was not on her side, did not wish her success, did not share her passions, did not approve of her proceedings. The fact was so; Englishmen could not deny it; they could not alter it. And it was this which irritated the people of the North. It was an irritation which, unhappily, it was simply impossible by all their efforts and all their caution to allay.[1] The consciousness of this difference asserted itself so vigorously that in March, 1865, an absurd panicky fear seized Englishmen of the large middle class because they imagined the North was about to launch war on their country.[2] In such a state of feeling effective desire on the part of English subjects to place large loans in America could not have been expected. All phases of America's activities, and of course those of monetary and financial significance, were criticized adversely. No good thing could ever issue from Secretary of the Treasury Fessenden because he advocated a high protective tariff. His successor (McCulloch) was reported to be sound on the currency. But, it was contended, he could not be sound on the currency unless he were sound on taxation, and this soundness the *Economist* doubted. Even though he were sound he would be practically helpless in the existing state of congressional wisdom at Washington.[3] Such was the attitude of Englishmen before the close of the war.

Favorable Attitude after the War

But when the news of the fall of Richmond reached him, the English investor began at once to face about. It was still impossible not to feel a sympathy with the Confederates. There is an attraction in vanquished gallantry which appeals to the

[1] Cf. London *Economist*, February 11, 1865, pp. 160, 161.

[2] *Ibid.*, March 11, 1865, pp. 279–280.

[3] *Ibid.*, March 25, 1865, p. 340.

good side of human nature. But, too, English sporting blood asserted itself and every Englishman felt a kind of personal sympathy with the victory of the Federals. They had won, as Englishmen would have won, by obstinacy. They would not admit the possibility of real defeat; they felt all along that they had in them latent elements of conclusive vigor which, in the end, they should bring out, though they were awkward and slow in doing it.[1] This turn of the tide in favor of the American government could not for long be checked even by the assassination of Lincoln. Englishmen recognized in the great President that "power and responsibility visibly widened his mind and elevated his character" and altered "the very style of his public papers," till his final inaugural "extorted from critics so hostile as the Saturday Reviewers a burst of involuntary admiration."[2] Neither was this tide of favorable feeling substantially checked by the quarrel over reconstruction between President Johnson and Congress. Confidence seemed to prevail then as in later years that the difficulty would be overcome in due time, and that "the reconstructed legislatures will, after a short spasm of conflict, agree that the easiest way to deal with the irrepressible negro is to leave him alone and permit the strong compulsion of hunger to act upon him as upon all other human beings."[3] Even when impeachment of President Johnson was insistently proposed and later accomplished, the English capitalist did not suggest that the controversy across the Atlantic would affect business relations between his country and America.[4] As the struggle proceeded it was said that the President was "barely mad enough to act against the advice of his Northern Councillors. . . . Still, on the whole, we think we are justified in expecting a great and pacific vic-

[1] Cf. *ibid.*, April 22, 1865, p. 461.

[2] *Ibid.*, April 29, 1865, p. 495.

[3] *Ibid.*, June 17, 1865, pp. 719, 720. Notwithstanding the flow of increasing confidence toward America, we find occasional—but only occasional—lapses, as when on September 23, 1865, reconstruction is deemed by the *Economist* practically an insuperable problem. A war to liberate negro slaves was righteous enough, but a war to "restore" a federal union had seemed always an absurd war. "It seemed like beating a man to make him like you." See issue of September 23, 1865, p. 1144.

[4] *Ibid.*, October 20, 1866, pp. 1217–1219.

tory of Congress over the violent and superficial policy of President Johnson for the reconstruction of the Union."[1] It was declared[2] to be a curious indication of how little the English had understood the United States that for four years they prophesied a revolution and a dictatorship to follow upon the heels of the first sweeping success of Northern arms. It was only when General Sherman completed his famous march to the sea—and neither he nor General Grant nor the people even thought of a dictatorship—that the greater part of the English public acknowledged one more evidence that they had underestimated the sober reserve and steady character of the American people.

Similarly, the perplexing problem of the Alabama Claims, to which reference has been made, was not permitted during the years 1865–66 to becloud the vision of responsible banking and financial interests. Although the injuries inflicted by the Confederate cruisers on American commerce and the asserted responsibility of England for those injuries assumed after the close of the war a superficial aspect not altogether free from the menace of hostilities, there was, Bagehot asserts, in October, 1865,[3] "no ground of anxiety in the temper of our own foreign minister or the American diplomatist" (Charles Francis Adams). By the exercise of "the utmost prudence . . . not only by the Governments, but by the people of both countries," serious ground for fear of disruption of friendly relations would be avoided. The affair seems not to have assumed much importance in Lombard Street, and therefore, we are justified in inferring, not much in the mind of the English investing public. Thus, in November, 1866, Bagehot was convinced[4] that Lord Stanley, as foreign minister, had a "singularly good opportunity of repairing the—errors, we will not say, but—mischances of this country in our relations with America during the late

[1] *Ibid.*, September 29, 1866, pp. 1136–1138. See also *ibid.*, April 21, 1866, pp. 471–472, and September 8, 1866, p. 1050, for evidence of realization of difficulties involved without discouragement as to final results.

[2] *Ibid.*, May 13, 1865, p. 561.

[3] *Ibid.*, October 14, 1865, pp. 1234–1236.

[4] *Ibid.*, November 3, 1866, pp. 1277–1278.

civil war." His predecessor, Lord Russell, had, in the face of a popular spirit of defiance on the part of his countrymen, handled the difficult problem with firmness and dignity. The natural effect of his temperate conduct was that he became thoroughly hateful to America and far from popular in England. "The Americans could not endure the tone of calm, if not haughty, self-respect in which he declined to accede to their unreasonable, and to one at least of their reasonable, demands." In consequence he was obliged to leave to some statesman who had incurred less odium at home and abroad the task of successful negotiation. Lord Stanley, on the other hand, was now reaping the advantage of his excessive reticence during the war. On the *Alabama* question, he came to the foreign office with the advantage of a good blank record, and the public opinion of both countries, with the usual ingratitude of public opinion, was far more favorable to him than to Lord Russell. The financial and banking interests saw quite clearly that in view of possible similar depredations upon her own commerce in the event of any future war it was the interest as well as the duty of Great Britain to set a precedent to prevent such mischief on the high seas. With such a view of the case it was not difficult to anticipate the reversal of popular opinion in England and the ultimate friendly settlement of the dispute.

Equally important with these more purely political difficulties, as influences affecting the willingness or unwillingness to lend us capital, was the state of mind of English investors toward our financial and industrial conditions and policies. Investors were sure to be interested in the trade relations between the two countries, for these relations gave them not only a source of profits, but also a means of judging America's capacity and trustworthiness in financial and industrial affairs. In its "Commercial History and Review of 1865" the *Economist*[1] records that as soon as men were finally certain that the war was ended "there was a rush on all sides to import goods from Europe. The American markets were bare, the warehouses empty, prices rising, and demand vehement.

[1] See issue of March 10, 1866, "Commercial History and Review," p. 1.

Agents arrived in England who bought not by bales and cargoes, but who took at a stroke the contents of entire warehouses." The revival of trade promoted friendly relations and opened the way for renewed mutual confidence. In midsummer, 1865, our federal bonds as a safe security were much discussed in Europe.[1] It was recognized that the North was not exhausted, that war does not exhaust countries which are not its theatre and whose credit is not ruined, albeit in such cases part of the annual production is withdrawn from uses economically advantageous and devoted to warlike and destructive ends. It was further recognized that "the earning power of an average American is far greater than the average earning power of any one in Europe." Therefore, the conclusion was, the American people had the means to pay their huge indebtedness if they wished to pay. On the other hand, Englishmen and other Europeans recognized that they contemplated conditions in a young and therefore untried nation with, as they thought, a most peculiar and wholly experimental constitution.[2] They were free to say that the answer to the question whether or not America would wish to pay her debts could only be completely given by one who felt he could foresee her whole future history. Notwithstanding a hesitancy thus indicated, they were certain that the Americans had "a singular reserve of character and power for a day of difficulty." Just when the Old World proved the case of the American people to be hopeless, "on a sudden they exert an energy which no one had expected, which has never been exerted before, which they themselves could not explain, yet they possess. . . . We must give credit to an almost unlimited extent to the wonderful capacity of the nation with the greatest faculty of earning which the world has ever seen, placed in the most productive place which the world has ever contained. . . . If they can only get capital they can do anything: they ought, therefore, to be borrowers from all the world. If they can establish their credit they will borrow as they like, for they have the means of paying higher interest

[1] London *Economist*, August 12, 1865, pp. 969, 970.

[2] *Ibid.*, October 28, 1865, pp. 1300–1301.

than all the others. But," Bagehot adds, "if they lose their credit at this critical juncture they will lose it for indefinite years."[1] What more definite statement of confidence in their ability could Americans, under their circumstances, have desired than this from the keenest observer, the most profound analyzer of economic facts, and the most influential financial writer of the time? And what more certain and effective method of establishing their credit, on the necessity of which he insists, than by resumption of specie payments at that time?

Confidence in America on the part of England's bankers and investors, whose opinions the *Economist* both led and reflected, steadily grew. As has just been intimated, the *Economist* did not leave out of account the weaknesses in the American situation. These were frankly and painstakingly stated. Yet the net result through the two years ending December, 1866, was an attitude of open-mindedness and of increased expectation of large things to come from the United States. Thus it was in October, 1865, that rumors of war between France and the United States excited the fears of certain sections of the English people, but "the City" flatly discredited such an event as thoroughly improbable. Some people would insist upon being absurd. "If the *Times* correspondent telegraphed that Mr. Seward had just written a dispatch 'recognizing' Ireland as an independent republic, we doubt whether it would not find a certain number of believers."[2] Not only did the English investor exhibit a growing confidence in American sanity on political matters, but he exhibited the same confidence on financial questions as well. He was not without direct means of information concerning the attitude of the American people themselves as to their ability and willingness to pay their enormous public debt. After visiting America in 1865, Sir Morton Peto carried back with him opinions which reinforced the *Economist's* belief in the ability of the American people to pay and in the excellent existing "state of the social mind to which voluntary repudiation is an impossibility. . . . The

[1] *Ibid.*, August 12, 1865, pp. 969–970.
[2] *Ibid.*, October 21, 1865, pp. 1267–1268.

truth is, we have absolutely no idea in England of the wealth of a population whose average means are probably over £100 a year for every family in the land."[1] "Their economic position is the best the world has ever seen. The productiveness of their industry is greater than the productiveness of any industry ever was before."[2]

In discussing McCulloch's annual report of December, 1866, the *Economist* discloses the same element of confidence in America's ability and willingness to pay her obligations and conserve her credit. The editor declares:

> That a government which one year ago had no *internal* revenue at all, whose tax-gatherer never came to the homes, or intervened in the dealings of the people, should be able to raise £60,000,000, or any such sum, is a miracle. In any other country the bare attempt would have caused a revolution. But in America these taxes are borne as patiently as taxes are ever borne in *any* country. There is no more idea of resisting them than of declaring a monarchy. . . . The Americans, too, have the money; everybody is well off, and everybody seemingly wishes that the Government should be well off also.[3]

Within a year from the conclusion of peace, and in spite of reaction from time to time, on foreign markets our securities had improved[4] until it could be said that "England and Europe have been large buyers of American securities, and these railway debentures and 5–20 [government] bonds are, in fact, the imports which balance our exports."[5] Indeed, investments in America had been carried to such an extent as to cause numerous warnings to be sounded in Great Britain against the movement. Although the *Economist* agreed in a measure with the appropriateness of such warnings, it was of opinion that "there are some counter considerations which must not be overlooked and which go far to mitigate any national anxiety. People who do bad business with America will lose their money as those who

[1] *Ibid.*, November 18, 1865, p. 1398.

[2] *Ibid.*, December 23, 1865, pp. 1549–1552; December 22, 1866, p. 1481.

[3] *Ibid.*, December 22, 1866, pp. 1481, 1482. See also the *Times* (London), August 13, 1866, p. 8.

[4] London *Economist*, January 27, 1866, p. 100.

[5] *Ibid.*, January 13, 1866, pp. 30, 31; and see the *Times* (London), October 9, 1866, p. 8, for a letter from the Philadelphia Correspondent.

do bad busines with other countries, or at home. But if we manage properly ourselves, we do not believe their bad business need hurt us."[1] So far from discouraging investments in America, Bagehot freely criticizes Secretary McCulloch for entertaining the mercantilistic fear of creating a debt to foreign countries through an excess of imports over exports, and he insists that English lending and American borrowing constitute the effective rôle of each nation respectively. "Why he [McCulloch] should fear being in debt we do not indeed comprehend. He says that international balances ought to be settled as soon as possible. We say, on the contrary, that the more an old country like England, where it is so difficult to use money, can lend to a new country like America, where it is so easy to use money upon good security, the better. America ought to be the greatest borrower in the world. She ought not to fear foreign debt, but covet it."[2] At the same time that comments and advices of this nature were expressed by the *Economist*, the belief was held that the condition of our national banks gave evidence of "amazing solidity. Perhaps no banks in the world on the same scale show as much. . . . The inference is plain. A nation in which the banks are so sound is particularly unlikely to suffer from a collapse of credit."[3]

Conclusion

From the evidence thus presented the conclusion seems warranted that, in the opinion of Bagehot, the financial editor who admittedly moulded and reflected the views of the British financial public, the English capitalist was, in 1865 and 1866, not only able but willing to lend capital to America in large amounts. With these loans in hand the government could have proceeded with the resumption of specie payments and saved the country from the turmoil and loss entailed by more than a decade of further experience under a paper money standard.

[1] London *Economist*, January 13, 1866, p. 30.

[2] *Ibid.*, April 14, 1866, pp. 439–441.

[3] *Ibid.*, February 24, 1866, pp. 217–219.

CHAPTER VII

A DECADE OF DEBATE AND DELAY, 1865–1875[1]

HAVING failed to seize the opportunity of resuming specie payments in 1865–66, the country moved rapidly into a decade of bitter strife and debate for a legislative act providing for resumption.

ECONOMIC CONDITIONS 1865–1875

The economic conditions prevailing from 1865 to 1875 form the background for the play of the various forces and influences which affected progress toward a sound monetary basis. It was in this period that America became important enough to compel the beginning of recognition in world finance and that many of her great national problems arose. At the close of the war a million men from the disbanded army, and an annual average from 1865 to 1874 of 326,000 immigrants,[2] were absorbed by an unprecedented development of trade and industry. Of prime importance in this development was the rapid growth of railway mileage. During this ten-year period nearly 40,000 miles of tracks were laid, thus practically doubling the country's railway facilities. Although the Pacific roads crossed the continent at this time and increased the mileage perceptibly, the great bulk of the new facilities permeated the rich agricultural lands of the interior. By these means a vast territory was opened for development, a population rapidly increasing through natural means and by immigration was given opportunity to earn a livelihood, European capitalists quick to realize the most favorable opportunities for investment poured into that region an abundance of loans, and America was raised to

[1] Aside from the sources cited in the footnotes in this chapter and in the following chapter, I have had some suggestions from an unpublished essay on "Resumption of Specie Payments in 1879," written several years ago, by Wilfred Eldred.

[2] Report of Immigration Commission (1907), Vol. I, p. 56, 61 Cong., 3 Sess., Doc. No. 747.

the first rank among producers and exporters of foodstuffs. These various developments had a marked influence upon the discussions and decisions on monetary and financial debate and legislation.[1]

The most important channel through which these developments exercised their influence on currency questions was the course of the price of grain. During the Civil War the average price had been raised to an unusual point, and in 1867 wheat sold in the Chicago market at $2.85 per bushel. That this advance was not due entirely to our inflated paper money was evidenced by the high price which prevailed in England also. No sooner had our agricultural communities begun to adjust themselves to this high level than forces were set in motion which compelled a serious decline in price, with corresponding hardship to farmers and all those immediately dependent upon them. The acreage devoted to the five small grain crops increased 33 per cent from 1867 to 1875 and 55 per cent to 1878. The increase in the yield of these five crops was even greater than the increase in acreage, the annual wheat crop having more than doubled in the longer period. Although the increase in the production of grain greatly exceeded the increase in population, a fall in price was temporarily prevented by shortage in Europe. But when Europe, in the early part of the eighteen-seventies, attained a reasonable degree of freedom from active warfare the increase of cereal production in the fertile valleys of that continent, added to that in the Mississippi Valley, was bound to have its effect in a decline of prices. The problem for America was not to feed a rapidly increasing population, but to market at paying prices its abundant crops of grain. The relation between prices of grain and legislative proposals for dealing with the greenbacks was warmly debated. Which was cause and which was effect? Did currency legislation cause a decline in prices, or did depressed prices impel men to seek a remedy for their hardship through currency legislation? Large numbers of persons seriously injured by the abundant pro-

[1] A. D. Noyes, *Forty Years of American Finance*, New York and London, 1909, pp. 1–3.

duction of grain were almost sure to be confused in their thinking on monetary and financial questions.[1]

While at the close of the war free public lands afforded a satisfying outlet to a growing population and served to mollify the discontent of many who found irksome their economic existence farther eastward, as the years advanced the more available and more valuable free land of the West became scarce. Urban population was increasing relatively to that of rural districts, and tendencies toward the industrial development of the country were more and more in evidence. The unrest consequent upon changes in economic conditions and in settling a new country manifested itself in monetary and financial heresies, and especially in a desire for inflation of the currency.

McCulloch and Contraction

It was under such conditions that the government and the leaders of the public press undertook the tasks of the resumption of specie payments, of funding and refunding the public debt, and of the revision of the system of taxation.

Hugh McCulloch became secretary of the treasury in March, 1865, and brought to that position experience of great importance as a banker and as a public official in another department of the treasury. His report for 1865[2] was anticipated with much interest by both the friends and the enemies of an early resumption movement. Influential daily papers had taken pains to impress upon the new secretary the necessity of presenting to the country some definite systematic plan for ridding the country of the paper standard.[3] Although it was a source of keenest regret to the friends of resumption that some movement had not already been set on foot before December, 1865, the report of the secretary issued in that month cannot be said to have been disappointing to them. In fact it was quite the opposite. In an intelligent manner he covered the whole range of treasury problems, including the currency, the public debt,

[1] *Ibid.*, pp. 3–5.

[2] Report of the Secretary of the Treasury, December 4, 1865.

[3] *New York Tribune*, October 16, November 3, 23, and 29, 1865; and *Boston Advertiser*, October 18 and November 4, 1865.

and the revenue. He declared that the existing inflation of prices was the result of heavy expenditure in the prosecution of the war and of the introduction of the new measure of value in the form of United States notes [greenbacks] and of treasury notes as lawful money. The immense volume of paper money in circulation must, in his opinion, be contracted if disastrous financial crises similar to those of 1837 and 1857 were to be avoided. He reviewed the history of the inflated currencies in order to point out the futile objections ordinarily advanced against contraction of the currency, and he insisted that the process of contraction could not, in the nature of the case, be injuriously rapid. It would not be necessary to retire more than $100 millions to $200 millions of greenbacks, in addition to the compound-interest-bearing notes, before the desired result of bringing paper money to par with gold could be attained. The first thing to be done was to establish a policy of contraction, and then the country would readily accommodate itself to the proposed change, and specie payments could be restored without a shock to trade and without diminution of productive industry or of public revenues. He therefore recommended: first, that Congress declare that the compound-interest notes should cease to be a legal tender from the day of their maturity; and, second, that the secretary be authorized, in his discretion, to sell bonds of the United States bearing interest at a rate not exceeding 6 per cent, and redeemable and payable at such periods as might be conducive to the interest of the government, for the purpose of retiring not only the compound interest notes but the greenbacks as well. The management of the debt, the revenues, and the currency were interrelated and inseparably bound together. He believed that when the whole debt should have been put in such form that interest charges could be met and regular and faithful payments on the principal made resumption would naturally take place. Proving himself an excellent prophet, he warned Congress against the continuance of the policy of an inconvertible currency, predicting that, unless remedied, the question would become a political one, creating untold disturbance.

The report was favorably received by the public and the press. Its recommendations secured the dubious support of President Johnson, who said in his annual message of December 4, 1865: "It is our first duty to prepare in earnest for our recovery from the ever increasing evils of an irredeemable currency without a sudden revulsion and yet without an untimely procrastination. For that end we must each, in our respective positions, prepare the way."[1]

As the year 1865 wore on a considerable number of public men were inclined to cast doubt on the obligation of the government to pay the war debt in full, because the government had received depreciated currency for a great mass of its bonds. But when Congress met in December, 1865, the feeling was still such that the House, with but one dissenting vote, "resolved (as the sense of this House) that the public debt created during the late rebellion was contracted upon the faith and honor of the nation; that it is sacred and inviolate, and must and ought to be paid, principal and interest; and that any attempt to repudiate, or in any manner to impair or scale the said debt, should be universally discountenanced by the people, and promptly rejected by Congress if proposed."[2] And later, on the eighteenth of the same month, after McCulloch had already retired some greenbacks by means of the surplus revenues, the House, by a vote of 144 to 6, adopted a resolution of cordial concurrence "in the view of the secretary of the treasury in relation to the necessity of the contraction of the currency with a view to as early a resumption of specie payments as the business interests of the country will permit," and pledged its coöperation to that end.[3] This resolution records the high-water mark in the policy of contraction so far as public opinion was concerned. At no time thereafter was there anything resembling such a universal sentiment in favor of the contraction method of approach to the specie standard.

[1] J. D. Richardson, *Messages and Papers of the Presidents*, Vol. VI, H. of Repres., 53 Cong., 2 Sess., Mis. Doc. 210, Part 6, p. 365.

[2] *Congressional Globe*, 39 Cong., 1 Sess., p. 10.

[3] *Ibid.*, p. 75. Also see Report of the Secretary of the Treasury, November 30, 1867, p. vii.

The sentiment for contraction having reached and passed its climax, those opposed to resumption on any terms grew rapidly in number. There were several reasons for this, chief among which was the unfortunate fact that McCulloch, in spite of his acknowledged abilities, was not especially gifted with tact in dealing with men. Furthermore he was, as a member of Johnson's administration, subjected to attack on account of the President's unpopular course in regard to reconstruction of the Southern states. Doubtless the reversal of opinion was strongly influenced also by business men, whose economic interests might be damaged by a vigorous policy of contraction. But if McCulloch's tact had been equal to his knowledge of money and finance, and if he had been able to stand more aloof from the purely political contests of the day, he might have carried out his policy successfully.[1] However, partly at least as a result of the unfortunate political situation into which he was naturally drawn by his loyalty to the President, he was thrown into a false attitude of hostility toward Congress. And so it happened that Congress, within four months after the cordial resolutions of the House in December supporting contraction, passed an act[2] seriously limiting the rate of retirement of greenbacks. It forbade the secretary to retire more than $10 millions of those notes within the following six months, or more than $4 millions in any one month thereafter.

Although this act of April 12, 1866, was received with satisfaction by many who favored resumption, it was a victory which showed the influence of politics. McCulloch later declared[3] that the act was ineffective and defeated its own purpose since the small amount of contraction permitted was practically offset by the increase in the national bank-note circulation. While even this limited authority to retire greenbacks was not used to its full extent by the secretary, he did, under the funding provisions of the act, convert or pay

[1] Cf. C. F. Dunbar, *Quarterly Journal of Economics*, Vol. XI, p. 227.

[2] Act of April 12, 1866, 14 Statutes at Large, 31.

[3] Annual Report of the Secretary of the Treasury, 1866, p. 9.

off short-term treasury notes to an amount surprising to both Americans and foreigners.[1]

Some years later, referring to this law, McCulloch wrote[2] that it was not what he wanted, for he knew there would be months in which much more than four millions of greenbacks could be withdrawn without affecting the market and other months when the withdrawal of a much smaller amount would cause considerable stringency. What he did want was authority to retire the greenbacks as rapidly as it could be done without affecting injuriously industry and trade. The contraction of $44 millions, which took place under the law, he believed so little affected the markets by reason of the reduced amount in circulation that no one outside of the department would have known contraction of any kind was going on but for the monthly statements issued by the treasury. And Sherman, thirty years afterwards, held the opinion[3] that it was "the most injurious and expensive financial measure" ever indulged in by Congress, since it both compelled the continuance of high war rates of interest for many years and postponed specie payments until 1879.

Reaction and Tendency Toward Inflation

Public sentiment was becoming increasingly hostile to contraction as a means toward resumption, and demands were already heard for the payment of 5–20 bonds in greenbacks. The arguments[4] against contraction arose from various quarters and sooner or later, in one form or another, were accepted by perhaps a strong minority. It was held that business interests would be adversely affected. Prices would be reduced with injurious effects upon trade, even to the extent of inducing a

[1] *Ibid.*, pp. 3–7.

[2] Hugh McCulloch, *Men and Measures of Half a Century*, New York, 1889, pp. 211, 212.

[3] John Sherman, *Recollections of Forty years in the House, Senate, and Cabinet*, New York and Chicago, 1895, vol. I, pp. 375, 384 (Hereafter quoted as Sherman, *Recollections*.); Sherman, *Selected Speeches and Reports on Finance and Taxation*, New York, 1879, p. 417.

[4] See D. R. Dewey, *Financial History of the United States*, 4th ed., New York and London, 1912, pp. 338–339.

panic. Values and business had adjusted themselves to an expanding currency, and contraction could not be undertaken without affecting credit contracts and injuring the debtor class. Moreover, an increase of the currency would promote foreign trade and would supply needed support for the development of the South and West, where the monetary medium was deficient. The government could not afford to resign the issue of paper currency to the banks. These institutions had their share of responsibility for the depreciated state of paper money, and if contraction was to be forced upon the country it should take effect first upon national bank circulation rather than upon government issues. The government itself would suffer from contraction, since public revenues would be reduced through slackening business, diminished consumption, and hence through a reduction of imports. The public credit would be endangered, since the funding of the short-term interest-bearing notes into bonds would be checked. Even Sherman, in one of his periodic lapses into weakness, argued that the very abundance of the currency facilitated the funding of the debt. Thus ran the arguments from a number of quarters. As already suggested, this change of sentiment was due largely to political conditions. But economic considerations were marshaled in support of the play of politics. The panic of 1866 in England, the chief feature of which was the failure of the Overend-Gurney banking house, was much talked about, and the temporary depression which was feared in this country added its impetus to the opposition to contraction. The opinion generally prevailed, and still prevails, that the English disturbance caused a heavy strain on the American markets. But facts seem to support the view that the effect was almost negligible. Few, if any, American houses in London and Liverpool were so affected by the crisis as gravely to compromise any interests on this side of the Atlantic.[1] So far as our credit abroad and the export of our securities were concerned, its effect was temporary. The course of American government

[1] *Commercial and Financial Chronicle*, May, 26, 1866, p. 644, and July 28, 1866, p. 100.

bonds abroad during these years was reassuring.[1] At no time was the English market effectively adverse to them except on occasions of threat by Congress to pay maturing bonds in greenbacks. Moreover, in December our 5–20 bonds were listed on the London Exchange.[2] At the close of 1866 McCulloch estimated that upwards of $600 millions of American government and industrial securities were held abroad.[3] Within the three years ending October, 1867, foreigners had absorbed $200 millions of our 5–20 bonds.[4] Nevertheless, English financial difficulties were made an excuse to help turn the tide against McCulloch and his plan of contraction. As usual, the blame for a slight stringency in the money market was saddled upon the treasury[5] in spite of the fact that little real contraction had occurred. During the two years following the authority given to contract the currency, $44 millions of the greenbacks were retired, but at the same time the national bank currency was expanded in practically equal amount.[6]

A wave of economic heresy had struck the people, especially in the West.[7] The fear of contraction was used as a political expedient to catch votes. Playing upon this fear, the opponents of resumption held the whip hand much of the time. The greenback movement, which took form at this juncture and the followers of which regarded inflation of the currency as a means of curing all economic ills, found encouragement in crop failures, high prices of nonagricultural products, speculation, and business troubles. The democratic party became the special advocate of inflation. Senator Pendleton, of Ohio, who had

[1] *Commercial and Financial Chronicle*, July 28, p. 104; August 11, p. 167; August 25, p. 231; October 20, p. 490; November 3, p. 551, 553; December 15, p. 754 all for year 1866; February 23, p. 229; April 6, p. 424; August 3, p. 137; August 17, pp. 197, 203; October 19, pp. 485–486 all for year 1867.

[2] *Ibid.*, December 15, 1866, p. 756.

[3] Report of the Secretary of the Treasury, December 3, 1866, p. 12.

[4] *Commercial and Financial Chronicle*, October 19, 1867, p. 485.

[5] Noyes, *op. cit.*, p. 15.

[6] Report of the Secretary of the Treasury, December 3, 1866, p. 9; and Dunbar, *Quarterly Journal of Economics*, Vol. XI, p. 228.

[7] A. B. Hepburn, *History of Coinage and Currency in the United States*, New York and London, 1903, p. 210.

formerly vigorously denounced the legal tender acts,—now aiming for the Presidency in 1868,—led the movement in favor of perpetuating the greenbacks. Then in the same direction, some republican leaders, fearful of party defeat, modified their views. Senator Sherman, for example, who in more than one speech had predicted that resumption would take place before 1868, now expressed his belief in the propriety of paying bonds in greenbacks, and was willing to stop all movements toward contraction.[1] This change of front, participated in by many men of both parties, resulted in a congressional enactment in February, 1868, suspending altogether the secretary's authority "to make any reduction of the currency by retiring or cancelling United States notes."[2] In this way the limited power previously granted to retire greenbacks was taken away, and the first movement for a return toward coin payments was all but effectively throttled. The notes outstanding had been, in the meantime, reduced from $400 millions to $356 millions, simultaneously, albeit, as just stated, with a corresponding increase of national bank notes. Happily in the following May the majority of the republicans, expressing themselves in national convention, took a firm stand on the question of the payment of the 5–20 bonds. In their platform they "denounce all forms of repudiation as a national crime; and the national honor requires the payment of the public indebtedness in the utmost good faith to all creditors at home and abroad, not only according to the letter, but the spirit of the laws under which it was contracted. . . . The national debt, contracted as it has been for the preservation of the Union for all time to come, should be extended over a fair period for redemption; and it is the duty of Congress to reduce the rate of interest thereon, whenever it can honestly be done.

"That the best policy to diminish our burden of debt is to so improve our credit that capitalists will seek to loan us money at lower rates of interest than we now pay, and must continue to pay so long as repudiation, partial or total, open or covert,

[1] *Ibid.*
[2] 15 Statutes at Large, 183.

is threatened or suspected."[1] On the other hand, the democratic party in its national convention in July was still controlled by inflationist sentiment. It declared for the "payment of the public debt of the United States as rapidly as practical; all moneys drawn from the people by taxation, except so much as is requisite for the necessities of the Government, economically administered, being honestly applied to such payment, and where the obligations of the Government do not expressly state upon their face, or the law under which they were issued does not provide they shall be paid in coin, they ought in right and in justice to be paid in the lawful money of the United States [i.e. in greenbacks]. Equal taxation on every species of property according to its real value, including government bonds and other public securities. One currency for the government and the people, the laborer and the office holder, the pensioner and the soldier, the producer and the bond holder."[2]

As the platforms indicated, the presidential contest between the two political parties was waged on the question of repudiation. Although Governor Seymour of New York, who was opposed to repudiation, won the democratic nomination over Pendleton, who was an advocate of that financial and political error, the republicans, possessing a great war hero as candidate, were successful at the polls. The election of Grant meant payment in coin, at least so far as the matter was settled by the exciting campaign of 1868. This was the first great national political contest for the maintenance of the monetary standard.

The reactionary legislation enacted by Congress had been discouraging to McCulloch, yet in his report for December, 1868, he again urged the necessity of reëstablishing the specie standard and recommended additional measures to abolish the "dishonored and disreputable currency."[3] Numerous business men were anxious to avoid the fluctuations and uncertainties due to depreciated paper by making their contracts specifically payable in coin. Believing that such practice would advance the

[1] Edward McPherson, *Political Manual for 1868*, Washington, 1868, p. 364.
[2] *Ibid.*, p. 367.
[3] Report of the Secretary of the Treasury, December 1, 1868, pp. iii-viii.

movement toward resumption both by bringing greater quantities of gold into circulation and also by habituating the people to the use of coin, McCulloch insisted that such specific contracts, executed in coin, should be legalized. He also recommended that after January 1, 1870, Congress should withdraw the legal tender quality from the greenbacks as to private debts subsequently contracted; and further, after January 1, 1871, the notes should, except for government dues, cease to be legal tender for any purpose whatsoever. The privilege of conversion of greenbacks into bonds at the will of the holder, provided in the first legal tender act of February, 1862, but revoked in March, 1863, he now urged should be reënacted. Sherman tells us in his speech in the Senate on March 6, 1876, that his vote in 1863 in favor of revoking this privilege brought to him the keenest regret of his official life. He, with other statesmen and publicists at this later date, fully realized that, had this privilege not been withdrawn, contraction of the currency would have gone on apace with the advance of the national credit after the close of the war, and resumption would have been accomplished by a natural process as the greenbacks in due course disappeared through the process of conversion.[1] These efforts of McCulloch and those of his sympathizers added strength to the transient enthusiasm for sound money which was forced upon large numbers of republicans by the political exigencies of the campaign.

Having assumed the attitude of virtue, it became necessary for republicans to show a semblance of sincerity by promoting congressional action. Furthermore, in his December message[2] President Johnson openly advocated repudiation of the public debt, and this position of a President now discredited by Congress made pronouncement of some forward step psychologically inevitable. The astounding statements from the chief executive in favor of repudiation brought forth a sweeping

[1] While statesmen of that day felt great confidence in the possibilities of this natural process of resumption, we cannot ignore the effect which such a contraction might have had on public sentiment. If contraction resulted in a drop in prices, agitation for the repeal of the conversion clause might have had a fair chance of success.

[2] Richardson, *Messages and Papers of the Presidents*, Vol. VI, p. 678.

condemnatory resolution in the Senate[1] by a vote of 43 to 6, wherein that body, "properly cherishing and upholding the good faith and honor of the nation, do hereby utterly disapprove of and condemn the sentiments and propositions contained in . . . the late annual message of the President." The House,[2] by a similar resolution and a vote of 155 to 6, supported the upper body. After passing an act, February 19, 1869,[3] which forbade national banks making loans on greenbacks or on national bank notes as collateral security, for fear of causing contraction in the currency, Congress, on March 3rd, passed a bill[4] to strengthen the public credit through a promise to pay bonds in coin and to legalize coin contracts as suggested by McCulloch. But Johnson defeated the measure by a pocket veto. Grant, in his inaugural address[5] the following day, came out squarely and unreservedly for payment in gold. Thus prodded, Congress finally registered the popular verdict, given in the recent presidential election, in an "Act to Strengthen the Public Credit," which was promptly approved by Grant on March 18th.[6] This act represented a reaction against the persistent drive of inflationists in favor of payment of government bonds in greenbacks instead of coin. It declared the faith of the United States to be pledged to the ultimate payment of bonds in coin, except when the law expressly provided otherwise, and also "to make provision at the earliest practicable period for the redemption of the United States notes in coin."

But promises and pledges were easily made. True to the shifting sentiment in Congress which underlay the virtuous assumption of fidelity to contract during the recent campaign and afterwards, nothing was done toward giving effect to the provisions of this law. The new secretary of the treasury, Bout-

[1] *Congressional Globe*, 40 Cong., 3 Sess., pp. 123, 128.

[2] *Ibid.*, pp. 71, 73.

[3] *Ibid.*, p. 1422.

[4] *Ibid.*, p. 1842.

[5] Richardson, *Messages and Papers of the Presidents*, Vol. VII, p. 7, H. of Repres., 53 Cong., 2 Sess., Mis. Doc. 210, Part 7.

[6] 16 Statutes at Large, 1.

well, and Congress apparently soon developed an understanding that the policy of contraction should finally be abandoned and that the country should be allowed to "grow up" to a currency admitted to be excessive. During the succeeding six years, hundreds of pamphlets,[1] mostly worthless, were written on the currency problem, and scores of bills of every shade of financial and monetary opinion were introduced at Washington.

Yet in the midst of heated discussion in Congress and in the country at large, which revealed remarkable weaknesses in economic thought and moral standards, it must be remembered that Congress enacted some measures for refunding the debt which disclose the leavening influence of sound judgment and wholesome desire. Boutwell, opposed to the contraction policy and convinced that the method of resumption through accumulation of a gold fund was impossible so long as existing large exports of that metal continued, fell back upon a process of careful refunding of the public debt as the best means in the long run of improving the state of the currency.[2] He believed that the condition of the currency would improve as the credit of the nation improved. Possibly as a result of the resolve to strengthen the public credit, recorded in the act of 1869, or possibly because inflationists did not fully agree with Boutwell's belief in the relation between the state of the depreciated currency and the state of public credit, Congress was induced to pass the important refunding legislation of July 14, 1870, and January 20, 1871. In order to refund the debt, these acts[3] authorized the issue of $500 millions of bonds at 5 per cent, $300 millions at 4½ per cent, and $1000 millions at 4 per cent, but a total issue not exceeding $1500 millions, all to be paid in coin and exempt from taxation. Not only were these enactments of importance at the moment, but they proved later to be a comfort and mainstay for Sherman in the actual accomplishment of resumption, and for a still later secretary in

[1] The best collection of pamphlets and speeches on the greenback period in this country is to be found in the New York Public Library. Oddly enough, a collection, possibly still better than this one, is housed in London, in the British Museum.

[2] Report of the Secretary of the Treasury, December 6, 1869, pp. xiii, xiv.

[3] 16 Statutes at Large, 272, 399.

battling with a redundant silver currency. Legislation once placed on the statute books is difficult to remove, and it is not too much to say that these acts, clearly pledging payment in coin, laid a foundation for right thinking on the subject of the public credit which even the intense craze of the inflationist propaganda from 1868 to 1874 was unable to subvert.

The Crisis of 1873

The men of that decade, however, constituted "a sorry audience . . . to which to address appeals for economy, retrenchment, and a rigid preservation of the public faith."[1] Socially, financially, and politically, they were on one of the lowest levels of our national existence. It was the decade of the Tweed Ring in New York, of the impeachment of a President for party purposes, of Black Friday and plundering raids upon private and public purses through the gold conspiracy and railway financing of Jay Gould, James Fisk, and their kind. In sum, it was a time when men preferred to revel in the gambling uncertainties of paper money rather than to face the sacrifice which recuperation from a monetary debauch required. In spite of these adverse conditions, industrial interests flourished remarkably, and the country experienced one of those great forward movements in industry and trade which every generation of business men has for a long period of time enjoyed. In 1869 it was declared[2] that since the close of the war more cotton spindles had been put in motion, more iron furnaces erected, more iron smelted, more bars rolled, more steel made, more coal and copper mined, more lumber sawed and hewed, more houses and shops constructed, more manufactories of different kinds started, and more petroleum collected, refined, and exported, than during any equal period in the history of the country. The increase of the railway net mileage from 1869 to 1872 was over 25,000 miles.[3] Not only had new roads been built for the purpose of transporting the increased production of

[1] Noyes, *op. cit.*, pp. 17, 18, gives a succinct statement of conditions of this period.

[2] See Dewey, *op. cit.*, p. 358, for this summary of a government report.

[3] Poor, *Manual of Railroads of the United States, 1873–74*, p. xxvii.

coal, iron, and wheat, but the old roads had increased their facilities. This building, in turn, stimulated larger production in iron and steel, leading to further investments in this industry. The stimulus felt in iron and steel, with their prices advanced from 12 to 40 per cent, was communicated to other fields of industry.[1] The situation was reflected in our foreign trade. Imports of merchandise exceeded exports in 1870 by $43 millions, in 1871 by $77 millions, and in 1872 by $182 millions.[2]

Conditions were shaping themselves for a financial recession. In agriculture, manufactures, and transportation much real progress had been made, but the movement was carried too far. In this period of great prosperity, as in similar cases, the majority of men who exercised controlling influence over business policy were not those who controlled during the preceding period of great prosperity and of severe crisis in 1857. A generation of business men had, for the most part, passed away, and their bitter experience in carrying a great forward movement to the breaking point was lost upon their successors. Plans were laid and contracts made for the extension of productive enterprises for which capital could not be found. The dearth of capital and other influences, aside from those flowing from the greenbacks, brought a reaction in business which culminated in the severe crisis and violent panic of 1873. The existence of a depreciated paper money was, therefore, not the cause of the crisis, although it was responsible for the wild and dramatic speculation in gold in 1869, and for misgivings throughout the period. The supply of money for the period 1869 to 1873 was a fairly fixed quantity. Gold, except in negligible amounts, was not used as a means of payment, and hence we could not secure our varying share of the world's production by means of the international flow of the precious metals. Greenbacks stood continuously for the four years preceding the crisis at the sum of $356 millions, bank notes at approximately $300 millions, and 3 per cent certificates at $46 millions. Of this aggregate of approximately $700 millions

[1] Rhodes, *History of the United States*, New York and London, 1910, Vol. VII, pp. 37–38.

[2] See Graham's table in *Quarterly Journal of Economics*, Vol. XXXVI, p. 231.

of hand-to-hand currency, the greenbacks and certificates were available as bank reserves and therefore could be made the basis for the creation of an enlarged deposit currency in support of expanding business. But this process could have been carried on at least as effectively and as rapidly under a gold standard, because the supply of gold would have been elastic while the supply of greenbacks, though redundant, was fixed. Furthermore the banks pursued a conservative loan policy during these years and cannot be held in any important degree responsible for creating unhealthy conditions.[1] The entire experience was characterized by the familiar succession of events which has taken place in each of the more important cycles of trade during the past hundred years. The usual ease in the New York money market was cut short in the winter of 1872–73, and earlier than usual country banks began to withdraw their funds. During the winter and spring fears of a crisis were frequently expressed, although, as the "summer torpor" seized upon Wall Street, a feeling of improvement pervaded financial circles. Notwithstanding warnings of every sort, the country permitted itself to be surprised by the suddenness and extremity of the crisis which occurred in the third week of September, 1873.[2] The most surprising and the most important failure was that of Jay Cooke and Company, the leading investment banking house in the country. Its attempt to float Northern Pacific Railway bonds under adverse conditions finally involved it in ruin, and its failure was the signal for a general collapse of the country's business interests. Within a few days a score of large brokerage firms, several banks, and some trust companies suspended. In consequence, the New York clearing house was called upon to issue certificates to tide over the monetary stringency.

The Inflation Movement and Grant's Veto

The significance of this devastating crisis for our greenback experience does not lie in the relation of paper money as a

[1] O. M. W. Sprague, *History of Crises under the National Banking System*, pp. 1–6, Senate, 61 Cong., 2 Sess., Mis. Doc. No. 538.

[2] *Ibid.*, pp. 29–33.

cause of the upheaval, but rather in the effect of the crisis upon the agitation for more issues of greenbacks and the inflation craze of 1874. As always happens in a financial breakdown, business men found themselves without the means of payment. In their desperate situation great pressure was brought to bear upon the treasury to relieve the stringency by the reissue of the greenbacks which had been retired by McCulloch under authority of the act of April 12, 1866. Secretary Richardson had already paid out a large part of his cash balance for the purchase of bonds in a vain effort to relieve the money market. Then in October, 1873, he found himself so crippled by the decline of revenue consequent upon the breakdown in trade that he felt compelled to pay out the retired greenbacks in order to meet the ordinary expenses of government. This reissue was made with doubtful legal authority but with the consent of President Grant, who was influenced by the representations of New York business men. In all, $26 millions of greenbacks were released, raising the total in circulation to $382 millions.[1] In this manner McCulloch's contraction plan was finally set at naught.

The country passed through a sudden and violent process of liquidation and of change in our foreign trade. The large importations ceased, falling from $642.1 millions in 1873 to to $533 millions in 1875, and to $451.3 millions in 1877. In 1874 the merchandise balance in international trade was in our favor, and by 1876 the outflow of gold was checked.[2] McCulloch had said, in his report of 1865, that in his opinion the realization of two conditions was absolutely essential before resumption could take place. These conditions were that the unnaturally high range of prices in America must be reduced to come more nearly to the European level, and that the balance of trade which had been running so strongly against America should be turned in our favor. As has already been stated, the seriousness of these conditions thus laid down by the sec-

[1] Report of the Secretary of the Treasury, December 1, 1873, pp. xi–xvi; Dunbar, *Quarterly Journal of Economics*, Vol. XI, p. 229.

[2] See Graham's table in *Quarterly Journal of Economics*, Vol. XXXVI, p. 231.

retary is doubtful. Their importance is lessened by two other considerations: first, the chief element of difference between the American and European price levels was due to the existence of our depreciated paper standard, and, second, the apparently unfavorable balance of trade was to a certain extent due to the large sums borrowed from Europeans in order to promote our industrial and governmental undertakings. At any rate, after the crisis of 1873, these two conditions were realized. But their realization did not weigh heavily upon the public mind, and there was little disposition shown on the part of Congress to take definite steps toward specie payment. The economic advantages for a movement toward resumption were not fully understood, and it was easy to make political capital out of the discontent which naturally thrived in the reaction following a crisis and panic.

Although the country was beginning to recover from the acute stages of the panic when Congress met in December, 1873, men were still clamoring for a greater output of means of payment. Schemes of all sorts were brought forward to relieve the monetary pressure. The plain business men from all parts of the country insisted that it was only right that the government should exert itself to make money plentiful for them in their time of trouble since it had come to the rescue of the banks during the trying days of the preceding September. When the question came up for debate in the Senate the opposition to inflation was led by Sherman, Thurman, and Schurz,—a republican, a democrat, and an independent,—but apparently they could make little headway against the rising tide of soft money sentiment. The House, on March 23, 1874, voted down by an overwhelming majority a bill to limit the legal tenders to $356 millions, and it was plainly shown that the members would not be content to let them stand at $382 millions, the amount outstanding at the time including the questionable reissues by Secretary Richardson during the preceding summer and autumn.

Another bill was soon afterwards introduced by a northwestern senator with provision to increase the amount of greenbacks to $400 millions. This was the "inflation bill." It was referred to the finance committee, from which it was later reported by the chairman, Senator Sherman, but with the total amount reduced to $382 millions. Since this proposal would legalize the reissues made by the treasury, it was a concession to the inflationists. The move served as a signal for bombarding Congressmen with indiscriminate inflation schemes from every point of the compass. The Senate forthwith proceeded to amend the bill to make it read $400 millions instead of $382 millions, and to give further advantage to the inflationists an additional issue of $46 millions of bank notes was provided. The bill now passed the Senate on April 6th by a vote of 29 to 24. The House concurred in it on the fourteenth by a vote of 140 to 102. Thus did Congress take its stand in time of peace for a fresh issue of paper money. In this session the republicans had a large majority in each House, but the measure did not pass by a strictly party vote. Approximately 60 per cent of the party in Congress voted in favor of the bill. As reported by the Senate committee the bill provided for the conversion of notes into gold at par or into 5 per cent bonds at the option of the holder, after January 1, 1876. Judging Senator Sherman by his more conservative speeches, this provision may reflect his views as to the possibility of speedy resumption. Unfortunately, however, the gold redemption section was not permitted to stand. Everbody knew that the bill was an inflationist measure, and the people at large, as well as men in the financial centers, were keenly watching the attitude of President Grant. In his annual message in December, 1873, and in other public utterances, he had reflected the popular desire for an increase in the currency and was considered to be in favor of moderate expansion. When the inflation bill was presented to him for his consideration he is known to have written a message favoring it, wherein he attempted to explain that the bill did not, in fact, mean expansion, and that it need have no adverse effect upon the government's credit. But a systematic campaign was launched among the more conservative men throughout the country to create a well-defined opinion against inflation, with the result that telegrams and letters poured into the President's office in such number that Grant faced about and vetoed the bill on April 22nd.[1] Thus, by an assertion of wholesome public opinion, was the inflation movement brought up with a sharp check. The message was a reasonable one, and was doubtless the turning point in the movement away from paper money.

Soon after this event the House passed a bill providing for free banking—that is, for the removal of the limitation placed upon the total amount of bank-note issues. This bill, however, was defeated in the Senate. A compromise was concluded by which those states having more than their proportion of the total bank-note issues should relinquish their excess in favor of those states having, under the law, a deficiency. The bill now, accordingly, provided that $55 millions of bank notes should be withdrawn from eastern banks and distributed among those of the South and West, which had suffered in the original distribution of the privilege of note issues. But the measure also provided that the $382 millions of greenbacks then outstanding should be retained in circulation. In this form the measure received the signature of the President on June 30, 1874.[2] Although in this manner the inflationists had been defeated, they received an expansion of currency to the extent of the millions of greenbacks which had been illegally reissued in order to ease the stringency during the panic of 1873. The amount of greenbacks remained at this figure until withdrawals began once more under the Resumption Act of the following year.

The inflation bill probably did not represent the real sentiment of all of the men voting for it, but, as Noyes remarks, it was "an anchor thrown desperately to windward" at a time when a majority of the people seemed to favor this movement.

[1] Report of the Monetary Commission of the Indianapolis Convention, Chicago, 1898, pp. 424–425; Richardson, *Messages and Papers of the Presidents*, Vol. VII, pp. 244–246, 268; Edward Atkinson, "Veto of the Inflation Bill of 1874," *Journal of Political Economy*, Vol. I, pp. 117–119; Rhodes, *History of the United States*, New York and London, 1910, Vol. VII, pp. 55–63.

[2] 18 Statutes at Large, 123.

It was a bid for popular favor. The republicans felt that they were facing almost certain defeat at the ensuing autumn election. They well knew the fate of the administration party in past periods of business depression. Yet their political game proved a failure. The congressional election of 1874 was lost. The republican plurality in the lower House of 110 in the 43rd Congress was changed to a democratic plurality of 74 in the succeeding Congress.[1]

A full decade had now been consumed in useless backing and filling on the money question. These years reveal an unsteadiness of purpose, an ignorance of fundamental economic conceptions, and a willingness to subordinate public welfare to private advantage which are disheartening and revolting.

[1] Noyes, *op. cit.*, p. 20.

CHAPTER VIII

THE RESUMPTION ACT: ITS ORIGIN AND INTERPRETATION

Republicans Face toward a Resumption Act

Out of the desperate straits in which a political party found itself after the public had pronounced its verdict upon it at the polls came a move toward a sane solution of long-standing difficulties. After the congressional election in November, 1874, the old Congress still had the short term before it. Here was an opportunity for republicans to recover favor with the best element of the country by enacting conservative and sane legislation looking toward resumption, albeit the inflationists of the party might stultify themselves by this sudden reversal of policy. They felt nothing was to be lost politically by such action, and they argued, furthermore, that it would be impossible after March 4, 1875, for any financial measure whatsoever to be agreed upon by a republican Senate and a democratic House. By Grant's veto of the inflation measure the hands of those men who were in favor of an early return to specie payments had been greatly strengthened. Led by Senator Edmunds of Vermont, they were determined to set on foot the resumption policy while republicans still held a majority in both houses. In their enthusiasm they, in turn, assumed some doubtful positions. They accepted, for example, the specious argument that the stringency in the money market which was suffered during the recent panic and which was caused by hoarding the inelastic paper currency could not have occurred under a coin standard. A coin standard, they insisted, would have met every demand in a similar crisis without creating a stringency. Clear thinking on economic subjects was not, upon the whole, characteristic of that day.

Senator Edmunds Author of the Act

In order to survey the whole situation and bring it to an issue, a caucus of republican senators was held in December,

1874. The caucus appointed a sub-committe to draft a resumption bill. In all of the literature covering this period, including even Sherman's *Recollections*,[1] the impression is given that the resumption act was drawn by Sherman himself. This is an error which has been perpetuated for more than a generation. He did nothing of the kind. He was, at the particular time at which the act was drawn, laboring under one of those spasms of uncertainty which so frequently marred his career in the Senate. Senator Edmunds of Vermont was the author of the essential provisions of the resumption bill. He was one of the ablest and most consistently sound public men of the resumption period. He entered the United States Senate in 1866 and served continuously there for the next twenty-five years. Among his notable legislative achievements and evidences of leadership were those connected with the reconstruction of the Southern states, the impeachment of President Andrew Johnson, the suppression of polygamy in Utah, the Hayes-Tilden Electoral Commission of 1876, the resumption of specie payments in 1875, and the anti-trust law of 1890. He was a great parliamentarian and a great jurist, and in these capacities he left his mark on the work of Congress for a full generation. His indifference to the enjoyment of personal credit for his most important efforts has led historians, even to the present day, to attribute to others the authorship of some of those memorable and far-reaching enactments. No act of Congress exerted finally a more profound influence upon the country's monetary, financial, and economic future than the Act to Provide for the Resumption of Specie Payments, passed on January 14, 1875.[2]

Correspondence with Edmunds

On the origin of this remarkable piece of legislation I had some interesting correspondence with Senator Edmunds. At the time of writing the correspondence quoted he was the only

[1] Vol. I, pp. 509, 510.

[2] *New York Evening Post*, February 28, 1919—an editorial on the work of Senator Edmunds, written at the time of his death at the age of 91; the *Burlington Free Press and Times* (Vermont), March 6 and May 8, 1919.

surviving member of that history-making caucus called to devise means to rid the country of a paper standard. In reply to my inquiries he wrote, under date of February 5, 1914:

The action of republican senators in confidential conference occurred a short time preceding the passage of the bill. All the papers, memoranda and propositions embraced in the confidential meetings of the republicans were carefully preserved by me until my resignation in 1891 from the Senate, when with other similar accumulations they were destroyed as no longer of any use.

At the meeting of that session of the Senate the views of many republicans were widely different from each other touching the policy or possibility of then acting harmoniously upon the subject. As the good custom then was, each republican was entitled without loss of his party standing or the good will of his associates to finally act as he should feel himself compelled to do in respect of the passage of the bill for the resumption of specie payment. Senator Anthony, the chairman of republican conferences (we did not hold caucuses in the technical and compulsory sense), at the request of two or three eastern republicans called a meeting of us all to consider whether our respective views could be harmonized in such a way as to result in effective legislation which we could all cheerfully vote for. Such a meeting was held, and a committee of eleven senators was appointed to consider the subject and report to a later meeting. That committee was so composed and appointed that the various conflicting views of senators should be represented. The committee sat for nearly three weeks, more than three evenings a week in discussing, first, whether we should act at all, and, second, if we did, what we should propose in the form of a bill.

Finally the committee came to an agreement upon the general propositions in favor of resumption which we would recommend to the full meeting of all the republicans. This meeting was held and the propositions were ratified by the votes, I think, of every republican excepting Senator Morton of Indiana. Senator Logan of Illinois and myself were appointed to draw up a bill accordingly; which became the Act of Congress above referred to. Senator Logan drew up the first and second sections and I drew up the remaining section, which we submitted, of course, to another meeting of the republican senators; and the whole draft was, with the exception before noted, unanimously agreed to. The subject was such a delicate one that we all agreed that the bill so prepared should be voted upon as it stood without any amendments by whomsoever offered, lest any change in it should disarrange or confuse the meaning of the language that Senator Logan and myself had employed in the draft of the bill. The draft was then placed in the hands of Senator Sherman as chairman of the finance committee to be reported from that committee to the Senate. He accordingly reported it. My recollection is that every amendment offered was disagreed to, and the bill passed, I believe, with the unanimous support of all the republicans present excepting, possibly, Senator Morton.

Of course, in view of the great diversity of views and the fear on the part of several senators that if the bill became a law resumption of specie payment could not be maintained, some republicans voted for it with deep solicitude, which I think was shared in by the chairman of the finance committee.

An interesting thing, and a wonderful thing, about it is that during all that time I believe no newspaper made mention of these conferences of the republicans.

As to your second question, I do not wish to express any opinion.

As to your third question, I think that no genius in a secretary of the treasury was required to carry the resumption act into effect so long as the honesty of the American people and of their officers should preserve the financial credit of the United States, as the third section of the act provided in effect that so long as the United States could borrow money specie payments would continue.

. . . The date of resumption was postponed in order to harmonize the views and relieve the anxieties of those republicans who doubted (of whom I was not one) respecting the possibility of resuming at all.

Senator Edmunds and Senator Sherman were both members of the sub-committee of eleven caucus members who were charged with the duty of drawing up general propositions on resumption for the consideration of the caucus as a whole. Edmunds was foremost in proposing the positive steps which should be incorporated in the proposed act. Sherman was hesitant, and was not a member of the still smaller subcommittee which did the real work of drafting the bill. A reading of the final form of the act as drawn by Edmunds and Logan will show that the provisions which Edmunds indicates were drawn by himself, who represented the conservative wing of republicans, were those referring to resumption of specie payments, while those drawn by Senator Logan, who represented the inflationist tendencies of the party, were of subordinate importance and did not refer directly to resumption. Senator Edmunds's authorship seems unquestionable.

Sherman Introduces the Bill

As Edmunds states in his remarkable letter, the bill was handed to Sherman, as chairman of the finance committee, in order to be reported to the Senate. This was on December 21st. It was taken up the next day, and after discussion, chiefly by democratic members, it passed without change by a strict party vote of 32 to 14. On the seventh of January the bill was considered in the House during one day only, when it passed by a vote of 136 to 98, receiving its entire support from the republican party.[1] It became a law by the President's signature on January 14, 1875. Thus, at last, was an act on the statute books providing payment in specie, under the title "An Act to provide for the Resumption of Specie Payments."[2] Criticism of this piece of legislation was immediately very active, and it was freely declared that resumption under it was an impossibility. It was plainly evident that the democrats and those republicans who were in reality opposed to the measure would attempt to overturn this work in the new Congress of the following winter.

Provisions of the Act

The measure covered a variety of subjects and conferred extensive powers on the secretary of the treasury. (1) The date for resuming coin payments was definitely fixed at January 1, 1879. (2) The legislative limitation of a fixed total amount was removed from the national bank circulation and a provision was made for the retirement of legal tender notes (greenbacks) to the extent of 80 per cent of future issues of national bank notes until the legal tenders were reduced in amount to $300 millions. (3) The mint charge for the process of coining gold was abolished. (4) Fractional currency was to be withdrawn and subsidiary silver was to take its place. (5) In order to carry out the purpose of resuming specie payments the secretary of the treasury was given power, first, to use any surplus revenues not otherwise appropriated, and, second, to issue bonds of the classes described in the refunding act of July 14, 1870. The two sections providing for subsidiary silver and the abolition of the mint charge on gold coinage were, although excellent in themselves, to a large extent merely concessions to the inflationist and mining interests. These were the provisions formulated by Logan. The provision dealing with the removal of the limitation on the issue of national bank

[1] Sherman, *Recollections*, Vol. I, pp. 511, 518.

[2] 18 Statutes at Large, 296.

notes was designed to placate those portions of the country which had not received their due share of the circulation privilege under the old plan of note restriction made necessary by the existence of an inconvertible paper standard. The earlier acts[1] in regard to such restriction fixed the total amount of issues at $300 millions, which was later increased to $354 millions by the act of July 12, 1870.[2] In the confusion of the time the treasury had poorly managed the affair, and some states received more than their legal proportion of bank-notes in relation to their population, banking capital, and resources. Frequent attempts had been made to adjust the awkward situation and a prospect of relief was now welcomed. The new act, in abolishing the restriction on the amount of bank-notes as a whole, required no limitation on the note-circulation of an individual bank except those relating to the 90 per cent United States bond requirement and to the reserve requirement in the original National Bank Act. In this sense "free banking" was part of the plan for banks to resume on the same day that the government proposed to pay in coin.[3] Section 3, in providing, further, for the redemption of "the legal tender United States notes" (greenbacks), required the secretary to limit the amount redeemed to 80 per cent of the sum of bank-notes issued by newly organized banks or by old ones thereafter increasing their capital, but to continue such redemption until there should be outstanding the sum of $300 millions of such United States notes and no more. Thus the secretary was given authority and required as opportunity afforded, to reduce the greenbacks from the amount of $382 millions to $300 millions. And then the chief provision, later vigorously debated, was added, authorizing the secretaryon and after January 1, 1879, to "redeem" in coin United States legal tender notes upon presentation for redemption. To enable the secretary to "prepare" and "provide" for redemption he was authorized in the sweeping terms above mentioned to use any surplus in the treasury not otherwise

[1] 12 Statutes at Large, 665, and 13 Statutes at Large, 99.

[2] 16 Statutes at Large, 251.

[3] C. F. Dunbar, *Economic Essays*, New York and London, 1904, pp. 359, 360.

appropriated, and "to issue, sell, and dispose of, at not less than par, in coin, either of the descriptions of bonds" authorized in the act of July 14, 1870—i.e. 5 per cent ten-year, 4½ per cent fifteen-year, or 4 per cent thirty-year bonds.

Controversy over the Meaning of the Act

Though ample powers were thus given to the secretary, the actual operations by which the purposes of the law were to be attained were left almost entirely to his discretion. When the bill was before the Senate, several members of that body attempted to force an explicit statement as to the meaning of some of these broad, indefinite powers. Particularly was the question pressed as to whether greenbacks once returned to the treasury for redemption would be reissued. The question was of vital interest to both inflationist and conservative. The able democratic Senator Schurz and others persistently inquired into this matter. They were bent upon learning what the word "redeem" meant as used in the bill—whether or not the law would be interpreted to mean that after January 1, 1879, greenbacks presented to the treasury for redemption would be retired and cancelled and not reissued, and that the amount outstanding would be reduced below the $300-million limit mentioned in the bill. Answer to these questions was steadily refused by Sherman, who, as chairman of the finance committee, was in charge of the bill on the floor of the Senate. Any explicit answer to such questions would drive away one wing or the other of the expected majority for the bill, and it was the first business of the sponsors of the bill to carry it through by whatever means.[1] Evading the point at issue to the last degree, Sherman was finally forced to declare that the bill left that matter open and that "we might leave to the future those questions which tend to divide and distract," and that it was wiser "for the present to hold to the main purpose of accomplishing the great work of resumption." The divergence of opinion, inside of Congress and throughout the country, was so pronounced that it was deemed best to make no statement for

[1] *Ibid.*, p. 212; Sherman, *Recollections*, Vol. I, pp. 512–518.

or against the policy to reissue notes that might be "redeemed" according to the law after January 1, 1879. It was only by a compromise of this sort—or rather by an agreement on a policy of silence—that it was possible, in the first place, to bring the bill before Congress and then to secure its passage. Here again a communication from Senator Edmunds gives the real intention of the republican caucus committee. In February, 1898, he wrote that, in the minds of the committee of the caucus and of the caucus itself, the greenbacks could not, in point of law, be reissued, but that western and other sensibilities recoiled from having that feature specifically mentioned in the bill. As previously stated, the bill was passed exactly as framed by the committee. Edmunds states again that he was a member of the caucus committee and had a vivid recollection of these events, that "some of the amendments proposed on the floor were good amendments, but I knew that if the door to amendment was once opened, that was the end of the effort to pass a useful bill." "I knew as a lawyer and congressman that Logan's part of it provided for circumstances which would never arise, whereas my part was copper-riveted and could not be shaken."[1] Silence on the part of the members of the caucus naturally produced confusion in the use of the term "redeem." Obviously, when applied to the section relating to bank-note issues, it meant actual cancellation and retirement until there should be no more than $300 millions of greenbacks outstanding. But as to the disposition of notes to be redeemed on presentation after January 1, 1879, nothing having authority of statutory enactment was advanced until three years later.

A further confusion of the currency problem related to the provision of the act making contraction of greenbacks dependent upon the issue of national bank-notes by new banks, or by old ones increasing their circulation. From the standpoint of resumption there was no logical connection between the two operations. In some quarters the removal of the bank-note restriction was considered a matter of conciliation offered to inflationists. Some went so far as to characterize the whole

[1] Quoted by the *New York Evening Post*, February 28, 1919.

resumption measure as an inflationist scheme. It is quite clear that this provision represented another compromise embodied in the bill. It was generally expected that an increase in bank-notes would come, and in order to secure the support of those desirous of such an increase in favor of the provisions for the reduction of the legal tenders to $300 millions it was necessary to make the two processes dependent upon each other. However, as it happened, the enforcement of this provision was accompanied by an actual reduction of the total bank-note circulation of the country. There was no provision for such a contingency. The bank-currency was not expanded but contracted, owing to an unexpected surrender of bank circulation under the pressure of the times. Depression in business, and a rapid rise in the value of United States bonds, occasioned by the betterment of the government's credit after the passage of the Resumption Act, were responsible for the shift.[1] The inflationists were naturally dissatisfied with this course of events and persistently strove for changes in the law. In January, 1875, the volume of bank-notes in circulation was $352 millions, and of greenbacks $382 millions. By April 1, 1878, $43 millions of new bank-notes had been issued, while $74 millions of earlier bank-note issues had been retired, leaving a net reduction of $31 millions. Meanwhile the United States notes had been redeemed to the extent of $35 millions, thus making for the period a total contraction, as to these elements of the currency, of approximately $66 millions.[2] These were facts well known to the enemies of resumption, hence their repeated attacks upon the act. They insisted that it was not resumption but more money that was needed. The sentiment against resumption was now so strong that a concession to paper money sentiment became necessary. Congress therefore hurriedly passed a measure on May 31, 1878, prohibiting any further contraction of greenbacks, and directing the reissue of those received by the treasury in the ordinary course of business.[3] This was a momentous act, scarcely less

[1] Dunbar, *Economic Essays*, New York and London, 1904, pp. 213, 359–361.

[2] Report of the Monetary Commission of the Indianapolis Convention, Chicago, 1898, pp. 207–208.

[3] 20 Statutes at Large, 87

important than the Resumption Act itself. It finally, after three years of uncertainty, settled the meaning of the term "redeem" as used in the Resumption Act, and fixed upon the country a permanent currency of greenbacks. The amount of greenbacks stood at that moment, as it has stood ever since, at $346,681,016. Thus the notes "redeemed" or "presented for redemption" were not, as in 1866, under McCulloch, cancelled and retired, but were reissued and kept in circulation as a never-ending drain—so thought the Cleveland administration—upon the resources of the secretary of the treasury during periods of insufficient revenue or of a persistent demand by the public for gold. The secretary was required to redeem them in gold as often as presented, without regard to any previous process of so-called "redemption."[1]

Extraordinary Powers Given to the Secretary

It is evident that the act of January 14, 1875, did not prescribe a definite plan or process of resumption. In leaving that to the discretion of the administrators of the law, Congress perhaps reflected in some degree the popular belief that resumption could not be accomplished under the act. The date set for the redemption of greenbacks on demand was far off, and the general feeling was that during the intervening four years many influences might turn up to cause a further postponement of a return to the specie standard. However, the authors of the act perfectly understood then, as we do now, that extraordinary powers were granted to the secretary of the treasury. Sherman said it placed "the whole credit and money of the United States" in the hands of the secretary. The discretionary power to issue bonds in order to accumulate gold was granted not only to prepare for resumption but to maintain it, and therefore it could be used by any future head of the treasury. In later years Sherman thought that probably the most serious defect of the act was the provision requiring bonds to be sold for coin and not for greenbacks directly. This requirement necessitated extensive dealings with banking syndi-

[1] Grover Cleveland, *Presidential Problems*, New York, 1904, p. 123.

cates in order to secure coin, which of course was not at that time in general circulation. The impossibility, under these conditions, of selling bonds directly to the people gave opponents of resumption opportunity to appeal to the public prejudice against banking and bankers and caused much ignorant criticism. The future secretary of the treasury was accordingly subjected to violent attacks on account of his negotiations with brokers and syndicates to secure gold. A plan to sell bonds for greenbacks, Sherman believed, would speedily have brought the paper money up to an equality with coin, and this was his favorite method of approach to coin payments. Such a policy was opposed by inflationists on the ground that contraction of the currency would be the result.[1]

The extent of the discretionary powers given to the secretary to "prepare and provide" for resumption is apparent when one pauses to consider the mischief he might commit in creating and maintaining a coin reserve. As Noyes remarks in his *Forty Years of American Finance*,[2] by literal compliance with the law the secretary might demoralize the entire operation of the money market through a policy of hoarding gold in the treasury vaults. He might, on the other hand, through deliberate choice or by force of necessity, make such inadequate provision that when the date for redemption appeared he would find his entire specie reserve withdrawn for purposes of private hoarding or for export. Exclusive of what might be obtained through the sale of bonds, the only source of gold supply then available to the government was import duties, which, by the law of February 25, 1862, were payable in coin. The supply of gold in the United States was thought to be entirely inadequate for the redemption of $382 millions of legal tender notes (greenbacks) in addition to the regular demands of trade. In 1877, the director of the mint estimated that, exclusive of the amount held by the treasury, there were less than $100 millions of gold in the country, and of this amount only $22.6 millions were held by the 2000

[1] Sherman, *Recollections*, Vol. I, pp. 591–593; Report of the Secretary of the Treasury, December 1, 1879, p. xi; Dewey, *op. cit.*, p. 374.

[2] Pp. 24, 25.

national banks upon which the treasury would have to rely in the event of its desire to float a domestic loan.[1] Furthermore, the task confronting the treasury loomed still larger because of the "scramble for gold" on the part of Germany and France during this period. But exports of gold were checked by the middle of 1876 and the international trade balance soon became more favorable to the United States.

Hostility to the Act

Although a resumption measure was now on the statute books, it was by no means safely there. The passage of the act was followed by an interesting campaign in Sherman's own state of Ohio during the autumn of 1875. There the election turned on the resumption issue. The democrats, in their platform, denounced the policy of contraction and demanded the abandonment of a "forced resumption of specie payments." The republican platform, on the other hand, endorsed the action of Congress in general terms and nominated Rutherford B. Hayes as their standard-bearer. The democratic governor, Allen, stood for reëlection. Owing perhaps largely to Sherman's speeches in the campaign upholding the resumption act, Hayes was elected governor. Since Ohio was then regarded as a pivotal state, this success was supposed to forecast the result in the presidential contest in the following year. This situation brought to Hayes the republican presidential nomination in 1876. But during this time and for more than two years the act of 1875 remained inoperative so far as positive action for ultimate redemption of greenbacks was concerned. Bristow, secretary of the treasury from the summer of 1874 to the summer of 1876, did not favor the policy of accumulating a gold reserve. He claimed such a policy would embarrass both foreign and domestic trade and would meet with the opposition of the financial powers of the world. He made much of the loss of interest which would be incurred by a reserve policy, and believed that there were inherent difficulties too great to be overcome in maintaining a fund sufficiently large to redeem over

[1] *Ibid.*

$300 millions of legal tender notes. Secretary Merrill, who succeeded Bristow, held the same view. Both urged upon Congress the alternative proposition that greenbacks be made convertible into bonds bearing a low rate of interest, thus reducing the amount of gold required for redemption purposes. Bristow maintained that the legal tender quality of greenbacks kept gold out of the country and stimulated specie exports. He suggested, as McCulloch had seven years before, that Congress should abolish the legal tender quality for all contracts made after a fixed date, which he designated as January 1, 1877. Nothing, however, came from these recommendations.[1] Furthermore, western congressmen of both parties were hostile to the law, and the democrats freely talked of repeal. Their attack upon the measure was begun during the winter of 1875–76, when the democratic party controlled the lower House. It was when Bristow's report in December, 1875, showed an appreciable contraction of greenbacks up to November 1st that bills were introduced for repeal.[2] In August, 1876, the house passed one such bill repealing the vital clause for the redemption of United States notes in coin on and after January 1, 1879, by a vote of 106 to 86.[3] During these years the gold premium on greenbacks rose from an average of 111.2 for 1874 to 114.9 for 1875, and fell again in 1876 to 111.5, but the fluctuations in the premium were due chiefly to other causes than the attacks upon the Resumption Act.[4]

It was as evident to men of that day as it is now to us that the work of resumption was only fairly begun. The actual test of ability to carry it through depended upon what a secretary of the treasury could do toward marshaling and executing the broad powers granted to him by the act and toward keeping in control the public opinion of the day.

[1] Annual Report of the Secretary of the Treasury, 1875, pp. xx–xxii; and 1876, pp. xiv–xvii.

[2] *Ibid.*, 1875, pp. xxiv, xxv.

[3] *Congressional Record*, 44 Cong., 1 Sess., pp. 5218–5232.

[4] See Mitchell's tables, *Gold, Prices, and Wages*, pp. 4, 11, 12, and compare p. 14.

CHAPTER IX

RESUMPTION ACCOMPLISHED, 1877-79

John Sherman

The important duties to be undertaken by the secretary of the treasury in the Hayes administration were to accomplish resumption and refund the debt, and Sherman's appointment on March 4, 1877, as the finance minister was natural and fitting. He was intimately known to the President as a resident of his own state, and his appointment was in conformity with the usual desire and practice of the chief executive to have at least one intimate and trusted friend[1] in his official family. In the public eye, if not in the view of the best-informed men either in public or private life, he was the most conspicuous, experienced, and well-informed financier of the day. From the viewpoint of private life and material gain, his career had been eminently successful. Starting as a young lawyer in a small city with slight opportunity for gaining a competency, he accumulated a comfortable sum from his practice within the first three years. With no well-founded suggestion of suspicion of corruption[2] or of undue advantage taken by reason of his position and influence in public office, and in the midst of engrossing duties of a public nature, he had, at the end of life, accumulated a considerable private fortune.[3] In spite of his unusually tall and slender frame, he was throughout his almost fourscore years possessed of a rugged physique which, as in the case of most men of achievement, enabled him to spend long hours at hard labor with telling results.

The charge of inconsistency and vacillation in public policy throughout one of the longest periods on record of service in House and Senate has frequently been preferred against Sher-

[1] Sherman, *Recollections*, Vol. I, pp. 561–563.

[2] Senator Hoar's eulogy in the Senate.

[3] T. E. Burton, *John Sherman*, Boston and New York, 1906, pp. 17, 18.

man. Unfortunately the charge can be substantiated. From the time of his first speech in the House on a financial subject,[1] in May, 1858, he was often found on different occasions on opposite sides of the same great question. In 1862 he finally brought himself to vote for the issue of the first $150 millions of greenbacks, but with the provision that they should be convertible at the pleasure of the holder into United States bonds. Such was the importance of this privilege that it was regarded as the pivotal point in the legal tender act. In 1863, however, he voted to repeal this clause for conversion. Later still, as already stated, he regretted this vote for repeal more than any act of his official career.[2] He alone among the members of the Senate finance committee opposed[3] the limited amount of contraction of the currency provided for in the act of 1866, although on both previous and later occasions he had warmly advocated such a measure. Again, in 1868, knowing full well that the ills of business were not caused by the process of contraction, he acquiesced in the popular demand that Secretary McCulloch's power gradually to retire the greenbacks should be taken from him.[4] And in 1875, to select but one more instance, he scarcely favored the resumption bill itself at its inception in the republican caucus[5] in spite of his earlier advocacy of such a measure. Such vacillation gave small promise of the steadiness and persistence needed to carry resumption to a successful issue.

This unfortunate wabbling in Sherman's opinions and activities was doubtless due in part to the extremely complex and inherently difficult nature of the currency problem, which involved economic, financial, political, and social considerations, and in part it was due to the fact that, prior to 1877, he usually favored a method of approach to resumption different from McCulloch's contraction policy—viz., the elevation of greenbacks to par with gold by improving the public credit through

[1] Sherman's *Recollections*, Vol. I, p. 154.

[2] Speech in Senate, March 6, 1876.

[3] Sherman's *Recollections*, Vol. I, p. 378.

[4] *Ibid.*, pp. 433–435.

[5] See above, Chapter VII, Senator Edmund's letter.

well-devised processes of refunding the public debt. It probably is not true that his inconsistencies were due to an overweening desire to curry favor with the public. In spite of his cold exterior and lack of personal magnetism, he seldom had real difficulty in securing his district's vote for election to the House, or favorable action by the Ohio legislature for election to the Senate. Rather, his inconsistencies were due to the fact that he represented the uncertain state of mind in which most men of his day found themselves in the face of some of the greatest problems the nation had ever been called upon to solve. One of his ablest colleagues, Senator Hoar,[1] regarded him as the "very embodiment of the character and temper of his time" and as representing "the limitations as well as the accomplishments of the people" about him. He knew what the people would bear and he sought within limits to give them what they wanted. This is not to say that Sherman was weak and subservient, but that he was an opportunist, and, while he bowed a little to popular opinion in the paper money struggle, he was not a mere thermometer registering the rise or fall of the public temperature. If he refused to drive his views to their logical conclusion and to force legislation to the highest point of excellence, it was because he thought in the long run the end could be better accomplished by less drastic action. But this writes him down as a compromiser—and that undoubtedly he was throughout his legislative career.

But as secretary of the treasury different and less willowy characteristics revealed themselves. The event proved the wisdom of his appointment. He had served as chairman of the ways and means committee of the House, and as successor to Fessenden he had been for a decade chairman of the finance committee of the Senate.[2] This experience, together with the development of unsuspected latent ability and firmness in executive capacity, made him an ideal man for the place. His intimate knowledge of the inner manœuvering of legislative procedure and struggle enabled him better to secure legislation

[1] Burton, *op. cit.*, pp. 428, 429.

[2] Sherman, *Recollections*, Vol. I, pp. 395–396.

needed, and, what was more important in the circumstances of the time, to overcome and block legislative movements hostile to resumption.

Gold Reserve Plan Adopted

As implied in a preceding chapter, several plans for accomplishing resumption were proposed and warmly controverted during the decade from 1865 to 1875.[1] The most important of these were: first, the accumulation of a gold reserve for the daily redemption of greenbacks, thus bringing them to par with gold and maintaining them at that level; second, contraction of the paper currency by retiring such amounts of greenbacks and circulating treasury notes as might be necessary; third, a waiting policy whose purpose was to permit the business of the country to "grow up to the currency," thus appreciating the greenbacks by reason of continuously increasing demands for means to exchange goods; fourth, the plan to take immediate and drastic action in accord with the policy laid down in the slogan, "The way to resume is to resume"—the plan to begin specie payments and depend upon the natural international flow of the precious metals to secure for us our share of the world's supply of specie; fifth, the plan of a graduated scale for resumption providing for starting the resumption of greenbacks at the current market gold-premium and then by a predetermined and gradually lowering rate of equivalence to reduce and abolish the premium; sixth, to bring the greenbacks to par with gold and remove them eventually from the country's circulating medium by an improvement of the public credit through a careful refunding of the public debt and by gradually converting the greenbacks into United States bonds.

So far as there was consistency in Sherman's own choice for an approach to resumption, it is to be found in a rather persistent advocacy of the sixth plan just mentioned—the plan to bring the greenbacks to par with gold by converting them into United States bonds whose principal and interest were payable in coin.[2] This was the red thread that he undoubtedly tried to

[1] For three of these plans, see Sherman, *Recollections*, Vol. I, p. 517.
[2] *Ibid.*

follow throughout the decade ending with the enactment of the resumption bill in 1875. At the close of the war the argument that the amount of greenbacks was in excess of the needs of currency in time of peace and that the amount should be reduced was firmly opposed by several senators, among whom Sherman was to be found.[1] As early as 1866 a wide difference was apparent between the views of Secretary McCulloch, who advocated contraction of the currency by direct and rapid withdrawal of greenbacks from circulation, and those of Sherman, who favored maintaining them in circulation as an aid to the smooth working of the process of funding all forms of interest-bearing securities into short-term bonds at a low rate of interest. They were both in favor of resumption of specie payments, the one by contraction, the other by a gradual improvement of the public credit. With McCulloch the primary object was resumption, with Sherman the point of supreme importance was an advantageous refunding of the debt. The latter believed that direct contraction would derange the business of the country and make funding and refunding more difficult, but that, on the other hand, if the greenbacks were retained in circulation they could be made to flow into the treasury through the sale of bonds and out again through various disbursements until, as bonds in which they were thus redeemable improved in status, they would gradually reach parity with gold.[2]

Yet Sherman found himself at intervals favoring the plan of accomplishing resumption through the establishment of a gold reserve. Concerning opinions held by him from 1865 to 1868, he writes[3] that McCulloch, by availing himself of the power to refund the interest-bearing treasury notes into bonds bearing a low rate of interest,[4] and by leaving the greenbacks undisturbed to circulate as money, might have saved millions of dollars for the government. This done, he should have urged the redemption of greenbacks in coin at some fixed period, reissuing

[1] *Ibid.*, p. 378.

[2] *Ibid.*, Vol. I, pp. 375–376, 385; speeches in the Senate, January 16 and March 24, 1874.

[3] Sherman, *Recollections*, Vol. I, pp. 387, 438.

[4] McCulloch was, in fact, doing this at the time.

them as occasion demanded, and maintaining them at par by a reserve of coin. In other words, these views indicated that Sherman, at any rate in December, 1867, felt that resumption of specie payments could have been successfully begun and maintained by means of a gold reserve. In the early spring of 1874[1] he was ready and anxious for the government to fulfill its pledge to redeem these notes—but not in coin. While acquiescing in the decision of a majority of the Senate finance committee to introduce a bill providing for a twofold process which called for a gradual payment of greenbacks in coin or in 5 per cent bonds at the option of the secretary of the treasury, he now declared that he had always doubted our ability and strength to fix upon a date for the full and complete resumption of payment in gold and to maintain payment.[2] He again insists that, if his favorite plan had been adopted of wedding the legal tender notes "to any form of gold bond by being made convertible into it, they would have been lifted to par in gold by the gradual advance of our public credit, leaving the question of contraction to depend upon the amount of notes needed for currency."[3] Although contrary to his long-continued inclination, economic conditions and the urgent opinion of the republican caucus committee which drew the provisions of the resumption act of 1875 decreed that, as the future secretary of the treasury, Sherman must plan and execute resumption by means of a gold reserve. As has been already stated, very broad and discretionary powers were granted to the head of the treasury by the act of 1875. Yet in one respect, at least, it was absolutely definite. The act specifically required that on and after January 1, 1879, the secretary should "redeem, in coin, the United States legal tender notes then outstanding on their presentation for redemption," and also that he must sell bonds for coin—and not for greenbacks—in order to "prepare and provide" for such redemption. Sherman would have preferred power to accomplish the great result by other means, and he did not hesitate to criticize

[1] Speech in the Senate, March 24, 1874; and *Recollections*, Vol. I, pp. 495–504.

[2] Sherman, *Recollections*, Vol. I, p. 502.

[3] *Ibid.*, p. 495.

this feature of the act as its most serious defect. Bristow, who was secretary of the treasury when the act of 1875 was passed and for a year and a half succeeding that event, was, to repeat, opposed to the program of a gold reserve, and refused to take any steps looking toward its accumulation. He accomplished nothing toward a final realization of actual resumption. He preferred to leave to other hands positive preparation for coin payments. Precedent and personal inclination, however, did not deflect Sherman from the path of sound policy. It was the gold reserve plan that he was legally bound to follow, and which he did follow with such marked success during the eventful years from 1877 to 1879.

Difficulties to be Overcome

Although the secretary had been given unprecedently broad powers to enable him to effect coin payment on a fixed date, the difficulties in the way seemed almost insurmountable. The premium on gold must be reduced. Instead of falling, however, with the enactment of the resumption measure, the premium had advanced and continuously remained at a higher figure for the space of eighteen months following. And although the premium declined from June, 1876, until the following March, when Sherman assumed office, no one could foretell what direction fluctuations might take in the future. In fact, for several months following March 4, 1877, the premium tended to advance.[1] The sources of gold supply were extremely problematical. Exports of that metal had been greater than the production of our mines. As already stated, the gold supply in the country, exclusive of the amount held in the treasury, was probably less than $100 millions. The national banks held in their vaults somewhat more than one-fifth of this total. Evidently, to build up an adequate reserve for the daily redemption of almost four hundred millions of greenbacks domestic sources were not sufficient, and reliance upon the domestic market was plainly futile. The foreign market must form the principal dependence. But at that same period European governments

[1] Mitchell's tables in *Gold, Prices, and Wages*, pp. 11, 12.

pursuing their own purposes to establish the gold standard for themselves were making great drafts upon the world's gold supply. It was to be expected that those governments through their centralized banking agencies would take every precaution known to the international money market to prevent gold leaving their shores. Then, too, preparation for resumption in the midst of the financial depression which continued for five years after the crisis of 1873 had its serious disadvantages as well as advantages. It was well enough that the resultant fall in prices came to accelerate the change in the balance of trade in our favor, thus influencing the international flow of the precious metals toward us; but the fact itself of falling prices was disturbing and disheartening to the business community, making it suspicious of the resumption movement lest prices should be forced to still lower levels. Standing in April, 1873, at 137, Mitchell's quarterly median index number for relative wholesale prices[1] declined steadily, save five slight quarterly recoveries, until it stood at 88 in January, 1879—the date of actual resumption. This decline and the accompanying business depression were reflected in business failures, which were "more numerous and serious in 1877 than in 1874 . . . and in 1878 the record of insolvencies far exceeded even that of the panic year 1873."[2] These were unpromising conditions on which to base an appeal to improve the currency.

Moreover, adverse monetary and economic conditions were not the only obstacles to be overcome. Political conditions were also extremely unfavorable. The republican administration's very title to office had been called in question by the Hayes-Tilden controversy and had been settled by a commission of fifteen men, eight of whom were republicans and seven democrats, who voted strictly in accord with their party affiliations, but who, remaining honest and intelligent citizens, could have cast their votes individually in the opposite direction—such was the complexity of the controversy. Thus hampered, the administration of Hayes faced other difficulties. It was com-

[1] Mitchell's tables in *Gold, Prices, and Wages*, p. 24.

[2] Noyes, *op. cit.*, pp. 34–35.

pelled to face an opposition majority in the House while the Senate was republican by the narrow margin of six votes. The administration party itself seemed hopelessly divided on currency and financial questions, with the net result that inflationists were in control of both houses. So great was the confusion of thought and party dissension that more than one determined attempt was made to repeal the Resumption Act itself. In the campaign of 1876 the democratic platform called for repeal on the ground that the act was "a hindrance to a speedy return to specie payments," and in the following year a repealing measure with the aid of republican votes passed the House, but fortunately failed in the Senate. Into the midst of this confuson and opposition was thrown the silver controversy. Inflationists and silver-mine owners made common cause in threatening the monetary system with a deluge of cheapening silver. And the so-called "crime of 1873," alleged to have consisted in secretly omitting the silver dollar from the coinage act of that year, was shouted from the housetops. The assaults made upon the public credit were by no means the least of the obstacles faced by Sherman. The result was that more than once resumption operations were brought to a standstill. Investors at home and abroad were of necessity his chief dependence in accumulating a gold fund. But domestic bondholders were frequently denounced on the floor of Congress, and foreign investors were made the object of especial attack. The safety of their investments in government bonds was seriously threatened during the winter of 1877–78 by three warmly debated legislative controversies. The Bland silver bill provided for free and unlimited coinage of silver and passed the House in November, 1877, by a vote of 164 to 34. If the silver advocates had been able to push this measure through the Senate and to override a presidential veto, the country would have been placed upon a silver standard basis. The market price of silver at the time would have given the country a legal tender dollar worth less than ninety cents in gold. Resumption of specie payments in silver would have been easy to accomplish because the gold value of the bullion in a silver dollar was then worth less than the gold value of the greenback dollar. In fact, "trade dollars" which contained more silver bullion than the standard silver dollar came into circulation at that time—a peculiar case of Gresham's Law inverted. Slipping to the silver standard would have been a debasement of the monetary standard, and such was the intent of its supporters. Creditors of the government would have been injured. In December the Matthews resolution, introduced in the Senate by Sherman's own successor in that chamber, declared for the payment of all government bonds, of past as well as of future issues, in the Bland silver dollar, which no one doubted would be depreciated. The third controversy—first in order of time—involved the effort, already mentioned, to repeal the Resumption Act, which of course formed the basis of Sherman's action for several months past and of his plans for the future. Four bills were introduced in the Senate and fourteen in the House, each providing for partial or complete repeal of the act.[1] Upon the whole, these were grave dangers which surrounded Sherman, and they threatened to wreck the entire plan of resumption.

Various Aids and Supports

On the other hand, in the prosecution of his task the secretary of the treasury enjoyed certain advantages and supports, partly of his own making, partly due to social and natural causes. Particularly fortunate was his selection of trusted assistants to carry on delicate negotiations and operations necessary to success in resuming payments.

Among these men were Conant, Gilfillan, Hillhouse, Knox, and French. Charles F. Conant was appointed funding agent of the treasury department and Sherman's personal representative abroad in negotiations with foreign bankers and syndicates. It was his mission to manage and supervise all business arising in or passing through London. With discriminating intelligence, he kept his chief fully advised concerning the course of the foreign market as to both American securities and foreign securities, received the new bonds from Washington, which he

[1] *Ibid.*, pp. 37–40.

delivered to Rothschilds and others of the banking syndicate in exchange for bonds redeemed, and proved in every way "a competent and faithful agent."[1] James Gilfillan, at that time treasurer of the United States, Thomas Hillhouse, assistant treasurer at New York, John Jay Knox, comptroller of the currency and Assistant Secretary H. F. French were all reliable assistants with whom the secretary of the treasury conferred freely on the technical phases of measures pertaining to the change from a paper currency to one of coin. Not less important was the support given the treasury by American bankers, and especially those of New York City. In the early stages of preparation domestic bankers were reluctant enough to take a share in what they considered heavy risks involved in the attempt to resume. So soon, however, as they were brought to realize that the head of the treasury—no longer the pliant politician and compromising legislator of past years—was an executive with knowledge of men, of firm convictions and resolute purpose, their patriotism as well as their financial interest insured their enthusiastic support of the government.[2] The motive prompting the foreign members of the banking syndicate was of course one of self-interest. They were made to feel that they could not afford to lose the prestige coming from participation in such an important monetary and financial achievement. Again, the attitude of the public was of great consequence to Sherman. Although at times lapsing into opposition, the trend of opinion throughout the larger part of the country and in Washington, earlier so hostile to the administration and its monetary and financial program, finally turned a sharp corner. In the summer and autumn of 1878 political conventions showed an unmistakable tendency to credit the treasury department with sanity and a measure of success in its operations. Members

[1] Sherman, *Recollections*, Vol. I, pp. 568–569. See also numerous letters passing between Sherman and Conant in *Specie Resumption and Refunding of the National Debt*. This collection of letters, contracts, circulars, documents, and accounts is an invaluable source of information on the actual process of resumption. It appears as Vol. XVII, No. 9, House Executive Documents for the 2nd Session of the 46th Congress. It will be referred to hereafter as *Specie Resumption*.

[2] Sherman, *Recollections*, Vol. II, p. 636 *et seq*.

of Congress were not slow to adjust their attitude to this change in public sentiment.[1] This meant an assurance that no legislative ghosts would again be raised up to block the way to the initiation, at least, of coin payments on the date required by law. Other favoring circumstances were the state of general prices and the balance of trade, forces quite beyond the control of the administration. What McCulloch and his fellow contractionists had not been able to accomplish by way of a gradual revolution in these forces, the financial crisis of 1873 and the harvests at home and abroad brought about suddenly and effectively. American prices, even when reduced to a gold basis, and therefore more properly comparable with European prices, stood well above English and German price levels from 1866 to 1873.[2] The shock of the crisis burst the bubble of inflated prices. Our price level coming more into conformity with foreign price levels removed what had been considered an important obstacle to a readjustment of our foreign trade. Excessive imports were discouraged and exports encouraged. Thus, two conditions laid down years before by McCulloch as essential to successful resumption were secured—*viz.*, prices had approached a normal level, and the balance of trade was turning in our favor. But of all the elements making for success—if one can say that one influence is greater than others when every influence involved is essential—Sherman's own latent executive powers and force of character constituted the dominant element in the entire movement.

Actual Process of Resumption

In the foregoing statement of important conditions and influences which either promoted or hindered the movement toward resumption, several events intimately connected with the actual process of resumption have been anticipated. We now proceed, at the risk of some repetition, to a more detailed

[1] Noyes, *op. cit.*, pp. 43, 44.

[2] J. L. Laughlin, *Principles of Money*, New York, 1903, chart opposite p. 220; Mitchell, *Gold, Prices, and Wages*, p. 28; and Falkner, Senate Report, 52 Cong., 2 Sess., No. 1394, Part I, p. 100.

account of the technical procedure and means employed in accomplishing a return to coin payments on January 1, 1879.

Attitude of Sherman's Predecessors

For more than two years after its enactment, the resumption act remained practically inoperative so far as any action toward ultimate resumption was concerned. Both Bristow and Merrill, the immediate predecessors of Sherman in the treasury portfolio, regarded the provisions of the law with disfavor and practically contented themselves with suggesting changes which met with no response on the part of Congress. However, when Sherman assumed office on March 4, 1877, he found in force a contract[1] which Secretary Merrill had made with a syndicate of New York and London bankers, composed of August Belmont and Company, who also represented the Rothschilds of London; J. and W. Seligman and Company; Drexel, Morgan, and Company; Morton Bliss and Company; and the First National Bank of New York. The syndicate, entering into the contract August 26, 1876, agreed to subscribe for $40 millions of 4½ per cent bonds authorized by the resumption act, $10 millions of which were to be taken by September 1, 1876, and the remaining $30 millions by March 4, 1877. The syndicate had also the exclusive right to subscribe on or before June 30, 1877, for the remaining $260 millions of the projected loan. The secretary, on his part, had the right to terminate the contract with ten days' notice at any time after March 4, 1877. The bonds were to be paid for in gold coin, matured United States gold coin coupons, or any 6 per cent 5–20 bonds which had been called for redemption. The proceeds of these sales of bonds were to go solely toward redemption of the 5–20 bonds then in process of refunding, a subordinate provision only being made for the sale of bonds to redeem or retire the greenbacks (United States notes). The syndicate received a commission of half of one per cent, and was to assume and defray all expenses connected with the issue and sale of the bonds. Here, then, was provision looking toward refunding the debt, but not especially for resumption except in

[1] *Specie Resumption*, pp. 2–4.

so far as good financiering and improvement in the public credit would aid that process.

For a time, Sherman was content to follow this plan, but he soon made known his desire to reduce the burden of interest payments. He therefore wished to float 4 per cent bonds as soon as there was a market for them. In a letter of April 6th to the Rothschilds he informed them that when $200 millions of the projected $300 millions of 4½ per cent bonds were sold he hoped to discontinue their issue and substitute therefor the 4 per cent bonds, which were also authorized by the resumption act. Into the 4 per cents he hoped all of the United States debt would in time be converted. These bonds Sherman considered a very desirable investment, running thirty years from the date of issue and protected by every safeguard and security that had been given to any bond of the United States. Success in this policy would both indicate and insure improvement in the credit of the government. Even Sherman himself had at this moment some hope that the surplus revenue would be sufficient to enable him to carry out the policy of resumption with the sale of only a small amount of bonds. In the contrary event however, he felt reasonably secure in the authority granted by the resumption act to sell 5, 4½, or 4 per cent bonds to prepare for gold payments. If resort to bonds should be made for this purpose, he assured the bankers that in the execution of their issue he desired to avoid disturbing the exchanges between Europe and America.[1] At this juncture, war between Turkey and Russia was imminent, but for the time being no great fear was felt for the standing of American securities at home or abroad, although, as was evident, some capital in London would doubtless be taken up by securities of the belligerent nations. The price of 4½ per cent bonds continued good and the demand fair, $135 millions having been sold by May 1, 1877.[2]

Contract with Syndicate of Bankers

In May, Sherman proposed to change[3] the syndicate contract in order to substitute more quickly the sale of 4 per cent for

[1] *Specie Resumption*, pp. 14, 15. [2] *Ibid.*, p. 27.

[3] *Ibid.*, pp. 39, 46, 60, 85: Sherman to Conant, May 14, 1877; Sherman to

the 4½ per cent bonds. This change was such as would enable him to begin more adequate and more economical provision for resumption through sales of bonds for gold, and it would enable him to look forward to the time when a popular loan might be launched and the exclusive right of sale by the syndicate modified. The syndicate agreed to the withdrawal of $100 millions of the 4½ per cents and to substitution of the new 4 per cents, but owing to the increasingly gloomy outlook for European war the Rothschilds were not sanguine concerning the success of the step. Conant wrote from London that the newspapers had much to say about American credit, that a great amount of English money had been lost through visionary enterprises in America, and that the old state debt of Virginia, much of which was still held in England, was of offending memory. All this, however, did not seem greatly to affect our national credit. The new contract[1] with the syndicate was signed on June 9, 1877. Under its terms the secretary was free to fall back upon the remaining $100 millions of 4½ per cents for resumption purposes if the sales of 4 per cents for refunding and resumption through the syndicate should prove a failure. The syndicate agreed to take $25 millions of 4's at par, and to make payment in gold coin or 5–20 bonds, and to offer the 4's in turn to the people of the United States as a popular loan. They were to be offered at par and accrued interest in coin, for a period of thirty days, at times and places designated by the secretary. Further, the syndicate was given exclusive right under certain conditions to subscribe for the remainder of the 4 per cents and other bonds authorized by Congress. The secretary agreed to use not more than $5 millions of the loan for resumption purposes, the remaining $20 millions to be applied to refunding operations, and agreed that any additional sales of bonds, either for resumption or refunding purposes, should be made through the syndicate or with its consent. At frequent intervals, Sher-

---

Belmont, May 14, 1877; Conant to Sherman, May 26, and June 9, 1877; and Sherman to Morton, Bliss and Company, June 20, 1877.

[1] *Ibid.*, pp. 61, 62; also pp. 36, 52, Belmont to Sherman, May 8, 1877, and Sherman to Conant, May 31, 1877.

man, under similar conditions, now secured $5 millions in gold per month for resumption purposes, thus accumulating his reserve.[1]

Although the syndicate acceded with great reluctance[2] to the reservation of the right of subscription on the part of the public, the Rothschilds soon saw that a successful popular sale of bonds in America would materially help sales in London.[3] Sherman at once requested the New York bankers to issue a subscription circular to the public, setting forth the mode of conducting the popular loan, the deposit required of subscribers, the places at which the loan was to be opened, the description of the bonds, and other necessary and convenient information. That he laid great store by this popular loan was evident.[4] The results were, under the prevailing conditions, quite gratifying. Subscriptions came in from all parts of the country, totalling $67.6 millions within the thirty days' time limit, while in Europe $10.2 millions were sold.[5]

Influence of the Silver Question and the Attempts to Repeal the Resumption Act

Unfortunately, almost immediately upon the signing of the new contract, the silver question began seriously to influence financial progress. The *New York Times* of June 12, 1877, commenting upon a dispatch from Conant relating to the favorable reception in London of the new 4 per cent bonds, threw doubt upon the government's final payment of principal and interest of the bonds in gold. The bonds had great advantages, but one serious point of weakness. If the silver ring should succeed in having Congress authorize an unlimited issue of legal tender silver dollars, this bond would be payable, principal and interest, in that coin. At that moment, the *Times* estimated the strength

[1] In addition to references given above, see *Specie Resumption*, pp. 28–31, Sherman to Belmont, September 29, 1877.

[2] *Ibid.*, p. 68, Sherman to Merchants' National Bank of Cleveland, June 14, 1877.

[3] *Ibid.*, p. 63, Conant to Sherman, June 11, 1877.

[4] *Ibid.*, pp. 67, 69, Sherman to Belmont, June 12, 1877, and Belmont to Sherman, June 14, 1877. For copy of circular proposed, see *ibid.*, p. 71.

[5] Sherman, *Recollections*, Vol. I, p. 580.

of the silver movement to be small, but pointed out that if this estimate proved to be mistaken the 4 per cents would suffer. Such a statement coming from a republican journal gave alarm to bankers on both sides of the Atlantic. In regard to this vital question of payment in gold the act of July 14, 1870, authorizing the bond issues, was altogether vague. It provided that bonds should be "redeemable in coin of the present standard value." Assistant Secretary French had been requested by Sherman to inform himself upon the question of whether "coin" meant gold or silver. He, the attorney-general, August Belmont, and other bankers, came to agreement and insisted that the provision meant gold coin. An act of April 1, 1873, had declared that silver was not a legal tender for payment of the bonds in question.[1] Belmont, for himself and his associates, expressed in June the urgent fear that the discussion of the silver question would, if permitted to continue, seriously affect progress toward resumption and the success of the treasury's financial measures generally. He pleaded[2] with Sherman, as of vital importance, that he over his own signature should publicly proclaim his conviction that the principal and interest of the bonds would be paid in gold coin. The misrepresentation of the views of the President and the secretary by leading organs of the administration made such an avowal of opinion "absolutely necessary." "The silver heresy is a worse heresy, more directly dishonest in defrauding the public creditor, than the inflation [greenback] heresy. . . . . The first actually proposes to pay at a discount of *fourteen per cent* what the government is now borrowing (at four per cent) *at par.*" Numerous other letters were received by Sherman beseeching him to make known his position.[3] Sherman, however, refused to make a public statement that bonds would be paid in gold, saying that such an act on his part would be inexpedient and defeat the very object the bankers had in view. Financial and political excitement would be aroused. Besides, parties and factions, such as the silver contingent,

[1] *Specie Resumption*, pp. 24, 64, 67, 69, 70.

[2] *Ibid.*, pp. 69–71, 81–82, Belmont to Sherman, June 14 and 19, 1877.

[3] E.g. see letter of Seligman Brothers, *ibid.*, p. 67, June 12, 1877.

might for a time raise and contest questions, but they were bubbles and would pass away, and these questions, like all others affecting the public credit, would be rightfully settled in due time by Congress and the people. In his private as well as in his official correspondence, he expressed the firm conviction that these bonds and others sold since 1873 would be paid, principal and interest, in gold coin. However, to pronounce publicly, as an executive officer, unauthorized "theses" or dogmas upon a question purely legislative or judicial would be indiscreet and disturbing in its effects.[1] The views thus expressed by Sherman as to payment in gold coin were "concurred in by the President and all his cabinet."[2] The bankers both in New York and in London felt encouraged at least temporarily by the assurance given through the expression of these views, and subscriptions for bonds increased accordingly.

The silver controversy was a great obstacle cast athwart Sherman's pathway. Still another was the threatened repeal of the resumption act itself. Of the two, some men responsible for administering the laws and restoring sound currency feared most, for the moment at least, the silver heresy.[3] In spite of Sherman's calling its agitation a "mere bubble," it shook the confidence of both English and American investors from the beginning. Conant from London wrote Sherman that "our credit would be absolutely ruined" in that city if silver were made legal tender in large payments.[4] Two days later Assistant Secretary French wrote from New York that unlimited coinage of silver would cause gold to disappear and the inevitable decline of silver would perpetuate a depreciated and fluctuating currency, with all its attendant evils. Even the limited coinage of silver, if we still continued to pay gold on the bonded debt, would cause an odious discrimination between bondholders and other creditors, and invite constant assaults against the "fa-

[1] *Ibid.*, p. 76, Sherman to Belmont, June 16, 1877; also *ibid.*, p. 79, French to Sherman, June 18, 1877; p. 80, Sherman to French, June 19, 1877.

[2] *Ibid.*, p. 81, Sherman to Belmont, June 19, 1877.

[3] *Ibid.*, pp. 84, 88, French to Sherman, June 20, and Conant to Sherman, June 21, 1877.

[4] *Ibid.*, p. 77, Conant to Sherman, June 16, 1877.

vored class." There should be but one dollar for the bondholder, for every other creditor, public or private, and for the workingman, and that dollar should be gold.[1] In reply to these correspondents, Sherman adhered to his conviction that, whatever system of coinage might be adopted, the essential element of good faith in preserving the equality of value between the coinage in which the government receives funds from sale of bonds and that in which it repays bonds would be sacredly observed by the government and by the people.[2]

In both the obstinate controversy on the silver question and the one on the repeal of the resumption act, the administration was bereft of its own party supporters. In the House, many republicans voted for the Bland free-coinage bill and for repeal of the resumption act, both of which passed that body without difficulty or delay.[3] In the Senate, Matthews introduced a resolution declaring that, in the opinion of Congress, all bonds "issued or authorized to be issued" were payable in Bland silver dollars. It passed both houses. On financial questions party chaos during the session of 1877 and 1878 was complete. Voting divisions were sectional and not partisan. The West and South voted almost solidly in favor of measures designed to block the way to resumption, and the East as solidly supported the administration. Fortunately, disagreement in the Senate defeated the bill repealing the resumption act, and the free-coinage bill was shorn of much of its evil by a compromise which provided for purchase and coinage by the government of two to four million dollars of silver per month. Although "limited" coinage only was thus permitted, President Hayes forthwith vetoed the bill. But the veto was equally expeditiously overridden by a two-thirds majority of both houses. Unable by resolute purpose to overthrow entirely the silver mania, the President succeeded in stemming the tide sufficiently to save the gold standard and the national credit from ruin. Sherman did not agree with the President in his veto of the bill, yet he withheld alike

[1] *Ibid.*, p. 79, French to Sherman, June 18, 1877.

[2] *Ibid.*, p. 81, Sherman to French, June 19, 1877.

[3] The Bland bill passed the House by the overwhelming vote of 164 to 34.

his opposition and his approval of the step. This attitude, together with views expressed in a letter to Senator Matthews in September, 1877, has led to denunciation of Sherman as having suffered a lapse in moral stamina and having become again the weak and wabbling Sherman of earlier senatorial days. Although doubtless he was guilty of trimming his sails to meet the gust of popular opinion, the criticism is not altogether just. The secretary's attitude was, rather, one of staunch opposition to free coinage of silver, but reluctant acceptance of limited coinage as finally provided by the silver act of 1878. The political chaos of the day made imperative the allaying of opposition of every possible voter against the administration's financial measures. Resumption was of supreme importance. Sherman did not believe that limited coinage as provided for would definitely and eventually defeat resumption, and the event proved him to be in the right. Bonds did sell and resumption did take place in spite of the compromise silver act; albeit, by that act was sown the seed of trouble which bore bitter fruit in the crisis of 1893. In the meantime Sherman, by giving way to this extent, had disarmed many of his opponents within his own party.[1]

Financial and Economic Conditions, 1877–78

The situation confronting the treasury may better be appreciated through a brief statement of some facts regarding financial and economic conditions during the year 1877 and the early part of 1878. The chief thing to be guarded against was a disturbance of the gold market through the transfer of gold to Europe to meet bonds that were at frequent intervals "called" by our treasury in the process of refunding the debt. It was important alike for the operations of refunding and for those of resumption that as many bonds should be sold in London as would equal the amount of called bonds held there by investors. Any amount in addition that could be sold on that side of the water would by so much ease the process of

[1] Sherman, *Recollections*, Vol. I, pp. 593, 594 and Vol. II., pp. 603–626; *Specie Resumption*, p. 194, Sherman to Conant, November 24, 1877.

resumption. During April and May, 1877, some gold left our shores for England. The price of the 4½ per cents being lower on the London market than in New York, bankers bought $3 millions of them for shipment to America. Coincidently considerably more than $2 millions of gold went to London within a period of ten days in May.[1] The two events were regarded as cause and effect. In June and July money was plentiful in the English and French markets due to large shipments coming from Australia. Our exports were constantly growing larger relatively and the gold flow from us was checked. England imported as much beef from the United States during the first four months of 1877 as during the whole of the preceding year, and Conant estimated that she would need 48 million bushels of American wheat since her own crop was very poor. In August and September gold came to us from England to the amount, on the average, of one million dollars per week, and fear lest gold might be exported from America during the autumn months to pay for "called bonds" sent home from England was ill-founded. The "calls" were planned so that England would export bonds, if at all, in October and November. But those were the very months in which imports of cotton and grain from America naturally took place, thus preventing gold leaving America.[2] The French also were importing gold at this time in preparation for resumption of specie payments on January 1, 1878, the Bank of France holding in August more than $400 millions in coin. To protect itself from these drains of her gold, the Bank of England advanced her discount rate to 5 per cent.[3] Another similar obstacle hindering Conant's efforts to sell bonds in London was the accumulation of gold by the German government for purposes of securely establishing the gold standard.

While Sherman and his assistants were keeping close watch on the gold movement, certain unfavorable conditions of another character also developed at home. The unprecedented

[1] *Ibid.*, p. 48, Assistant Treasurer Hillhouse to Sherman.

[2] *Ibid.*, p. 125, Conant to Sherman.

[3] Correspondence between Sherman and Conant, *ibid.*, pp. 110, 111, 118, 127, 128, 130, 131.

building of railways which had taken place in the decade following the year 1868 had produced transportation facilities in excess of the country's needs. Especially was the oversupply felt during the period of depression following the panic of 1873. As a result the railways indulged in a severe struggle of competition and in consequence reduced themselves to an impoverished condition. In order to retrench, wages of employees were reduced. In 1877 the workmen revolted and started riots which assumed serious proportions. The disturbances influenced business and financial affairs unfavorably, and were consequently disquieting to Sherman and his fellow workers.[1] Business affairs in general were at low ebb during the first year of the Hayes administration (1877). The number and extent of business failures were greater than they had been in 1874, the year following the panic; and although the year 1878 was destined to mark a revival in business, a greater number of insolvencies took place in that twelvemonth than in the panic year of 1873. Politicians, therefore, who desired to saddle the blame for hard times upon the resumption operations of the treasury, found a ready response both in Congress and in the country.[2]

It was these difficulties, together with the "greenback" proclivities of both House and Senate, that lay behind the annoying attempt to revoke the secretary's authority to sell bonds for resumption purposes and to foist the silver standard upon the country. Under these circumstances the sale of 4 per cent bonds, after the close of the popular loan, was seriously checked. Strenuous effort had been made by Sherman and his staff to place these lower rate securities on the markets at home and abroad. They succeeded in some degree in August and September, but sales were then almost suspended. Not until the public was assured that neither the repeal of the resumption act nor the enactment of a free silver coinage law could pass both houses of Congress, or, if passed, that they would be vetoed by the President, did affairs take a more favorable turn.

[1] Correspondence between Sherman and Conant, *ibid.*, pp. 125, 126.

[2] Noyes, *op. cit.*, pp. 34, 35.

The London bankers advised against pushing sales, but to "wait patiently for the market to recuperate." On the tenth of November 4½ per cent bonds had fallen below par, selling for 99¼ in gold. While some bonds were sold, suspense and anxiety on the part of the administration and the bankers' syndicate continued throughout the remainder of the year 1877. It was under these conditions that Sherman wrote his first annual report[1] (December, 1877).

SHERMAN'S FIRST ANNUAL REPORT AND HIS POLICY

The absorbing topics of this report were, naturally, resumption and refunding. In spite of untoward conditions, the secretary was able to make a favorable showing of the financial situation. Although the receipts from different sources of revenue were largely diminished, expenditures had been reduced by corresponding amount and a surplus revenue of $30.3 millions could be shown. The surplus was applied to the redemption of greenbacks and of fractional currency, and to the purchase of outstanding bonds for the sinking fund. It will be remembered that the method and procedure to be followed in bringing about resumption had not been definitely specified in the act of 1875. The plans already adopted and to be executed were now explained in the report. The act required the secretary to redeem legal tender notes to the amount of 80 per cent of bank-notes issued by national banks, and to continue such redemption until there was outstanding the sum of $300 millions of such legal tender United States notes (greenbacks), and no more.[2] On and after January 1, 1879, the law also required the secretary to redeem on demand, in coin, these notes then outstanding. "To prepare and provide for the redemption in this act authorized or required," authority was given to use certain surplus revenues and to sell bonds of various kinds described in the

[1] Sherman, *Recollections*, Vol. I, pp. 598–601; Vol. II, pp. 606–607; *Specie Resumption*, Conant to Sherman, November 10, 1877; Belmont to Sherman, November 29, 1877.

[2] By the act of May 31, 1878, the reduction of the amount of greenbacks was actually inhibited when the total of $346 millions was reached. See above, Chapter VIII, pp. 189, 190.

refunding act of July 14, 1870. In pursuance of the powers thus granted to accomplish resumption, and in addition to his efforts to refund 6 per cent bonds, Sherman had begun the accumulation of a reserve by selling at par, for coin, $15 million of 4½ per cent bonds during the months of May, June, and July, and $25 millions at par, for coin, of 4 per cent bonds from August to December, 1877. Four millions of this coin, together with a portion of the surplus revenue, were used for redemption of the notes (greenbacks). The balance was held in the treasury in further preparation for resumption. During these operations the greenbacks advanced in value to 97⅜ per cent, or within nearly 2½ per cent of par. While taking to himself due credit for this gratifying result, Sherman readily acknowledged that favorable conditions of our foreign commerce gave indispensable aid in its accomplishment. He believed that, barring untoward developments, the practicability of restoring the greenbacks to par, in coin, was now (December, 1877) demonstrated and that this goal could be reached without disturbing either domestic or foreign trade or industry.

Whether greenbacks, when permanently reduced to the $300-million limit, could legally be reissued by the treasury and placed in circulation was a hotly debated question. Although the resumption act was silent on this point, Sherman now expressed the opinion that they could be so reissued, and founded his belief upon the authority given by the revised statutes[1] to use them in payments by the treasury "from time to time, as the exigencies of the public interest may require." Since, however, this construction of the legislation was controverted, he advised that the matter should be settled by distinct provisions of law. A decision by Congress would not only determine the construction of the law, but would tend to fix the policy of the country toward the maintenance in circulation of federal notes, strictly redeemable in coin. A maximum of $300 millions of legal tender notes (greenbacks) supported by a minimum reserve of $100 millions of coin was the plan. Such a feature of the currency Sherman approved. His approval was

[1] Section 3579, and Annual Report of the Secretary of the Treasury, 1877, p. xiv.

long criticized as tending to retain a harmful monetary element, good enough if redeemable, but continuously offering temptation to overissue and consequent relapse into an irredeemable paper currency. The criticism may have been justifiable throughout a generation. In those days the amount of greenbacks relative to the entire circulating media was of importance, and at the same time public opinion was all too easily swayed toward the issue of fiat money and its presence gave a temptation. A generation later the proportion of greenbacks to our enormously increased media of exchange is so small that it is immaterial whether we retain or eject the paper issues. Briefly, Sherman, in December, 1877, pronounced himself in favor of a currency (bank deposits aside) composed of gold and of national bank notes, greenbacks, silver dollars, and of token silver limited to the needs of business and to be kept at par with gold through prompt redemption in that metal. Issued under these conditions of limitation, both greenbacks and silver dollars would prove, in his opinion, a public advantage, but without such limitation a great public injury.[1]

Coming to the year 1878, we have already seen that in the early months progress toward resumption was hampered by the proponents of silver. While Sherman's repeated assurances that payment of government bonds would be made in gold stimulated bond subscribers, this pleasing result was weakened and at times entirely counteracted both by the practical repudiation of government obligation involved in the threat of free coinage of silver and in the open attacks in Congress upon bondholders at home and abroad. Yet the Matthews Resolution, favoring payment of all bonds in Bland silver dollars, was "a mere expression of opinion without binding force"; the bill to repeal the resumption act, which at no time influenced government creditors so adversely as did the fear of payment in silver,[2] failed to pass the Senate, and limited coinage only of silver was permitted. Although the opposing difficulties culminated in the congressional act of May 31, 1878, which

[1] Sherman, Finance Report, 1877, pp. xiv, xv; *Recollections*, Vol. II, pp. 607–619.
[2] Sherman, *Recollections*, Vol. I, p. 599.

suddenly terminated the process of reducing the greenback issues to the $300 million mark, Sherman persisted in carrying out the plans conceived by him upon entering office.

Sales of 4 per cent bonds during the last three months of 1877 were discouragingly few. As was his privilege according to agreement of the preceding summer, Sherman terminated the contract with the bankers' syndicate on January 26, 1878. His reason for taking this action was his desire to try a loan direct from the people of the country.[1] Such a loan, if successful, would tend to secure the sympathy of the public for the administration in its efforts toward resumption, and would lessen the criticism against it which the employment of a syndicate so obnoxious to many would excite. The sales of the 4 per cents had so far aggregated $75.4 millions, and the calls of the 6 per cent 5–20 bonds for purposes of refunding amounted to $50 millions, leaving a balance of $25.4 millions for resumption purposes.[2] Sherman's new plan for selling direct to the investor provided for:

1. Four per cent bonds, exempt from taxation, redeemable in 1907.

2. Two per cent of the purchase money to accompany the subscription and the remainder to be paid within thirty days.

3. A commission of a quarter of one per cent on subscriptions of $1000 or over.

4. Payment to be made in coin, gold certificates, or "called bonds."

5. National banks to be designated as depositories to receive deposits on account of this loan.[3]

Satisfactory arrangements for coöperation were made with the national banks, many of which throughout the country seemed eager to assist in the plan. The secretary was deluged with letters of inquiry. However, in spite of well-laid plans for a direct-to-the-people scheme, there was slight market for

[1] *Specie Resumption*, p. 224, Sherman to Belmont, January 14, 1878.

[2] *Ibid.*, p. 191, Sherman to Randall, November 19, 1877.

[3] *Ibid.*, pp. 226, 230, Treasury circular, January 16, 1878, and circular to National Banks, January 21, 1878.

these bonds during the early months of the year 1878. Kuhn, Loeb and Company, complaining that no offers came for 4 per cents, made a bid for $10 millions of 4½ per cents at 100¾, with a commission of half of one per cent. After considerable negotiation the offer was declined. Other New York bankers had counseled patience on the part of Washington, advising that 4½ per cents should await a better market and that if the 4 per cents did not have to compete with similar issues already in the market they would sell better. Sherman agreed to this suggestion, stating that he would not consider the sale of 4½ per cents until convinced that the sale of 4 per cents would not enable him to execute the policy of resumption which he had so much at heart.[1]

At the time of confronting this problem of selling 4 per cents Sherman found a great obstacle to his progress in the disposition of both houses of Congress to insist upon the payment of called bonds in greenbacks instead of coin. Nor did this seem to be a party question. Republicans and democrats alike favored the policy. Then, within the month of March (1878), the Senate finance committee and the House committee on banking and currency each in turn called Sherman before it expecting to subject him to a grilling interview, particularly upon what the committees deemed the impossibility of selling 4 per cent bonds and of accumulating the requisite gold fund for resumption. Pronounced "greenbackers" of both parties were on the committees, and they seemed to entertain honest doubts concerning the secretary's resumption plans. Color was given their opinion by the fact that the bond market was at the moment not responsive, and specie in the New York banks stood at only $40 millions on March 18th.[2] But Sherman welcomed this opportunity to win over the committees, and through them Congress and the public, to the saneness of his views on the sale of bonds and his ability to secure sufficient gold coin and bullion to meet the requirements of the treasury. He was con-

[1] *Specie Resumption*, pp. 267–286, *passim;* correspondence, March 5, 13, 14, 16, 18, 21, 22, 23, and 25, 1878.

[2] *Ibid.*, p. 280, Kuhn, Loeb and Company to Sherman, March 18, 1878.

vinced that the portion of the gold fund still required could be secured in the home market and that recourse to foreign countries was unnecessary. Sherman was completely successful in winning over his opponents. After these interviews most of the abler public men ceased to regard him as a visionary and an enthusiast. He was convinced that in the future serious and destructive opposition in Congress would not again occur and that his plans to resume on January 1, 1879, were reasonably certain of success.[1]

The public, however, persisted in its reluctance to buy the 4 per cents, and thus the second week in April (1878) found Sherman in New York for the purpose of making some contract, either with the old syndicate or with a new group of bankers, to obtain $50 millions for resumption purposes. After some clever bargaining and astute handling of bankers, Sherman agreed to sell to the old syndicate $50 millions of 4½ per cents at 101½, the syndicate to receive half of one per cent commission. Payment was to be made in gold and for resumption purposes only. Ten millions were to be taken by the syndicate at once, the remainder at the rate of $5 millions per month. The secretary retained the privilege of selling 4 per cents through other channels for refunding purposes, but not for the purpose of resumption. Sherman was well pleased with the outcome of these negotiations, and considering the status of the national credit and the jealousy of several non-syndicate bankers toward the syndicate his comfortable feeling was warranted.[2]

The policy of the treasury seemed now to be well launched and on solid ground. It involved, as it had all along, the twofold purpose, first, of improving the government's credit through wise refunding operations, and, second, of accumulating a gold fund to be used for redemption of greenbacks. Sherman had determined upon a gold fund equal to 40 per cent of the paper money outstanding.[3] With greenbacks out-

[1] Sherman, *Recollections*, vol. II, pp. 629–635.

[2] *Specie Resumption*, pp. 290–298, *passim*; correspondence, memoranda, and contract, April 7 to 13, 1878.

[3] Annual Report of the Secretary of the Treasury, 1878, p. ix, and 1879, p. ix.

standing to the amount of $346 millions, this meant a reserve of approximately $140 millions of gold.

Eliminating the Premium on Gold

During these negotiations and successes an absorbing question confronting the treasury was the elimination of the premium on gold. Various suggestions were offered for accomplishing this object, among which were: to decrease the demand for gold by substituting silver in transactions where gold was then used; to make it inconvenient to carry large stocks of gold by refusing to issue gold certificates, but to issue silver certificates in quantity desired; to bring the value of greenbacks up to that of gold by receiving them in all government transactions on an equality with gold; to recognize the fact that, while the power to buy gold was of the first importance both in preparing for resumption and in maintaining it, yet the hoarding of gold in the treasury tended to raise instead of to lower the premium.[1] These suggestions may have had some merit. As a matter of fact, the premium had shown an almost continuous and unbroken decline from 1876, and especially from the date of Sherman's accession to office, and the decline continued to January 1, 1879. The causes of this decline were doubtless to be found in the increasing need of a rapidly developing country for circulating media and in the growing confidence of business men in the redemption of greenbacks as provided by the resumption act of 1875. Confidence in government to redeem them probably meant the withdrawal from circulation of some of the greenbacks, which could profitably be held for a rise in value.[2] This confidence must have reflected also the stronger condition of the treasury. At all events, by the middle of May (1878) the bond market had begun to improve both in New York and in London. The sales of 4½ per cents for the gold reserve amounted to $35

[1] *Specie Resumption*, p. 379, Hillhouse to Sherman, September 9, 1878.

[2] Mitchell, *Gold, Prices, and Wages*, pp. 12–14; Irving Fisher, *Purchasing Power of Money*, New York, 1911, p. 261; Sherman, *Recollections*, Vol. II, p. 652, Sherman's letter to Peter Cooper.

millions by the twenty-fourth of the month, thus in a marked manner outrunning the requirements of the syndicate's contract.[1] At the same time the prospect was excellent for good crops, which, being in part exported, would help to secure the country against loss of gold through exportation to Europe. But, since gold was rapidly withdrawn from the market, a slight although temporary rise in the gold premium appeared. This led bankers and treasury officials to recommend the prepayment at once of interest due July 1, on the bonded debt, thus returning some gold to the market.[2]

Resumption Believed To Be Assured

By the middle of July, 1878, the position of the treasury was highly satisfactory to Sherman. Sufficient coin was held to cover coin liabilities of every kind and, in addition, to equal 35 per cent or more of the greenbacks outstanding. Moreover, $7 millions of fractional currency were available for current expenses. Of the $346 millions of greenbacks outstanding, at least $60 millions were held in the treasury under conditions which indicated no early diminution of the amount. The revenue, reckoning in both coin and currency, was more than sufficient to pay all current expenses covered by congressional appropriations. The greenbacks outside of the treasury were scattered over a vast territory and were in great favor and demand by the people. Gilbert, the assistant treasurer at Chicago, wrote on July 8 that as a rule payees in his region much preferred greenbacks to coin, provided there was no premium on the latter. Men of all shades of opinion about him agreed that the bridge of resumption had been reached and the sooner it was crossed the better.[3] Furthermore, of course, the secretary had authority to sell bonds in order to secure means to purchase coin or bullion, and he might use greenbacks for the same purpose. With this favorable showing, Sherman felt entire confi-

[1] *Specie Resumption*, Sherman to Buckner, May 24, 1878.

[2] *Ibid.*, Belmont and Company to Sherman, June 1; Sherman to Belmont and Company, June 5; and Hillhouse to Sherman, June 7, 1878.

[3] *Ibid.*, Gilbert to Sherman, July 8, 1878.

dence in the ability of the government to have on hand a sufficient gold reserve to resume specie payments on the following January 1st, and the leading bankers of New York were of the same opinion.[1]

Upon the renewal of the syndicate contract to sell 4½ per cent bonds for resumption purposes, Conant was again sent to London. By his frequent and luminous letters he kept the department at Washington well informed upon current financial conditions in Europe.[2]

Attacks upon Sherman and Final Preparation for Resumption

It was during the summer of 1878, when Conant was exercising effective influence upon our bond market abroad and when resumption seemed so surely attainable at home, that Sherman suffered in some quarters extraordinary unpopularity. Feeling the need of recuperation from the heavy strain under which he had been working, he decided upon a visit to Ohio, his native state. While the people of Mansfield, his home town, gave him cordial welcome and praise, the situation was quite the reverse at Toledo. He had promised to speak in the latter city on the financial issues of the day. This city had suffered severely from the panic of 1873 and had not fully recovered from that disaster. The people were sorely in need of capital funds, and, confusing in the usual popular manner the need for money and the need for capital and business activity, they denounced Sherman's preparations for resumption as depriving them of currency to meet their requirements. To hear him, three thousand persons were crowded into an auditorium designed for a much smaller number. Insults were hurled at the speaker from various parts of the house, and the meeting became boisterous and turbulent. When, however, the heckling process took the form of questions, which gave Sherman an opportunity to reveal to his fellow citizens what good had really been accomplished toward correcting the evils of the

[1] *Ibid.*, p. 343, Sherman to Groesbeck, July 15, 1878.

[2] Sherman, *Recollections*, Vol. II, p. 659.

currency, he drove his points home with telling effect. He secured control and turned the crowd in his favor. His carefully prepared speech was cast aside, and his extemporaneous address was so masterful and clever that it was selected by the state republican committee as a campaign document.[1]

Upon his return to Washington, Sherman proceeded to make final preparation for the redemption of paper money in gold on the first day of the coming year, 1879. He found a reluctance on the part of purchasers of 4 per cent bonds to pay coin into the treasury when, within a brief period, greenbacks could be used in such payments, but no such deviation from previous practice as payment in greenbacks would involve was permitted.[2] Payment for bonds must be made in coin until January 1st. The most important single step still to be taken in preparation for January 1st was to secure representation in the New York clearing house for the assistant treasurer of the United States in that city. As head of the treasury's business in the financial center of the country, membership in the clearing house would give the assistant treasurer means of facilitating the change in the basis of the currency through ability to pay the balances only of debits or credits in the transactions between the treasury and the public. This was not a new proposition from government officials, but the plan had never been previously adopted. Even now some of Sherman's associates were opposed to it. Knox, comptroller of the currency, and Hillhouse, assistant treasurer at New York, favored it. After a series of negotiations and conferences in which the clearing house committee and other bankers gave willing support, the assistant treasurer was admitted to membership on November 12, 1878. Thereafter, drafts drawn upon any bank represented in the clearing house association in New York and received by the assistant treasurer could be presented to such bank at the clearing house for payment, and drafts drawn directly on the assistant treasurer could be adjusted by him at the clearing house. The balances due from the United States could be paid

[1] *Ibid.*, pp. 661–664.
[2] *Ibid.*, pp. 668–670.

at the assistant treasurer's office to an agent of the clearing house in greenbacks or clearing house certificates. In brief, in making its exchange of checks and drafts through the clearing house the government now would conduct its operations practically as any member bank conducted its own business.[1] This was a remarkable innovation and a notable achievement on the part of Sherman. As Noyes has well said,[2] the arrangement with the clearing house was indispensable. While the city banks were anxious to give support to the government, the mere good will of those institutions was not enough. That good will proved "largely useless to the treasury on two not at all dissimilar occasions—in 1861 and in 1894—and at both those junctures the fault distinctly lay in lack of timely business management by the treasury. It is conceivable that with the vacillating policy of those two years applied in 1878, the government's financial schemes might even now have broken down." Sherman induced the banks to abandon their policy of keeping special deposits of gold because that policy would endanger the maintenance of the government's gold reserve fund. With the adoption of the plan of membership in the clearing house, a timid and blundering banker could have little opportunity to start a general drain of gold by presenting his drafts for payment directly over the counter of the subtreasury. By agreement, the banks were to accept greenbacks after January 1st, in payment of clearing house balances against one another and against the treasury. Customs duties were to be paid in coin or greenbacks at the importer's option, thus revoking the long-standing requirement of coin payment and taking away another reason for abstracting gold from the treasurer's reserve fund. In all these arrangements the Boston

[1] *Specie Resumption:* Sherman to French, October 29; French to Sherman, November 5; Knox to Sherman, November 5; Hillhouse to Sherman, November 7; Sherman to Hillhouse, November 9; Gilfillan to Hillhouse, November 9; Hillhouse to Sherman, November 11; Coe to Sherman, November 12; Hillhouse to Sherman, November 12; Manager of New York clearing house to Sherman, November 12; Sherman to Coe, November 13; Hillhouse to Sherman, November 14; Sherman to Hillhouse, November 16, 1878.

[2] Noyes, *op. cit.*, pp. 45, 46.

clearing house[1] was in full accord with the treasury, and with New York, and it was confidently expected that associated banks throughout the country would take similar action. On December 14th Sherman issued a circular letter[2] stating that after January 1st no distinction would be made between coin and greenbacks in settling the accounts of public officers for transactions subsequent to that date, and that the interest and principal of the public debt would be paid in coin or greenbacks at the option of the claimant. In the meantime, the assistant treasurer had been instructed to issue no more gold certificates, thus creating further use for greenbacks to circulate from hand to hand in place of cumbersome coin. In spite of attempts of cliques and combinations[3] in New York to perpetuate the premium on gold, greenbacks touched par with gold on December 17, 1878, for the first time since their issue in 1862.[4] After that date the premium did not reappear.[5] The first day of January fell upon a Sunday, hence Monday, January 2, was the crucial day. On that Monday anxiety was felt in the treasury department. On the ground of lack of authority the treasury had refused the solicitous request of the chairman of the New York clearing house committee for a deposit of $5 millions in gold with a New York bank as a means of preventing any attempt to corner the gold market.[6] As the hours of that Monday dragged on no news came to Washington from New York. Finally, in response to a telegram, Sherman was informed that all was quiet. At the close of the business day a laconic message from the New York sub-treasury told the complete story: "$135,000 of notes presented for coin—$400,000 of gold for notes." Greenbacks were preferred to gold by the business public and resumption was an accomplished

[1] *Specie Resumption*, Lamb, chairman Boston clearing house committee, to Sherman, November 15, 1878.

[2] *Ibid.*, pp. 421, 422.

[3] *Ibid.*, Hillhouse to Sherman, December 14, 1878.

[4] *Ibid.*, Hillhouse to Sherman, December 18, 1878.

[5] Mitchell, *Gold, Prices, and Wages*, table, p. 338.

[6] *Specie Resumption*, Vail to Hillhouse, December 30; Sherman to Hillhouse, December 31, 1878.

fact. The process of exchange on the basis of a reëstablished gold standard met with no significant disturbance. "By five o'clock the news was all over the land, and the New York bankers were sipping their tea in absolute safety."[1]

[1] J. K. Upton, assistant secretary of the treasury, quoted by Sherman, *Recollections*, Vol. II, p. 702. *Specie Resumption*, Hillhouse to Sherman, January 2, 1879.

CHAPTER X

COULD SPECIE PAYMENTS BE MAINTAINED?

THE PROBLEM NOT YET DEFINITELY SOLVED

RESUMPTION attained so successfully on the day fixed by the law by no means solved the whole problem. The difficulties connected with the future maintenance of specie payments had yet to be faced. The great danger lay in the possibility of the export of gold. That event would threaten the existence of the gold reserve held by the treasury for the redemption of greenbacks and set at naught all the painstaking effort expended in its accumulation. In addition to the importance of having an able secretary of the treasury in whom confidence could be placed to make the best of every opportunity to overcome difficulties, three factors were of primary concern in the effort to safeguard the reserve. One factor related to the absence of authority to hoard greenbacks in the treasury, another to the interdependence of the success of resumption and the refunding of the public debt, and the third to our foreign trade situation.

The natural method to be employed by a central bank of issue to protect its reserve against excessive demands for note redemption would be to hold in its vaults or cancel and destroy such notes as were presented for redemption. In this manner the money market would be tightened and a tendency to ward off the presentation of notes for redemption would be established. Had authority existed in law to enable the secretary to hoard greenbacks in the treasury when they were presented for redemption the withdrawal of gold from the reserve fund might have been checked in a similar way. But no such authority existed. The act of May 31, 1878, expressly provided that when greenbacks were redeemed and received into the treasury they should be "re-issued and paid out again and kept in circulation."

Hence, Sherman was compelled to proceed without the aid of this safeguard.[1]

Refunding the Debt and Resumption

In the view of Sherman and several other leading statesmen of that day, not only the accomplishment but the maintenance of resumption was closely related to a successful refunding of the public debt. Possibly they laid too much stress upon this interdependence. Yet it is true that the maintenance of resumption was closely bound up with the state of the government's credit. The government's credit, in turn, was closely related to the operations of the treasury. Successful refunding operations were a cause of improvement in governmental credit, and at the same time those operations were made possible by the fact that credit was improving. The interrelation of these forces seemed evident at the beginning of the year 1879. No sooner did resumption take place than an unprecedented ease was enjoyed in placing loans for refunding purposes. On the other hand, if refunding operations could be carried out successfully, bonds could the more readily be sold to obtain gold to replenish a possible depletion of the gold reserve. Large amounts of bonds bearing high rates of interest and destined to be refunded were at that time held in England. If refunding operations could be so conducted (so thought Sherman) that new lower interest-bearing bonds could be sold abroad equal to or in excess of the amount of old bonds called in and cancelled for refunding, no occasion would arise, at least on this account, for the export of gold from America to pay old bonds thus retired. Other influences might cause an export of specie, but it was the part of the secretary of the treasury to "call" no bonds in Europe the payment for which might compel an export of gold.

Conant was again stationed in London as agent of the treas-

[1] Sherman afterwards claimed in his annual report of December, 1879, p. x, that he had the power to retain greenbacks in the treasury, but a reading of the act of May 31, 1878, and of the debates in Congress of that period seemed to preclude this interpretation of the secretary's powers.

ury to act as an intermediary in financial negotiations and to keep Sherman informed on English and European financial affairs.[1]

On January 1st, the day fixed for resumption, Sherman issued a circular letter announcing a new plan for the sale of 4 per cents in this country. This differed from the former plan[2] in the amount and graduated character of the commission paid for sales to June 30, 1879, the commission being so graduated as to stimulate large subscriptions and thus hasten the refunding process.[3] Two weeks later he offered to enter into a contract with Seligman and Company, of New York, and their banking associates in the syndicate of this country and London, by which they would be the sole agent of the department for the sale of 4 per cent bonds in Europe. They were to pay for such bonds in gold or in foreign-held bonds called for redemption and refunding. By this means it was hoped that unnecessary gold exports from New York would be prevented. The offer was at once accepted, and the formal syndicate contract was signed on January 21, to continue to June 30 following, the syndicate's commission being a quarter of one per cent, with an additional one-tenth of one per cent on sales in excess of the sum of $10 millions.[4]

Following up the plans launched at home and abroad, a robust competition was created among the bankers of New York in the business of refunding.[5] Subscriptions for bonds poured in from all parts of the United States and from Europe. More than $60 millions were subscribed for in the first two weeks of January, and on February 21, 1879, Sherman informed a committee of the House of Representatives that $232 millions had been sold in this country since the first of the year. Called bonds held abroad were so far paid for without the exportation of coin. The secretary had placed the 4 per cents upon the

[1] *Specie Resumption*, p. 485, Sherman to Fry; Sherman, *Recollections*, Vol. II, pp. 706–707.

[2] *Specie Resumption*, p. 226.

[3] *Ibid.*, pp. 445–446.

[4] *Ibid.*, correspondence and contract, pp. 466, 468, 482, 483, 485.

[5] *Ibid.*, p. 464, Sherman to Fry.

market on existing terms against the advice of several leading bankers of New York and their prophecies of failure. The success of the operation, however, had been so great that during these weeks fears had been expressed by Sherman as well as others lest the rapid refunding process might really endanger the maintenance of resumption. Settlement for calls made for old bonds and for new bonds sold would be made on April 1st, and there was danger that transfer of such large amounts would create a stringency in the money market, and thus cause dangerous demands for gold at the treasury.[1]

Demand for Gold and the Status of the Gold Reserve

Meantime, however, the records of the assistant treasurer in New York showed very little demand for gold, either for redemption of greenbacks or for payment of other coin obligations of the government, including interest on the public debt. More than three-fourths of the amount of all checks for interest presented at the sub-treasury in New York was paid in greenbacks by request of the payees. There were, also, frequent applications for greenbacks in exchange for the more cumbersome gold. This situation satisfied treasury officials that, for the time at any rate, no drain of gold from the treasury would take place in ordinary disbursements, or on redemption account, or in refunding operations so long as the calls did not exceed the sales of the 4 per cents. In fact, the banks themselves in which the proceeds from the sale of 4 per cent bonds on refunding account were deposited insisted on paying these proceeds to the treasurer in greenbacks instead of gold, although coin was definitely required by the provisions of the departmental circular of January 1st.[2] Since refusal to receive greenbacks either in transfers on account of the 4 per cent loan or in other coin payments would have induced their immediate

[1] Sherman, *Recollections,* Vol. II, pp. 705–707; *Specie Resumption,* p. 523, Sherman to Atkins; p. 540, Sherman to Morrill; pp. 463, 495, Sherman to Fahnestock; p. 470, Hillhouse to Sherman.

[2] Later, March 26, 1879, Sherman ordered that these proceeds might be paid by drafts on depository banks and settled through the New York clearing house, at the option of the banks.

presentation for redemption, thus practically compelling the treasury to furnish the required gold, and since under the resumption act a tender of greenbacks at the treasury was practically the same as a coin payment, it appeared that nothing would be gained by requiring payment in gold. Consequently Sherman ordered the acceptance of greenbacks. Assistant Treasurer Hillhouse desired to pursue the policy of paying promptly all demands for gold at any treasury office in the country, as well as at the New York sub-treasury, on the ground that gold would be sought more eagerly in proportion to the difficulty in obtaining it.[1]

The membership of the sub-treasury in New York in the clearing house of that city afforded additional means for use of greenbacks in settlement of balances between that institution and the treasury, and therefore an additional means for relief of pressure on the gold reserve in proportion to such use. To facilitate further their use and safety in this manner Sherman consented that the sub-treasury should issue clearing house certificates in exchange for an equal amount of greenbacks, which would be transferred from the ordinary sub-treasury stock on hand to a deposit on account of the certificates, such certificates to be used in settling its balance at the clearing house. The operations between the sub-treasury and the clearing house were, so far as convenience of settlement was concerned, thus placed upon precisely the same footing as the operations between the banks and the clearing house.[2] The attitude of Sherman in this matter shows a remarkable and favorable contrast with that of Secretary Chase when, in the earliest days of the Civil War, the latter refused the importunate requests of the New York bankers for his coöperation in facilitating the transfer of funds through the use of the clearing house. Today, when the treasury uses the clearing house as a matter of course, it is difficult for us to appreciate the importance of taking the first step in its use which was taken by Sherman at that time.

[1] *Specie Resumption*, pp. 462, 467, Hillhouse to Sherman; and see pp. 470, 471, 503, 505, 546, for additional treasury correspondence.

[2] *Ibid.*, correspondence, pp. 521, 523, 528, 530, 543, 553.

On December 31, 1878, after deducting the gold certificates outstanding and liable for redemption, Sherman held in the treasury $114.2 millions of gold available for resumption of specie payments.[1] Of this sum $95.5 millions arose from the sale of bonds and the remainder from surplus revenues.[2] At the close of the first seven weeks of the next year, as a result of his continued refunding operations, improving the government credit, and further accumulation of funds, he wrote to the chairman of the ways and means committee that the balance of all moneys held in the treasury available for resumption purposes stood, in spite of improvident expenditures by Congress,[3] at $136.4 millions, while that balance had stood on December 31, 1878, at $126.4 millions.[4] In neither case, however, was the total available balance composed entirely of gold coin and bullion. The amount of gold coin and bullion held at the later date was $133.3 millions ($2 millions less than on the earlier date), but of the amount of gold certificates outstanding against this sum we are not informed. We do know, however, that the gold certificates outstanding diminished in amount from December 31, 1878, to October 31, 1879.[5] We may assume, therefore, that the treasury's position for the maintenance of specie payments was, at least, no less strong in the middle of February, 1879, than it had been on the date of resumption.

Yet at this precise time indications pointed to a change in the foreign trade situation which might lead to the exportation of gold from the United States. The sale of the 4 per cent bonds for the purpose of refunding the 5–20 6 per cent bonds experienced a somewhat checkered career during the month prior to April 4, when all 6 per cent bonds available for refunding were called for payment. Although they had sold freely in

[1] Annual Report of the Treasurer of the United States in Finance Report for 1879, p. 338. See table of coin assets and coin liabilities.

[2] *Specie Resumption*, p. 492, Sherman to Ewing, January 24, 1879.

[3] *Ibid.*, p. 521, Sherman to Wood, February 18, 1879; pp. 569, 570, Sherman to Conant.

[4] Annual Report of the Secretary of the Treasury for 1879, p. 338.

[5] *Ibid.* Compare tables given on pp. 338, 339.

January and February, during the month of March the sales declined in a marked degree, averaging about $1 million per day. This decline was due to several causes. The silver question was embarrassing to treasury operations on account of the absorption of revenues in the monthly purchase of silver bullion required by the silver act of 1878, and on account of a growing opinion in Congress in favor of a standard silver dollar at the ratio, approximately, of 18 to 1—which was the market ratio of silver to gold at that date.[1] In London the sales were slow, since investors, naturally having none of the sense of national pride in the improvement of credit from a 6 per cent to a 4 per cent basis, resented the loss of one-third of their interest and threatened to demand payment of their called bonds in coin. The London *Times* of March 15 remarked: "United States bonds continue rather dull, and it now seems probable that the conversion of the debt has been pushed with too much haste."[2] Unfounded charges of favoritism on the part of Sherman toward certain banks used as depositories of public funds added an additional hindrance to the sale of bonds. Upon the whole, a feeling existed, temporarily, on both sides of the Atlantic, that danger lay in such rapid refunding operations. The danger in some instances probably lay in the suspicion on the part of bankers and individuals that they had subscribed for bonds beyond their ability to pay. But the first of April, the date for settlement, was approached and passed without severe strain on the money market. Accounts were settled without difficulty. The foreign-held called bonds were met by the sale of 4 per cents in London and the anticipated export of gold which was feared did not occur. Immediately after the danger from the general settlement was passed, subscriptions to 4 per cents were made in such numbers and in such large amounts as to surprise the secretary himself. On April 4, as already indicated, Sherman had the satisfaction of issuing calls covering all outstanding bonds under the act of March 3, 1865, and the last of the 5–20

[1] *Specie Resumption*, pp. 569, 570, Sherman to Conant; Sherman, *Recollections*, Vol. II, p. 707.

[2] *Specie Resumption*, p. 571, Conant to Sherman; p. 545, Evarts to Sherman.

bonds. The subscriptions for 4 per cents more than doubled the amount of old bonds called. Desiring a free hand to make use of a different method in the sale of securities, Sherman now cancelled the contracts of January 1st with the national banks and of January 21st with the London syndicate for the sale of 4 per cent bonds.[1]

Congress had recently authorized the extension of the process of refunding to the 10–40 bonds, bearing interest at the rate of 5 per cent. Preparations were now made to carry this legislation, involving $195 millions, into effect.[2] In the meantime Congress had also authorized the issue of certificates of deposit[3] of denominations of ten dollars, bearing 4 per cent interest, and convertible into 4 per cent bonds. The purpose of the certificates was to afford opportunity to persons of limited means to purchase at par a 4 per cent governmental security. Both the pronounced demand for them and the obvious advantage in having governmental securities widely held among the people justified the issue of these certificates of small denominations.

On April 16th Sherman offered to sell to banks and the general public $150 millions of 4 per cent bonds at one-half of one per cent above par and accrued interest, and in addition to this amount $44.5 millions of these bonds were reserved for the conversion of the ten-dollar refunding certificates[4] which were also offered for sale at banks, post offices, and other public places. On the day following, telegrams poured into the secretary's office with offers to purchase securities on the terms published. The movement culminated in an offer from the First National Bank of New York, on behalf of an association of banks and bankers, subscribing for $190 millions of bonds and

[1] *Ibid.*, pp. 469, 490, 545, 550, 584–588, 595–596; Sherman, *Recollections*, Vol. II, pp. 709, 717–719.

[2] Act of January 25, 1879. The bonds here referred to were payable in forty, but redeemable at the option of the government in ten years, hence known as 10–40s.

[3] The act of February 26, 1879. For treasury circular relative to these certificates, see *Specie Resumption*, p. 583.

[4] *Specie Resumption*, p. 648; Sherman, *Recollections*, Vol. II, pp. 720–722.

certificates. The treasury's offer was thus oversubscribed in one day. This unexpected development caused such surprise to Sherman that he found it difficult to credit the correctness of the messages and he wired informally the following to the First National Bank: "Your telegram covering one hundred and ninety million consols staggers me. Your telegram for twenty-five million received, and entered at two o'clock. About thirty million from other parties were received and entered before your last telegram. Will wait till letters received. What is the matter? Are you all crazy?"[1] An equitable distribution of bonds was made among the buyers, final calls were made for all outstanding 10–40 bonds,[2] and refunding operations were practically at an end for the time.[3] Conant wrote from London that when the reports of these rapid and large-scale developments were posted in the London stock exchange "people were astounded at the information."[4]

During these later months the resumption of specie payments and its maintenance, rather than the refunding of the public debt, was the object of chief importance in Sherman's policy. The foregoing account shows how successfully, at least from the point of view of governmental financing, the prime purpose of that policy had so far been carried out. The public debt had been refunded to the full extent permitted by contracts contained in the bonds issued to carry on the Civil War. The public credit had steadily improved, both at home and abroad, with new bonds selling for refunding purposes at steadily decreasing rates of interest. The aggregate amount of bonds refunded from March 4, 1877, to July 21, 1879, was $845,345,950, and the annual interest saved by this operation was $14,290,-

[1] *Specie Resumption*, pp. 649–654, treasury correspondence.

[2] For departmental orders calling these bonds, see *ibid.*, pp. 632, 661, 662, 668; *ibid.*, p. 708, James, Postmaster in New York, to Sherman, for an interesting account of a turbulent struggle of more than 400 women and nearly 400 men to get in line at the New York post office, on May 20, 1879, for the purchase of the 4 per cent certificates.

[3] Sherman, *Recollections*, Vol. II, pp. 722, 723; *Specie Resumption*, p. 660, Sherman to Conant.

[4] *Specie Resumption*, p. 664, Conant to Sherman.

416.50.[1] The gold reserve for the redemption of greenbacks had throughout these operations been protected and maintained. On May 17, 1879, Sherman was able to write the president of the Senate that the "coin reserve of the treasury had been increased to $138 millions, that being about 40 per cent of the greenbacks outstanding and believed to be the smallest reserve upon which resumption could be successfully maintained."[2] So long as the public debt could steadily be reduced and the public credit improved, there was not the slightest doubt, as events proved, that specie payments could be maintained. Under these circumstances bonds could be sold, whenever occasion might demand it, to replenish the gold reserve.

Gold Exports Threatened in the Spring of 1879

But in spite of these favoring conditions, the treasury was facing serious difficulties. No one could know in the spring of 1879 that the public credit was secure and that bonds could find a market to any extent required for the purpose of maintaining a gold reserve. If an export of gold from New York had set in, as had been the case every spring season for the preceding eighteen years,[3] the gold reserve fund would have been endangered. This is precisely what threatened Sherman and his aides. They had done all that could be done by means of purely financial measures to secure and maintain specie payment. But no nation could afford to continue the process indefinitely of borrowing to maintain a gold reserve. Whether resort to such measures would continue for a time to be necessary depended upon the condition of foreign trade, the foreign exchanges, and the natural international movement of gold. From late winter and early spring fears were felt, as already indicated, that gold might leave our shores, although such fears were seldom even referred to in Sherman's *Recollections* or in the voluminous treasury correspondence contained in the public document, *Specie Resumption*. As early as February 22, Conant

[1] Sherman, *Recollections*, Vol. II, p. 723.
[2] *Specie Resumption*, pp. 702, 703, Sherman to Wheeler, President of the Senate.
[3] Noyes, *op. cit.*, p. 48.

reported from London that the Rothschilds and other bankers were confident "that there must soon be a shipment of gold from New York, and that it will at once lower the price of bonds." Since January 1, $43 millions of United States bonds and $7 millions of Erie and other railway stock had been sent from London to New York, while to offset this movement the banking syndicate and others were able to place abroad approximately only $25 millions of bonds and stocks.[1] Three weeks later, Sherman gives evidence of uneasiness in regard to the flow of gold. He had hoped for sales of bonds in London to an amount which, with the balance of trade in our favor, would be sufficient to cover the called bonds held there. The sales were not equal to his expectations, and he inquired of Conant whether an arrangement could lawfully be made for sterling exchange to the amount of $10 millions to be drawn upon, if necessary, in April and May. In case of a considerable shipment of gold, such a resource, he thought, might prevent popular alarm.[2] Again Conant's letter[3] of March 29 shows a continued uneasy feeling in London. He writes that the constant decline in the price of our bonds in New York, the strenuous efforts on the part of certain parties to sell American bonds in London at low rates on home account, the advancing rates of interest, and the condition of the exchanges, gave rise to apprehensions in the minds of many for the safety of America's money market and hence of its gold reserve. On the same date on this side of the water bankers[4] wrote Sherman of the "very nervous and uneasy feeling in the street about money," and reminded him of the fact that we were in the midst of a fair spring's business and that any serious disturbance in the money market would do great harm. There was, in fact, imminent

[1] *Specie Resumption*, pp. 524–526, Conant to Sherman.

[2] *Ibid.*, p. 569, Sherman to Conant, March 15, 1879. See also an interesting reply from Conant, *ibid.*, pp. 602, 603. On the other hand, a letter of March 15, 1879, from Conant to Sherman, *ibid.*, p. 571, expresses the writer's opinion that gold was not wanted in London and the reduction in the rate of interest which had taken place would prevent the shipment of it from New York.

[3] *Ibid.*, pp. 595, 596, Conant to Sherman.

[4] *Ibid.*, p. 597, Fry to Sherman.

danger that the natural course of international trade and of foreign exchanges might be such as to destroy the work for the maintenance of specie payments erected by Sherman and his assistants. Gold exports had exceeded imports during each year since 1861,[1] and now in the spring of 1879 foreign exchange hovered around the gold-exporting point. Would gold in quantity be exported, was the question asked by all concerned.

A brief survey of business conditions at home and abroad will show the nature of the threatened danger.[2] On January 1, 1879, the New York banks held but $19.7 millions in specie, a sum approximately equal to the excess of gold exports in the first half of 1877. With a slight rise in sterling exchange gold would leave our shores. In such event the natural source of supply for export by bankers would be the treasury's gold reserve. Under our existing banking system and under the law of May 31, 1878, providing for the reissue of greenbacks when paid into the treasury, no method, except an excess of revenues, was available to prevent an "endless chain" process of drawing gold from the treasury by presenting greenbacks for redemption, paying them out again for ordinary expenditures of government, and repeating the process until the gold reserve became exhausted. This was practically the case a few years later in Cleveland's second administration. Power to hold greenbacks, once redeemed, in the treasury, and to pay them out only in exchange for coin, would have avoided the danger, but no such power existed.[3] The treasury was thus deprived of the ordinary banking safeguard to protect its reserve. The success of the resumption experiment depended largely, therefore, as already indicated, upon conditions of trade and industry. These conditions were unfavorable and discouraging at the out-

[1] Finance Report for 1879, p. xxxi.

[2] For the following statement of the economic influences which brought such timely aid to Sherman and his associates, see, where not otherwise noted in footnotes, the excellent account of Noyes in his *Forty Years of American Finance*, New York and London, 1909, pp. 48–65.

[3] See Sherman's claim to such power, Finance Report, 1879, p. x. He had no occasion to put his interpretation of the act of 1878 into practice, and it was not followed in later years. Indeed, there seems to be no ground for his claim.

set. In 1878 the United States enjoyed a large favorable trade balance of merchandise, but during the first five months of the resumption year (1879) the trade balance decreased and threatened to reverse itself. A New York commercial firm, of which former Secretary McCulloch was the head, wrote that the foreign trade "figures indicate the beginning of a change in the relative volume of imports and exports." Business at home, in spite of the slight revival in 1878, had not yet recovered from the long period of depression following the crisis of 1873. The cotton-goods industry was declining, with wage reductions in prospect. Prices in the iron trade, long regarded as a barometer of business conditions, fell below the average cost of production. What was true of these two industries during the early months of 1879 was true of practically all the staple industries of the country. Complete stagnation prevailed. On March 8th, the New York *Commercial and Financial Chronicle*, commenting upon the resumption experiment, remarked: "'Where is the prosperity promised with the event?' is the question frequently coming to us. 'Wheat is no higher. Corn is no higher. There is no money in any of the earth's products. Where is the promised prosperity?'"

Although, as has been already stated, the domestic bond market improved with the resumption of specie payments, the recovery was irregular and was not much helped by the foreign market. Fifty million dollars of bonds and stocks were resold by London to New York in February. The unfavorable conditions continued until the climax was reached in the second week of June, when over a million of gold was drawn from the treasury and exported. The London *Statist* of June 7, 1879, expressed the feeling abroad: "The effect of resumption has passed off, and we may expect to find gold steadily drifting from that side to this."

In 1878, England enjoyed agricultural prosperity in great degree. The wheat harvest there, as on the continent of Europe, was one of the largest on record. This grain moved to markets continuously throughout the following autumn and winter, and at the end of March, 1879, Liverpool's stock on hand exceeded that of any for five years past. In similar fashion, every other cereal product had accumulated. While unfavorable weather showed that the English crop of 1878 could not be equaled in 1879 and the price of wheat advanced, grain in storage was abundant and no one anticipated a marked rise in price. In New York, also, wheat had advanced a few cents during the first weeks of the new year, but had dropped back again to $1.10 per bushel in the second week of April.

Harvests at Home and Abroad Avert the Danger

The foreign situation began to change gradually, but unmistakably. In May all indications pointed to a fair harvest in America, but in France the late spring brought a heavy snowfall, while in England a late and destructive frost, and rain which continued throughout the summer, brought gloom upon that country. Grain fields were soaked and threatened with ruin. The situation had assumed such grave national importance that the Archbishop of Canterbury directed the English churches to offer prayers on the first Sunday of July for fair weather.[1] Bad weather, however, continued, and in August it was clearly seen that all English crops were practically destroyed. "No such disaster had befallen English agriculture within the memory of living men." The wheat crop was several million bushels less than the poorest crop produced since the middle of the century. Across the Channel conditions for good crops prevailed until midsummer, when sunless skies and soaking rainstorms blighted the grain there as they had already in England. Each of the great countries of Central Europe, as well as Russia, yielded the smallest and poorest wheat crop within a period of several years. European countries were converted from wheat-exporting to wheat-importing communities. The London *Economist*, in the autumn, stated: "It is the American supply alone which has saved Europe from a great famine."

The American grain crop of 1879 was unusually large and it was an undoubted stroke of fortune for the United States. The

[1] *Specie Resumption*, p. 739, Conant to Sherman, July 12, 1879.

huge harvests were a guarantee for the success of resumption, and it initiated the rapid recovery of business from one of the most serious periods of depression the country had ever known. "All circumstances seemed to conspire in favor of this country. Sunny and favorable 'farmers' weather,' with the due proportion of rain, prevailed throughout the season." The acreage sown to wheat was increased over that of 1878, the total crop was the greatest yet harvested. Upon news of England's crop failure prices increased forty cents per bushel, and exports of this grain were the greatest ever known. Indian corn, from the largest crop on record; cattle from the grazing fields of the interior; oil, transported to the seaboard by the newly completed tidewater pipe-line; our cotton crop, enhanced in value by the partial failure of India's crop—all these were exported in huge volume.

The conditions thus detailed led to a complete reversal of international trade tendencies. Our exports of merchandise now greatly exceeded imports, the foreign exchanges declined, a flow of gold from abroad was assured, and fears that the fund accumulated for resumption would be taken from us were dissipated. With resumption secure, the country turned with a stout heart to the restoration of its torpid enterprises. The business revival which followed was, up to that time, the most remarkable in the country's history. Practically all American industries participated in the movement. The iron trade, paralyzed since 1873, gained such momentum during the resumption year that a profit of 100 per cent on current rates of cost was yielded. Cotton manufactures, in spite of the high price of raw cotton, enjoyed a complete revival. The spinning industry made a notable recovery during the year, and "print cloths, the staple of the dry-goods trade, not only advanced fifty per cent over their price of January first, but closed the year with stocks depleted, mills running at full pressure, and large orders booked ahead." What was true of iron and cotton was true also of almost every other line of business. By the middle of this remarkable year of 1879 the heavy demands for expanding trade led to a rise in rates for loans in the New York money market, thus making that market attractive to foreign capital.[1] With these various influences at work the importation of gold began on a scale unknown in our previous history. "Within three months, $20 millions had come from Great Britain, $30 millions from France, and $10 millions from Germany." But this gold was not suited for use in the trade of the interior, hence eastern bankers into whose hands it initially flowed exchanged much of it at the treasury for greenbacks, which better satisfied the pressing needs of the West for a currency at once safe and convenient. Here was the consummation for which the treasury had striven—greenbacks at a parity with gold and freely exchangeable therefor, and a gold reserve in abundance accumulating in the natural course of domestic business and of international trade. On January 1, 1879, New York banks held only one-third of their reserves in specie. On December 12th their aggregate amount of specie had almost trebled, standing at $53.1 millions and constituting nearly 80 per cent of their total cash reserves. To the dismay of treasury officials, early in the year, the customs duties at New York were paid almost entirely in greenbacks, but in November and December the situation was reversed and two-thirds of such payments were made in gold. The treasury's gold reserve accordingly increased from $114.2 millions in January to $119.9 millions in June, and to $157.1 millions at the opening of November. The estimate of a reliable London commercial firm placed the amount of gold sent to America from England, France, and Germany during the three months following July 1st at upwards of $50 millions.[2] As early as September, gold coin having accumulated in the treasury beyond the needs of the government, Sherman issued a circular letter to the agents of the treasury authorizing them "to pay out gold coin as well as silver coin and notes [greenbacks] upon current obligations of government, and upon advances to disbursing officers, as may be convenient and practicable."[3]

[1] *Ibid.*, pp. 724, 760, 761, Conant to Sherman, June 14 and August 30, 1879.
[2] *Ibid.*, p. 799, Conant to Sherman, October 4, 1879.
[3] *Ibid.*, p. 780; circular of treasury department issued September 19, 1879.

Within less than another month, the care of the large amount of gold flowing into the country became a pressing problem. The supply of greenbacks held in the treasury was almost exhausted by demands for them in exchange for gold. The secretary was compelled to refuse to issue gold certificates for fear the banks would, in exchange for them, transfer their large supplies of specie to the custody of the treasury. The banks apparently had no desire to accumulate actual coin in their own vaults.[1] In the absence of a better arrangement, they finally appointed the Bank of America to act as a depository for the care and custody of their gold, providing that this bank should issue certificates on deposits of gold by other banks which should pass current in the settlements at the clearing house.[2]

The prosperity of the resumption year was built upon a solid foundation. The five-year period preceding had been one of strenuous economy and of thoroughgoing liquidation. Artificial elements in business and inflation of the currency had disappeared. The extraordinary strokes of fortune for the United States in the way of huge harvests at home and shortage abroad gave an impetus to her business and to her foreign trade which would have carried resumption to a successful issue even if no further accidents of nature had been in store. But, as it happened, the two years following placed the country in similar circumstances. In 1880 favorable crops in Europe were matched by still more favorable ones in this country, and in 1881 the drought which destroyed much of our crops was paralleled by unfavorable conditions and a short harvest abroad, so that our farmers exported all the surplus grain they could spare and "at the highest prices in nine years." The substantial character of the improvement in business during these years had no better proof than that afforded by its quick recovery after repeated onslaughts of speculators. Daring speculations in the wheat market, in the iron market, and in

[1] *Ibid.*, Hillhouse to Sherman, October 3, 1879.

[2] *Ibid.*, Hillhouse to Sherman, October 8; Hawley to Hillhouse, October 10; Sherman to Hillhouse, October 18, 1879.

corporation shares, which were perpetrated upon the country at that time, would have wrecked the movement for recovery and for the maintenance of specie payments had the foundations been less secure. As it was, after each collapse and resulting punishment of individual wrongdoers values recovered and soon reached new high levels with healthful investments. The prosperity of the railways, in spite of the depredations of Jay Gould and those who imitated his methods, was pronounced, while other lines of business were equally successful, and "1880 was undoubtedly the most prosperous year of the generation."

Success of Resumption—Final Problems

The success of resumption and the strong upward movement in business exercised an inevitable influence upon the politics of the day. In both the state and the national elections of 1879 and 1880 the administration party won complete victories at the polls. The republicans were given credit, not only by their fellow-partisans, but by democrats as well, for establishing the currency on a solid basis. Yet in the last days of the administration President Hayes and Secretary Sherman, apparently enjoying each other's full confidence, gave conflicting advice to Congress concerning the future of the greenbacks. The President in his message to Congress on December 6, 1880, wrote: "The retirement from circulation of United States notes [greenbacks] with the capacity of legal tender in private contracts is a step to be taken in our progress toward a safe and stable currency which should be accepted as the policy and duty of the government and the interest and security of the people."[1] Sherman, on the same day, in his annual report, wrote: "United States notes [greenbacks] are now, in form, security, and convenience, the best circulating medium known."[2] This difference of opinion, singular enough in the circumstances, was in fact characteristic of the whole period of the greenback history. Apparently the best men of the time—

[1] Richardson, *Messages and Papers of the Presidents*, Vol. VII, p. 616, H. of Repres., 53 Cong., 2 Sess., Mis. Doc. 210, Part 7.

[2] Finance Report, 1880, p. xiv.

to say nothing of the public at large—continuously ranged themselves on opposite sides of every principle, legislative device, and business proposition that was ever brought forward in relation to the greenbacks.

Although the struggle for a specie standard of value had occupied much of the country's effort for almost a generation, raging incessantly during the last five years, and had at last issued in gratifying success, yet the currency problem of the country had by no means been brought to a final solution. The silver question loomed large in the minds of all classes of men during the last years of the resumption struggle and for many years afterwards. The greenbacks themselves were partly the occasion, although not the primary cause, of monetary and financial disturbance fifteen years after the resumption of specie payments was accomplished. By an act of 1882, controlling the issue of gold certificates, Congress had virtually fixed the legal minimum of the gold reserve for the redemption of greenbacks of $100 millions. When, a decade and more later, a continuing heavy deficit in revenue brought the treasury face to face with bankruptcy, this reserve was drawn upon to meet the ordinary governmental expenditures and its existence more than once threatened by the "endless chain" process of presenting greenbacks and treasury notes of 1890 at the treasury for redemption in gold. Undoubtedly the presence of the greenbacks in our currency system concealed from congressmen and others the real nature of the difficulty in hand, and in so far was responsible for damage done, but it should be clear that had the public revenues been adequate to meet expenses, and the flood of silver been checked, no trouble could have arisen under the circumstances from the existence of the greenbacks.

Until the end of the century two final controversies in regard to the greenbacks waxed warm. One related to the question of the power which brought the government to a position to enable it to resume specie payments. Was it the ingenious work of John Sherman and his associates, or was it a stroke of fortune from nature in the form of crops and sudden industrial advantage, which accomplished the great result? The reasonable answer seems to be that Sherman and his aides prepared for resumption and brought greenbacks to par with gold under industrial, commercial, and political circumstances which were adverse to success, that the fortunate turn in foreign trade in 1879 did, in fact, supply the great source with which to make resumption secure and maintain it, but that the treasury could have maintained specie payment of greenbacks so long as the public debt and public expenditures could be met, no matter what a season's crops had been. The other controverted question related to retaining the greenbacks as a permanent part of our circulating medium or abolishing them. Were they a continuous menace to a sound currency, or did they constitute a convenient form of currency and a good device for saving the government interest on $346 millions? The reasonable reply to this dispute seems to be that so long as the people were not convinced that the greenbacks must be redeemable in gold they were a menace, but when in the course of time they came to constitute a negligibly small element in our currency as a whole and their redemption was beyond doubt they could not be considered inconvenient or dangerous.

INDEX

INDEX